The Divine WABA

On The Hudson
Jung
BOOK SERIES

The Jung on the Hudson Book Series was instituted by the New York Center for Jungian Studies in 1997. This ongoing series is designed to present books that will be of interest to individuals of all fields, as well as mental health professionals, who are interested in exploring the relevance of the psychology and ideas of C. G. Jung to their personal lives and professional activities.

For more information about this series and the New York Center for Jungian Studies contact the Center at 27 North Chestnut St., Suite 3, New Paltz, NY 12561, telephone (845) 256-0191, fax (845) 256-0196.

For more information about becoming part of this series, contact: Nicolas-Hays, Inc., P. O. Box 1126, Berwick, ME 03901-1126, telephone: (207) 698-1041, fax: 207-698-1042, e-mail: info@nicolashays.com.

The Divine
WABA

(Within, Among, Between, and Around)

A Jungian Exploration of
Spiritual Paths

J. Marvin Spiegelman

NICOLAS-HAYS, INC.
BERWICK, MAINE

First published in 2003 by
Nicolas-Hays, Inc.
P. O. Box 1126
Berwick, ME 03901-1126
www.nicolashays.com

Distributed to the trade by
Red Wheel/Weiser, LLC
P. O. Box 612
York Beach, ME 03910-0612
www.redwheelweiser.com

Library of Congress Cataloging-in-Publication Data
Spiegelman, J. Marvin.
    The divine WABA (within, among, between and around) : a Jungian
exploration of spiritual paths / J. Marvin Spiegelman.-- 1st American
pbk. ed.
        p. cm. -- (The Jung on the Hudson book series)
Includes bibliographical references and index.
    ISBN 0-89254-077-X (pbk. : alk. paper)
    1. Psychology, Religious. 2. Jungian psychology--Religious aspects.
I. Title. II. Series.
    BL53.S624 2003
    200'.1'9--dc22
                            2003016020

Cover design and typesetting by Phillip Augusta
Typeset in Palatino Light

Printed in the United States of America

09 08 07 06 05 04 03
7   6   5   4   3   2   1

Contents

List of Illustrations   vii

Acknowledgments   ix

Introduction   xi

Chapter 1
     Circumambulating the Divine: The WABA System   1

Chapter 2
     Divine Among in Islam: The *Hajj* or Pilgrimage
     to Mecca   17

Chapter 3
     Divine Within: The Zen Oxherding Pictures   26

Chapter 4
     Divine Within: The Kundalini Path in Hinduism   66

Chapter 5
     Divine Within: The Tree of Life in Jewish Mysticism   96

Chapter 6
     Divine Between: Alchemical Relationship and
     Jungian Analysis   112

Chapter 7
     Divine Around: Nature, Art, and Synchronicity   140

Chapter 8
   Can Science Be a Spiritual Path? Jung's Inner Way   155

Chapter 9
   Combining Types: Stages in
   Hinduism and Catholicism   171

Chapter 10
   Combining Types: Women's Mysteries   199

Chapter 11
   A Modern Woman's Initiation onto
   the Shaman Path   216

Epilogue   241

Bibliography   259

Index   261

Illustrations

1. Multiple layers of the psyche   xv

2. The Rainmaker Model   2

3. The Community Model   6

4. The Alchemical Model   11

5. The Nature, Art, and Synchronicity Model   13

6. Oxherding picture 1   31

7. Oxherding picture 2   35

8. Oxherding picture 3   37

9. Oxherding picture 4   40

10. Oxherding picture 5   43

11. Oxherding picture 6   47

12. Oxherding picture 7   50

13. Oxherding picture 8   53

14. Oxherding picture 9   56

15. Oxherding picture 10   60

16. *Muladhara* chakra   72

17. *Svadhisthana* chakra   74

18. *Manipura* chakra   76

19. *Anahata* chakra   79

20. *Vishuddha* chakra   83

21. *Ajna* chakra   87

22. *Sahasrara* chakra   89

23. The lightning flash   101

24. The Tree of Life   104

25. Adam Kadmon   109

26. The mercurial fountain   117

27. The king and queen   119

28. Diagram of the opposites   120

29. The naked truth   122

30. Immersion in the bath   123

31. The conjunction   125

32. Death   126

33. The ascent of the soul   128

34. Purification   129

35. The return of the soul   131

36. The new birth   132

37. Soul and spirit united   134

38. Resurrection   136

39. Villa of Mysteries   201

40. Plan of the initiation chamber   203

41. Scenes 1 – 8a of the Villa of Mysteries   205

42. Scenes 8a – 10 of the Villa of Mysteries   210

43. The human energy system   243

Acknowledgments

I am privileged to thank all my teachers, including my analysands, for helping me to realize my ecumenical myth and live it as best I can. To Max Zeller, to C. A. Meier, to Marie-Louise von Franz and, above all, to C. G. Jung, I express my deep gratitude. Thanks, too, to my co-writers in my books, especially Mokusen Miyuki and Arwind Vasavada, and the other members of my psychoecumenical group: Tom Stehly, Lucia Van Ruiten, Levi Meier, and Noreen Cannon. A special thanks to Valerie Cooper who has proven to be a knowledgeable and careful editor. Finally, to my wife, Ryma, for love indomitable.

Introduction

During the Christmas season in 1951, the second year of my first personal Jungian psychoanalysis, I dreamed that a divine child was being born, and that a Christian priest, a Jewish rabbi, and a Buddhist priest were attending this event. I awakened moved and in wonder, remembering that during the previous day I had been humming the beautiful carol, "We Three Kings of Orient Are," and had sensed that I had at last resolved those lingering problems from childhood that people usually have to deal with in any kind of depth psychoanalysis. By then, I had realized that the archetypal level of the psyche, The Great Mother and Great Father, for example, had been influencing many of the images and experiences I had with my quite human and decent parents, and that I was ready to leave behind remembered childhood issues. In fact, I was able to deal more fully with the psyche itself, both personal to me and transpersonal in its general functioning.

The Self, the divine spark at the center of my own being—just as it is in everyone's psyche—was revealed to me in that dream in the form of the archetypal image of the Divine Child. This was quite valuable for the twenty-five-year-old graduate student in psychology that I was, a year away from my Ph.D., but it spelled the end of any ambition I had of being content with becoming an academic professor and behavioral scientist. I knew that I could no longer be happy if I were to abandon my exploration of the soul and its interiority. It was also the beginning of my awareness of an important part of my own myth, that of the pursuit of many spiritual paths, symbolized by the three men of religion in the dream, finding their common central focus in that image of the divine within the psyche itself.

That "child," now having achieved its 50th birthday, has grown a lot as a result of my studies, inner work, training, and functioning as a psychotherapist, analyst, teacher, and writer. It has also helped me produce many articles and books, a half-dozen of the latter on the theme of psychology and religion. It now seems time to translate some of that experience and study into something that could be useful to the nonspecialist in these fields. The book that you have in hand is the result. The reason that I think it might be useful is I believe that my dream was not only a "personal" one, as we Jungians say when referring to dreams shedding light on our own unconscious. We might also view it as a "big" dream, one that reveals aspects of the psychological condition of the group or tribe, something that shamans and medicine men have experienced in many cultures.

Everyone has the capacity to have "big" dreams, but these usually happen in times of great personal or collective stress and transition, such as much of the world is now undergoing, beginning both a new millennium and aeon. It is a time when belief systems, myths, and religions of the past become worn out, lose their meaningful and exclusive grip on us. At such times, we are compelled to go deeper, to search both outside and inside ourselves for what can sustain and nourish us in the way of significance and faith. We may thus be able to renew our born-into faith and/or discover our own myth. Perhaps needless to say to those who are attracted to this book, I understand "myth" in the sense of the many spiritual stories, both individual and collective, that give meaning to existence, and not in the sense of being "false" or illusory. Spiritual stories, as found in fairy tales and religions, are always "true" of the soul, whether true in a factual sense or not. Myths are thus stories of the soul.

I do not, of course, think that the divine child of my dream was equivalent to the Messiah of the Jews, the Second Coming of the Christians, or the Maitreya or future Buddha. The Source of all such beliefs and experiences was also working in me, I believe, and produced my own psyche's take on this ecumenical bent of our time. The world was transcended literally when Mr. Neil Armstrong set foot on the Moon ("one small step for man and one giant leap for mankind" is how he eloquently and accurately put it). I think our Earth was also transcended psychologically when Jung, in his old age and illness, before this Moon-landing occurred, dreamed that he had ascended in space and could see a beautiful blue light surrounding our precious planet, a vision subsequently verified by the astronauts.

We live in a syncretistic time, when peoples and religions are in powerful interaction, resulting in fragmentation of both people and beliefs, and we do not yet foresee how this encounter will play out. My own myth, the ecumenical one, has me going ever deeper into the various faiths by experiencing their stories—in dreams and fantasies and in waking life—without losing my commitment to the faith into which I was born. Indeed, all this circumambulating of paths has required that I deepen my roots into what I am, including what I brought into this world, biologically and psychologically, as well as what I imbibed culturally. I will tell more about that, and the problem of individuation, at the end of the book, after we have dipped ourselves into the various spiritual streams that many generations of religious seekers have navigated for us.

We shall examine these paths from a depth psychological perspective, particularly Jungian. In so doing, we will employ one of the meanings of the word *religio*, that of "careful observation of the numinous," indicating that we respectfully let the spiritually-charged material speak to us directly, without reducing it to some previously determined interpretations, particularly reductive ones. We use our knowledge and experience to amplify the symbols presented, as if we were examining the facets of a diamond, to grasp it from within, within ourselves and within the symbols—if we can—knowing that these ancient trails were traveled by many gifted faithful over long periods and that we, alas, are only spiritual tourists. Nonetheless, our current visits will deepen our own understanding of the spiritual path itself and we will bring to bear what a modern consciousness can contribute to them. We most definitely do not wish to do anything resembling a *psychology of religion*, which has the danger of inflation in it, reducing phenomena of the soul to some presumed "higher" wisdom, such as science ("scientism"). *Psychology and religion*, on the other hand, respects borders and differences, does not "colonize," but amplifies and interprets for the sake of deeper understanding. Reason, in this approach, becomes a "servant of the passions"—as Plato deemed it should be—namely to use this divine gift not to conquer or overcome, but to "understand" in the depth sense of the German word *verstehen*. In this way, that "divine child" will be served, nourished, and helped to grow, just as the child, in turn, merits our devotion, love, and will teach us.

That same "child" is seen here through a Jungian filter, naturally, since it was thanks to Jung's psychology that my own path was prepared and lit. Such a prism seems not to limit the perspective religiously, apparently, judging from my experience in editing a series of books on the theme of Jungian psychology and religion. In the most recent of these, *Psychology and Religion at the Millennium and Beyond*,[1] for example, there were contributions by some dozen Jungian analysts who were born into different religions and were surprisingly brought back to their natal source as a consequence of their analyses. Many had felt that they had previously "outgrown" their born-into faith, but after a time in their own personal analyses, they thought that Jungian psychology was amazingly like their natal Confucianism, Taoism, Buddhism, Hinduism, Christianity, or Judaism! How could that be? I think that this stems from Jung's example in deeply probing the psyche, which is the source of all our faiths, and that in so doing he helped us to find that ground of religious experience common to all peoples. Differences exist at every level as well, naturally. I person-

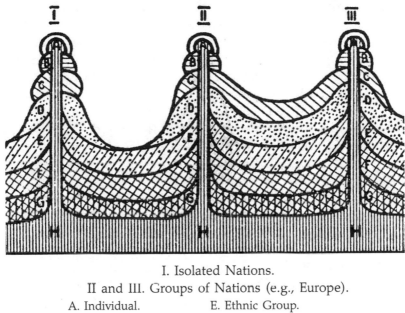

I. Isolated Nations.
II and III. Groups of Nations (e.g., Europe).

A. Individual.   E. Ethnic Group.
B. Family.   F. Primitive Human Ancestors.
C. Tribe.   G. Animal Ancestors.
D. Nation.   H. Central Energy.

Figure 1. Multiple layers of the psyche. From Jolande Jacobi, The
Psychology of C. G. Jung *(London: Routledge/New Haven, CT: Yale
University Press, 1942/1962), p. 34. Copyright © 1962, Jolande Jacobi.
Used with permission.*

ally like the diagram in figure 1 which illustrates both this
similarity and difference.

We can clearly see that at the deepest level—that ground
where matter and spirit are united—we are truly all alike. I was
astonished, many years ago, when I realized that the atomic structure of carbon, the most prevalent element in the human body, had
a valence of four, and that this number is also a symbol of psychic
wholeness (a geometric mandala) everywhere. It said to me that
the Self in its basic form (mandala) expresses itself in matter as
well as in the soul (psyche), perhaps in parallel manifestation.

We can also see that we humans share a common substructure with everything that lives. As we rise, in the diagram, to higher levels of psyche, variations begin to emerge. We discover the ethnic, national, local, and familial differences we all know about but have difficulty specifying without becoming racist, sexist, "religionist," or "familialist," since ethnocentrism is also natural to us.

Finally, our individual egos are at the top, making us feel special and different, but each of us rests, all the same, on that wonderful/terrible substrate that grounds us and limits us, yet also enables us to become aware of our own substance and depth. Our spiritual lives become ones of discovering those depths, adapting to and transforming that totality into which we are born but which requires our consciousness for our growth and individuation.

This book is a journey among some of the paths forged historically on that great substrate. In chapter 1, we shall begin the journey among the paths and faiths with the aid of a classification system that I have used successfully in my lectures, subsequently referring to these descriptions from time to time. The mnemonic I have used for this classification system is WABA, which is not the Women's American Basketball Association, but refers to the Divine Within, Divine Among, Divine Between, and the Divine Around. We shall dance among these categories, spending much time on various paths of the Divine Within, both because these are especially relevant for our time and because our psychological perspective, a late development in the evolution of the spirit, is naturally so focused.

Before embarking upon our journey, however, I'd like to answer the question you might have in the back of your mind: How does this book about religion differ from others? My immediate reply comes from my tale about a Knight, present for me since early childhood, maturing when I was 40, and becoming a grown-up version of that divine child I spoke of before. This is a story of a heroic journeyer on his own path of individuation, revealed in a tale that combined Jewish, Christian, and Pagan elements, so that a Jewish friend of mine asked me, with friendly Passover humor, "How is this

Knight different from all other Knights?" My reply was that he was a "psychomythological Knight," that he could enter into multiple myths from the "inside,"—from inside the myth and inside himself. This Knight was joined by nine other figures, thus representing ten different religions and paths, but all quite individual just the same. Their tales are found in my book, *The Tree of Life*,[2] all of them embracing interiority, at least in part. The modern spirit, I am suggesting, requires this kind of inward quest since conviction in matters of faith, which worked well in the past, has been weakened, even lost. Combined with our prevalent myth of scientific empiricism, this modern spirit demands that we rely on our own experience rather than on outer authority. I know of few books on religion that do this.

I am happy to recommend, however, three books (aside from those of Jung, of course, which are part of my own substrate) that have been especially valuable to me in this regard. The first book, published about 1938 and which I read during my analytic training in Switzerland in the late 1950s, is *Religion in Essence and Manifestation*, written by a great Dutch Protestant theologian, Gerhard van der Leeuw.[3] This book is phenomenological; it stays with the images and qualities that the religious symbols present to us with the aim of appreciating and deepening our understanding rather than reductively interpreting them. Van der Leeuw uses anthropological and psychological categories for this understanding, such as "Friendship with God" and "Enmity to God," which takes us beyond the conventional classifications of the various religions to the experiences that they address. This book, alas, is out of print, but reading it would do you a world of experiential good, to say nothing of learning a lot as well.

The second book that has been of great value to me is *The World's Religions* by Huston Smith, the scholar and teacher who became particularly famous as a result of a series of interviews with Bill Moyers on public television.[4] Seeing or reading this man, a son of missionaries, and glimpsing his faith, his broad-mindedness, his openness, his true spiritual capacity and achievement, is to be moved on the path toward enlightenment. That he is able to use the rituals, meditations, and prayers of several religions in his daily spiritual life, honoring each yet connecting to the Source, reminds me of the great Hindu saint, Ramakrishna, who also could do this. *The World's Religions*, reprinted many times, has a deserved reputation as both popular and academically sound. It is even sounder, coming from a man who knows the Source from "inside."

There are many books on the various particular religions themselves, of course, and I will mention some in due course. I do, however, want to mention an astonishing book by a man of faith, which has moved me greatly. It is *Halakhic Man* by Rabbi Joseph B. Soloveitchik.[5] It not only reveals the depth and breadth of one who might even be considered "fundamentalist," as an orthodox Jew, but like the previous two authors, he ends his scholarly work with deep obeisance to God and asking pardon for any error that he has committed.

Given these three excellent books, along with others that could and will be cited, why do I offer another? None of the three is particularly psychological, I think, either in attitude or in content. Present-day consciousness, in my opinion, needs to incorporate the findings of depth psychology for the religious life, without undermining the latter or becoming a religion in itself. This, I believe, is what psychomythology is about, and is what I offer here.

Let us turn, then, to our WABA classification system.

Notes

[1] J. Marvin Spiegelman, *Psychology and Religion at the Millennium and Beyond* (Tempe, AZ: New Falcon, 1988).

[2] J. Marvin Spiegelman, *The Tree of Life: Paths in Jungian Individuation* (Tempe, AZ: New Falcon, 1974/1993).

[3] Gerhard van der Leeuw, *Religion in Essence and Manifestation* (1933), J. E. Turner, trans. (London: Allen and Unwin, 1938).

[4] Huston Smith, *The World's Religions* (New York: Harper & Row, 1958).

[5] Joseph B. Soloveitchik, *The Halakhic Man* (Philadelphia: The Jewish Publication Society of America, 1983).

CHAPTER 1

Circumambulating the Divine: The WABA System

For me, the divine is a broad term, in some ways comparable to the "holy," but more specifically akin to what Rudolf Otto called "the numinous."[1] It is that experience of something beyond ourselves ("Wholly Other"), which moves us, awes us, can be both fascinating and frightening, or ecstatic. It brings us to a "creature feeling" within ourselves, which we attribute to divinity itself as its cause. It is *qadosh* in Hebrew and *sanctus* in Latin, but beyond "the good," and makes us shiver and quake. It also inspires and enlightens us. Almost everybody has at least one such experience in life, perhaps in religious ritual or prayer, in nature, while performing or hearing special music or seeing art, or reading inspired writing. Otto's term is especially useful because it is nonjudgmental, phenomenological (lets the event speak for itself) and, therefore, empirical or scientific. For our present purposes, however, I prefer the term "divine" because it is more generally understood. It is also not limited to any particular religion or spiritual path.

The Divine Within: The Rainmaker Model

Figure 2 (page 2), representative of what I call the Rainmaker Model, gives us a pictorial hint of what it's like to approach the Divine Within. It comes from a Taoist alchemical text

Figure 2. The Rainmaker Model. Taoist sage in meditation.
From Wilhelm and Jung, The Secret of the Golden Flower.

on stages of meditation, which can be found in Jung and Wilhelm's book, *The Secret of the Golden Flower.*[2] It looks like many pictures of Asian meditators—the Buddha, above all—who sit and contemplate either nothingness or their own center. This image of a seated Asian seeker, highly introverted, really, can be contrasted with our Western religious heroes, such as Moses, Jesus and Muhammad, who walked a lot! But even our extraverting Western monotheists spent much time alone, contemplating and dialoguing with the Divine as it presented itself to their solitary consciousness. Besides, the Buddha wandered a good deal before sitting stoically at the Bo tree. So, even here, there is commonality. But the differentiation, I think, is useful.

Of course, every experience of the divine has to occur "within." That is, it takes place inside our own psyches, although the example of the Rainmaker is not exclusively an inner event. All the same, this classification clearly has its focus on the manifestation or working with the divine energies, symbols, or experiences that arise from within the psyche itself. The Rainmaker Model comes from an experience witnessed by Richard Wilhelm, the famous Sinologist who translated the ancient Chinese oracular text, *I Ching,* for the West. Jung thought this story was so important that he suggested to his pupil, Barbara Hannah, that she tell it every time she gave a lecture.

Wilhelm was in a remote Chinese village that was suffering from a most unusually prolonged drought. Everything had been done to put an end to it, and every kind of prayer and charm had been used, but all to no avail. So the elders of the village told Wilhelm that the only thing to do was to send for a rainmaker who lived far from their village. This interested him enormously and he was careful to be present when the rainmaker arrived. The rainmaker, a small, wizened old man, came in a covered cart. He got out of the cart, sniffed the air in distaste, and asked for a cottage on the outskirts of the village. He made it a condition that no one should disturb him and that his food should be placed on the ground outside the door. Nothing was heard from him for three days. Then, everyone woke up to a downpour of rain. It even snowed, which was unknown at that time of year.

Wilhelm was greatly impressed, naturally, and sought out the rainmaker, who had now come out of his seclusion. Wilhelm asked him in wonder, "So you can make rain?" The old man scoffed at the very idea and said that of course he could not. "But there was the most persistent drought until you came," Wilhelm retorted, "and—within three days—it rains?" "Oh," replied the old man, "that was something quite different. You see, I come from a region where everything is in order, it rains when it should and is fine when that is needed, and the people are also in order and in themselves. But that was not the case with the people here, they were all out of Tao and out of themselves. I was at once infected when I arrived, so I had to be quite alone until I was once more in Tao and then naturally it rained."[3]

This story beautifully conveys the idea that we are to work within our self in order to produce or reproduce harmony therein, no matter whether the source of imbalance arises from within our selves or outside of us. Furthermore, it suggests that it is this inner work—perhaps *only* this inner work—that helps change the outer world, too, even in nature; that's why I call this category of spiritual path the Rainmaker Model, although the variations on this theme that I will examine later are more inclined to work on changing our self within, leaving the world to fend for itself. All the same, the divine is not to be found exclusively within, as we all know, and ultimately it transcends us in every way, thus affecting us and being affected at the same time. Hazrat Inayat Khan, who brought Sufism, the mystical form of Islam, to the West, echoes the Eastern experience of the Divine Within:

> "The One whom I have called God . . . has been seeing His life through my eyes, has been hearing through my ears . . . I did not realize that this body was the shrine of God." Not knowing that God experiences this life through man, one is seeking for Him somewhere else, in some other person aloof and apart from the world, whereas all the time He is in oneself.[4]

The Divine Among: The Community Model

The Divine Among is known to us all, and is familiar to us in the form of the religious rituals and liturgies that most people everywhere have grown up with. They take form in Sabbath services, in the Mass, high holiday prayers, or festivals of the year, celebrated in church, synagogue, mosque, temple, ashram, etc. Indeed, the main function of such rituals and prayers is to reconnect us to the divine when our daily lives have taken us far afield. Even if that is not the case, if we are not estranged from our Maker, the Divine Among is designed to enhance this numinous sense by sharing such holiness with others on a regular basis. For many people, everywhere, this is their exclusive form of the spiritual path, and one does not deviate or go outside it. Those who can honestly be so contained in a traditional faith are indeed fortunate, for they are already like the renewed rainmaker. Nor can one say that they are necessarily just "conventional," since in history many spiritually creative innovators or mystics continued to follow the practices of their born-into religion while courageously being directly open to the divine, without mediation by rituals or formulated prayers. I am thinking of Joseph Caro, Isaac Luria, and the Bal Shem Tov in mystical Judaism, for example, or St. Francis, Jacob Boehme, and Meister Eckhart in Christianity, Rumi, and Ibn al `Arabi in Islam.

The example I shall use for the Divine Among, which I explore at length in chapter 2, comes from Islam, that of the sacred collective journey to Mecca and the Ka'aba. There are beautiful examples from all religions, of course, but I chose this one just because most readers are likely to come from Judaism, Christianity, or perhaps Hinduism or Buddhism, and are probably less informed about this tremendously power-ful religion, which we encounter these days, alas, in a more political or military fashion than spiritually. By the same token, I shall not here explore all the wonderful mystical aspects of Islam, as revealed in Sufism, for example.[5]

I cannot limit myself to describing an aspect of God Among exclusively to Islam, however, since sacrament, involv-ing expected and somewhat codified religious experience at

Figure 3. The Community Model: Muslims praying.
Copyright © Getty Images. RL 000249 (RF).

different stages of life, is not only to be found in every faith, but is a fundamental aspect of every seeker's spiritual experience, even among those who depart from the parent faith in some manner. Let's take a brief look at the Christian sacraments, therefore, to round out our introduction to the Divine Among.

The Sacraments

The first sacrament, baptism, is truly an immersion into holy life, in which we are both named and inducted into family and community religious life. Without such "immersion," so to speak (partial, total, or however), we remain somehow apart from community, separate from glorious tradition, where God has spoken to the faithful and given them the sense of both individuality (naming) and togetherness. Without such induction, we remain something of an animal (in the sense of staying unconscious, not pejoratively but descriptively, unawakened to the human condition). Psychologically, without such baptism (however it is named in other faiths), we have nothing to even revolt against and alienation is ultimately a likely consequence. The community welcomes us into the experience of the Divine Among, even if we are so young and immature that we do not do this consciously. The communal act, Among, is the powerful event for all, joyfully noting individuality as well as commonality, even if the main participant is hardly aware of this religious act.

We also need to be aware of the tremendous importance of naming, everywhere and all the time. Mystical Islam has a wonderful image for this. It holds that each human being has his/her own Name of God, which needs to be realized during the subsequent life. This Name is even more important than the collective Name found in the faiths, such as monotheism. To name, then, is to make manifest particularity—divine particularity—but also in the context of divine generality.

Communion, the second sacrament in Christianity, is a movement beyond the acknowledgment of individuality and acceptance into a community toward the personal union with God. This is truly the beginning of an interior life of the soul, the approach to the Divine Within, via the particular ritual provided by the group. Now there is an Other to whom we speak, pray, ask for connection. Creatureliness is both affirmed and transcended, since it is indeed the very lowly "I" who "dares" (as one priest put it) to address the Most High as "Our Father."

Confirmation, the third sacrament, brings affirmation of individuality, once again, but in the context of adulthood, its responsibilities and privileges. That such a ritual takes place far earlier than actual maturity makes possible in modern life is not only because people entered adulthood more quickly in the past when religion and culture were one. It is also because both the inner and outer changes in adolescence are so profound that they must be marked as a third stage on the spiritual path for everyone in their relation to the divine. Confirmation can and should provide this. For many in the 20th century, alas, this did not occur, as C. G. Jung describes of himself in his very moving memoir, *Memories, Dreams, Reflections.*[6] A more conscious pursuit of individuation, of the realization of the divine in our self and in life, is now required. We are called upon to experience the Divine Within again, along with the Divine Among, in a group context.

For many people, confirmation often no longer has the desired effect (as it did not with Jung), and may become just an occasion for celebration of a person's or family's material success ("Today I am a fountain pen," is the classic joke of the bar mitzvah boy). When that initiation experience, which is common in every culture, fails to do its work, it will need to take place at some other time or locale. This can some-times transpire in military training, at schools or, when the psychological or inner spiritual dimension becomes necessary, in psychotherapy. So, the exploration of early adulthood in analysis is often just as important as early childhood.

Marriage, the fourth sacrament, also especially significant everywhere, brings union with our "other half," under God. Most people are not aware of the myth, told by Plato, that initially people were hermaphroditic wholes, but were insolent to the divine. As a result, they were split in half as a punishment and these "halves"—all of us individual mortals—seek their counterparts with lesser or greater success. From a psycho-logical perspective, marriage is a symbol of the union of the opposites, the *coniunctio* as it is called in alchemy, experienced concretely as outer marriage in youth and, usually later in life, inwardly as the coalescing of our total nature, masculine and feminine. Here is the first real collective representation of the Divine Between.

Confession, a fifth sacrament, formerly especially important to Catholicism, is less pursued in modern life, even among the faithful, probably owing to a profound shift in ethics and conscience going on everywhere, with concomitant danger and opportunity. This less frequent use of such a solemn and meaningful method of purification is not because of the rise of psychotherapy, wherein we confess to an impartial and nonpriestly guide, but because the struggle with conscience is becoming more of an interior matter. The great issues of sexuality, honesty, fidelity, etc. are more often being addressed to an inner authority and only secondarily in accordance with religious precepts handed down from the past. It is this decreasing use of the sacrament of confession, I think, that signals profound changes going on within the collective Christian psyche itself. This sacrament can also be viewed as a manifestation of the Divine Between, since the ritual has always been an intimate dialogue between confessor (priest) and confessant (parishioner).

The sixth sacrament, practiced in particular by Catholics, is that of the Eucharist, celebrated in the Mass.[7] Of course, people in most religions are mindful of the connection with the divine involved in sitting down to a communal meal, in being aware of what they take into themselves and being thankful for the divine energy that nourishes them. It is the Catholic understanding of the Eucharist, however, which transforms this event into a central celebration of the *imitatio Christi*, of enacting and experiencing the life and death of Christ. This ritual, taking place in the Mass, has both a human and divine aspect. From the human point of view, gifts and sacrifices are offered to God at the altar, on the part of priest and congregation, consecrating both. The ritual celebrates the Last Supper, the Passover feast, which Jesus shared with his disciples and it commemorates the incarnation, Passion, death, and resurrection of Christ. From the perspective of the divine, however, what is taking place is that the life of Christ, which exists non-temporally, manifests at the human level in time. Christ takes on human flesh and spirit in the form of the bread and wine, suffers, is killed, placed in the sepulcher, but rises again in glory. The human participants, therefore, conjointly experience what the divine undergoes, resulting in a transformation of all concerned—the people, the priest, the substances, and the divine itself. This is indeed a most powerful sacrament, enacted regularly and powerfully redeeming the participants.

Ordination, the seventh sacrament, is privileged to the clergy, of course, but this affirmation of a path of service is also available to all, in an inner sense. Its power is immense, as I can attest from my own analytic work with clergy. I have seen more than one priest who has given up his priesthood outwardly but is compelled to continue to examine his "calling" or lack of same, from within. I have been deeply moved to find that such individuals continue to follow their priesthood—or other commitment to outer religious life such as in spiritual communities—within themselves, despite being cut off from their previous official priesthood. In short, they are driven to find and pursue their religious path of service in a new way. Whether this contemporary mass exodus from the priesthood and religious orders will also ultimately lead to a change in the vocation itself (such as ordination of women and married clergy) is unclear, but the psyche, as I see it, is truly enlarging the spiritual life of service far beyond what we have traditionally accepted. This sacrament, again, has the character of the Divine Within (vocation, calling), but is collectively sanctioned (Divine Among).

Extreme unction, the eighth and final sacrament, is, of course, the ultimate union with God at death. The loving attention in Catholicism to the dying process is most beautiful and profound, matched perhaps by no other religion except Tibetan Buddhism, and reflects the Christian understanding that spiritual life is not only womb to tomb but lasts beyond this life altogether. It also encompasses the aspect of the Divine Between (union with God), facilitated by ritual.

The Divine Between: The Alchemical Model

The next category of the Divine in the WABA classification system is that of the Divine Between. The illustrative figure on page 11 comes, not from the traditional symbols of marriage as the age-old carrier of the numinous, but from alchemy, that relatively modern, mysterious precursor and underside of science, which discovered the psyche projected into matter. That discipline produced a plethora of symbols, methods, and ideas that we now realize were also a precursor to depth psychology. I therefore refer to it as the Alchemical Model. The picture I

Figure 4. The Alchemical Model. From Jung, CW 16, figure 12.

use as an illustration is a relatively late one from the alchemical period. It was produced at a time when at least some of the alchemists realized that what they were working with was not the transformation of base matter into gold, but was both their own personal darkness and the dark aspect of the divine in matter that was in need of transformation.

Our picture shows the typical pair of the alchemist and his *soror mystica* ("mystical sister") deeply and religiously at work in that transformational process. They are kneeling in devotion before a fiery furnace, symbolizing change, while above them are two angelic figures, also male and female, who support a container wherein the alchemists themselves are being transformed. A "third" person, who may be the Divine itself, guides them, in turn. Above it all is the symbol of the sun, representative of higher consciousness that sheds light on the path and is also enhanced by the work. That the maker of this woodcut was so enlightened, already in the 17th century, is amazing. But also amazing is the fact that alchemy soon afterwards was consigned to the scrap heap, since the experimenters could not, indeed, transform base matter into gold. Science itself, with its more materialistic foundation and empirical methods, accomplished so much more of tangible value in its experimental endeavor that it drove the proto-science out altogether. It took mid-twentieth-century depth psychology, one of the most recent of the sciences, to realize that it was the psyche that was being worked with—projected into matter, of course—and it was here that Jung found the historical amplification of his surprising discoveries in working with dreams. We shall explore this path of alchemy later on, but here we can recognize that the deeper meaning of the Divine Between is: "Together we can transform ourselves, matter, and God."

The Divine Around:
The Nature, Art, and Synchronicity Model

The fourth category of religious experience we will investigate is that of the Divine Around, and is called the Nature, Art (including music, of course), and Synchronicity Model. Figure

Figure 5. The Nature, Art, and Synchronicity Model.
"High Sierra" photograph courtesy of Ryma Spiegelman.

5, shown above, is a photograph of a place in the High Sierra where my family and I have been vacationing every summer for some 40 years. Most of us know the numinous experience in nature, in high mountains, or at the ocean or with a lovely flower, just as we know the Divine Among in ritual. Some, indeed, know the numinous only in nature. Others are privileged to experience the aesthetically moving in the arts to the point that they are even thereby linked to the Beyond. A most beautiful example of the latter is found in the oral tradition of singers from North India.

During the period when the Mogul emperor Akbar was ruling India, there was a very famous singer, called Tansen, who was the greatest of them all. Tansen was invited by the Emperor's courtiers to give a concert, during which the audience listened spellbound. Tansen's profound knowledge of structure and tempo, plus the almost magical quality of his voice made his listeners weep. His words were also redolent with passion and subtlety of meaning. His artistry, in short, was such that everyone was carried to such realms of pleasure that no one wanted the music to end.

Emperor Akbar, too, was so moved by Tansen that he left his throne and bowed deeply before the great musician. Overwhelmed with gratitude, he gave him a bag of ten thousand gold coins, the largest gift ever given a musician. The emperor noticed, however, that although everyone else was celebrating, Tansen's face was dark, even despairing. Emperor Akbar asked Tansen why he seemed so sad, but the musician did not answer at once. Finally, Tansen asked Emperor Akbar to come with him that evening to a special place where he would discover why the musician was so unhappy.

That night, the two walked under the bright full moon to Brindaban, the sacred park associated with Krishna. As they approached the park, they heard a man singing to the accompaniment of a tamboura, a drone instrument. They hid behind a bush and witnessed a miraculous scene. A man, who was obviously a devotee of Lord Krishna, was singing as if he were pouring out his heart, his love, his entire being. His voice was so full of ecstasy that neither Tansen nor the emperor could speak. And they were not the only audience. Other people were there as well, of course, but there were also monkeys and cows sitting silently, while parrots and parakeets, mynahs and cuckoos perched motionlessly, listening in the trees. Even the trees, vines, rocks, mountains, and the moon seemed to take part in the divine ecstasy of the singer's voice. Akbar and Tansen were both transported as well.

When the music ended, Tansen led the emperor back to the palace. After a time of silence under a tree, Tansen spoke: "Your Majesty, the singer that you heard in Brindaban is my master, Swami Haridaas. He is singing for Krishna, he is singing about Krishna, and when he is singing he is Krishna himself—such is his devotion! His music is that of ecstasy. My music is the music of pleasure, because I am singing for courtiers. I have not conquered my ego and neither have my listeners, have they? My music is not bad, and I do not mean to say that the music sung for enter-tainment is bad, but my guru's music is infinitely superior to my own. He was absolutely unaware of his audience or his surroundings. For him, everyone and everything had become Krishna. Earlier tonight, when you rewarded me, I was wondering whether I will ever sing as Swami Haridaas does, even once. That was why I looked so sad."

Tears streaking down his face, the emperor got up, and without saying a word, he embraced his favorite musician.[8]

With that, we will leave our introduction to the fourth cat-egory, the Divine Around, with the promise that in due course we will consider another of its aspects, namely, the area of synchronicity—the meaningful correlation between events that link nature or the world in some way with inner experience. Such small miracles happen to most people at least once in their lives. Their occurrence or impact cannot be ritualized, as can the Divine Among, but if we are sensitive enough and open, then the creative worlds of the arts and of God's work in nature will reveal the numinous as well.

This fourfold classification system, which came to me gradually over the years, is one of convenience only, of course. Other good ones can be found, as I mentioned in the intro-duction, in Gerhard van der Leeuw's *Religion in Essence and Manifestation* and in Huston Smith's *The World's Religions*. Their task was to teach about the religions in their totality, rather than dwelling on particular spiritual paths within them. That latter effort, making use of the psychological methods adum-brated in the last hundred years, is our engagement here. Now our *hajj* (the Muslim path of the approach to Mecca) will truly begin with the Divine Among in Islam.

Notes

[1] Rudolf Otto, *The Idea of the Holy: An Inquiry into the Non-rational Factor in the Idea of the Divine and Its Relation to the Rational*, John W. Harvey, trans. (New York: Oxford University Press, 1958), p. 6.

[2] Richard Wilhelm and C. G. Jung, *The Secret of the Golden Flower* (London: Routledge and Kegan Paul, 1931).

[3] C. G. Jung, *Mysterium Coniunctionis, The Collected Works of C. G. Jung,* vol. 14, R. F. C. Hull, trans., Bollingen Series XX (Princeton: Princeton University Press, 1970), p. 419, n. 21. Also, Barbara Hannah, *Encounters of the Soul* (Santa Monica, CA: Sigo Press, 1981), p. 14. Further references to *The Collected Works of C. G. Jung* will be cited as *CW,* with the volume number. See Bibliography for volume details.

[4] Hazrat Inayat Khan, *In an Eastern Rose Garden: The Sufi Message of Hazrat Inayat Khan,* vol. 7 (New Lebanon, NY: Omega Publications, 1991), p. 35.

[5] For a guiding introduction to Sufism, I suggest the book I edited, *Sufism and Jungian Psychology* (Tempe, AZ: New Falcon, 1991), which includes work by the great contemporary leader, Pir Vilayat Inayat Khan, the son of Hazrat Inayat Khan, who helped introduce the mystical Sufi path to the West.

[6] C. G. Jung, *Memories, Dreams, Reflections,* Aniela Jaffé, ed. (New York: Pantheon, 1961), pp. 53–55.

[7] For a detailed and respectful psychological understanding, see C. G. Jung, "Transformation Symbolism in the Mass," in *Psychology and Religion: West and East, CW* 11, pp. 201–296.

[8] This story was retold by D.K.M. Kartha, "A Singer for Krishna," in *Parabola* 23, no. 2 (1998):15–17.

CHAPTER 2

Divine Among in Islam: The Hajj or Pilgrimage to Mecca

Most everyone knows that every Muslim is expected to come to Mecca at least once during his or her lifetime. But apart from the aerial view of the great stone temple there, the Ka'aba, and its throngs of pious believers, few of us are aware of the details and significance of these rites. The great French scholar, Henry Corbin began to make such information available to Westerners less than a half-century ago and we shall now draw upon his sensitive and knowledgeable account for our understanding.[1]

As a preliminary to our accompanying the pilgrim in his rite, Corbin supplies us with information regarding the religious basis underlying it. We begin, theologically, with the spiritual fact common to Jews, Christians, and Muslims—the myth of our original parents' fall from Paradise. For Muslims, it is neither disobedient pride nor original sin that needs redemption—the *felix culpa* for Christians, for example, in which the "happy fault" is redeemed for everyone through the sacrifice of Jesus Christ. For the followers of Muhammad, Adam and Eve's eating of the forbidden fruit constituted a violence that consists in naturalizing the things of the spirit. This means that we endlessly perpetuate the act of taking concretely those spiritual qualities that are then meant to be experienced and understood symbolically. The entire pilgrimage is an initiation aimed at repairing this typically human failing.

What a most modern rendering of our human predilection to get things wrong! From depth psychology, we have begun to understand that addiction to alcohol, for example, is a misplaced concretization of the need for "spirit" or for relaxation, endlessly continued and resulting in destruction because—we now learn from Islam—of misplaced "naturalizing" (concretizing). Similarly, addiction to candy has the spiritual meaning of a longing for sweetness in life, only momentarily fulfilled in gorging, but resulting in guilt (*culpa*) and despair once more. Addiction to drugs or sex portray the human longing for Dionysian ecstasy and release from rules and taboos, normally achieved in ancient and native cultures through special religious rituals. Is it any wonder, then, that many modern people, cut off from spirit and religious meaning, thus "naturalize" their deep desire? Islam shows a path that we may take to attain such reparation or liberation.

Pilgrimage

We are told in the Muslim story that the angel Gabriel was sent to our first father, Adam, when he was in total despair about the exile from Paradise. Interestingly, Jewish lore has it that when Adam and Eve were in such darkness about their evil deed of disobedience, they sacrificed a unicorn (symbol of pride) and were thereupon reaccepted by the Lord, Hashem. In the Muslim story, Gabriel (the healing angel in all three faiths) led Adam to where the future temple (Ka'aba) was to stand. Our world (Earth) is constituted by the four elements (a symbol of wholeness): fire, air, water, and earth. The temple of God in heaven, the archetypal representation of wholeness and completion, is matched on earth by the to-be-constructed temple (Ka'aba). Following Gabriel's instruction, Adam traces with his foot a mark on the earth, which is the outline of the future Ka'aba, descending from that original spiritual heaven. Therefore the pilgrims, imitating our ancestor, are required to walk around the earthly temple once before visiting the places of devotion that surround it. After they have accomplished this initial act, pilgrimage—in the imagined company of the angel Gabriel—then proceeds.

Modern psychology may help us understand this Muslim repairing of the breach between humankind and the divine, caused by the former's lack of limit or restraint. We begin to heal the "breakage" of the initial image of wholeness and union with the divine through the religious rite of circumambulation—that is, making a circle on earth, another image of wholeness—that matches that archetypal one in the "beyond." It is an aspect of the divine itself and the angel Gabriel guides us on the way. Furthermore, this primordial breakage and its repair were always known (the mark of the eternal archetypal image). Thus, the known destructive tendency of human nature and the means of its repair is given form for at least once in a lifetime. This one circumambulation, however, is only the beginning of the pilgrimage, which requires subsequent visitation to the various places of devotion that surround the Ka'aba. These visitations constitute four steps. Again, wholeness is given numerical representation as four.

The First Devotional Visitation

The angel first takes Adam (and thus all of the pilgrims) to Mina, which is a valley near Mecca. Mina means "desire." Theological understanding has it that when we follow the road that leads back to God, or Allah, the first thing to manifest itself—ardent desire—lies in the heart, which is also the home of *Bayt Allahi'l Aikbar*, God's greatest temple. Thus Adam—humanity—is engaged, under the angel's guidance, in the heart's pilgrimage toward the personal, spiritual Ka'aba, based on the ardent desire to reconcile with the Divine.

Not stated here, but symbolically pushing out toward us to be understood, is the psychological truth that the cure for desire is desire. It is a spiritual homeopathy, so to speak, in which the lust after the tabooed or dangerous or destructive thing is repaired by the equally ardent desire for the divine itself! Sin or guilt means "missing the mark," not linking desire with divinity, for example. Perhaps people engaged in twelve-step programs like Alcoholics Anonymous might be aided by the realization that little rituals such as grace before meals or drinking, thus linking the desire with the divine, may help accomplish that union for the traditional believer.

The Second Devotional Visitation

After prayers at Mina, the angel and Adam go to Al 'Arafat, which means to have escaped from the place or level at which the pilgrim was located previously. This "escape" signifies that the pilgrim has now entered upon the Way, going from exile— cut off from God—to being on the path to reconnection. Was this in Palestinian leader Yassir Arafat's mind when he chose such a name? Typically, the pilgrim arrives at Al 'Arafat at sunset. At this point, a task is set. The angel says: "Now that the sun is on the point of setting, acknowledge your fault."[2]

This has the theological meaning that the spiritual sun (truth) is veiled to the pilgrim because of the human betrayal of the divine injunction. The pilgrim is enjoined to acknowledge that he or she "is estranged from your Friend only because you considered that you yourself were sufficient to yourself in order to be yourself."[3]

What a subtle and profound realization on the part of Islam, and how characteristic that requirement is from a religion that requires total abasement and worship before the Lord! Our great sin is not simply pride or limitless desire, but our ridiculous belief that we can become who we truly are without any help or connection with the Self (God) at all! Only the most recent depth psychology has arrived at the truth of that Muslim realization. Consider the implication: even to think about becoming who we truly are, we need divine partnership to help bring us there.

When we think of the typical ways of praying to God in Judaism, Christianity, and Islam, we can see further symbolic representation of this relationship. The religious Jew rocks back and forth on his heels, rarely kneeling, but both deeply bowing and standing tall, as if in dialectical song and communion with the God with whom he can converse and argue, as well as pray. The religious Christian kneels in submission to the power that utterly transcends him. And the religious Muslim falls flat on his face before Allah. The very word *Islam* means total surrender to God!

The Third Devotional Visitation

After this entry upon the Way, the pilgrim then arrives at Muzdalifah, a point halfway between Mina and Al'Arafat. The word *Muzdalifah* means "approach." The Koran (2:200) itself prescribes that one must here perform a rite of "recollection" of God, called *dhikr*. This is an allusion signifying that this mystical station, coming after the realization of separation, is meant to help us reunite with God. Prayers are said at both sunset (*maghrib*) and the coming of night, similar to the Christian Vespers and Compline. Here we experience the vigil in the night. As in the psalm chanted at the beginning of the holiest of days in Judaism, Yom Kippur, we are like a sentinel, "waiting for the dawn." This dawn is the Morning of the Presence, the "face" of the divine reality. At dawn, the angel instructs Adam to make a sevenfold confession of his fault, thus erasing darkness, and thereby asking God in sevenfold adjuration to "return to him." These seven acts are aimed at the removal of the seven veils between man and the Divine Face.

Psychologically, we understand the veil as both concealing and revealing ("re-veiling"). It both connects us and shields us from a great numinous power. Moses' face, for example, shone so powerfully when he returned from atop Mt. Sinai, that he was enjoined to veil it. Similarly, veiling in Islam is a most potent symbol: women, whose beauty and attractiveness are so great, must be protected from the immodest or intrusive gaze of others, particularly men, just as the latter require shielding from their beauty, which can engender dangerous desire once again. Allah's Face is even more overwhelming and we must be prepared to encounter it only in measured, successive stages, lest we succumb to madness or death. The opposites lie very close, here, just as we know that the Self, in its depths, contains those same opposites in extreme degree.

In the ritual, this purification and gradual preparation, through the long night's vigil and the seven acts of penitence, makes possible the realization of the Pearl, which is the angel within us. This angel or Pearl is the form assumed by God to reveal Itself to us. It is both gnosis (knowledge) and the soul, itself. Only at this point is Adam—humanity—worthy to enter into the temple. Only now can the pilgrim realize the Secret of the Black Stone, which is also connected to the white Pearl, or White Stone.

The Secret of the Black Stone

The Black Stone at the center of the Ka'aba was once an angel who reminded Adam of his initial covenant with God at the time of the betrayal. After the tragic event, God sent from Paradise this very angel, in the form of a white pearl, toward Adam. Adam saw this marvelous white gem but did not recognize it. For him, it was only a stone. Now, in the ritual of recovery, the Pearl speaks and reminds Adam (the pilgrim) of the initial covenant with God and that Satan had blotted out the memory that Allah was meant to be a companion of humankind, not apart. Now remembering this ancient fact, Adam (the pilgrim) weeps and kisses the Pearl, thus renewing his agreement and promise. God then once again gives the Pearl an appearance of a stone, which Adam is to carry on his shoulder. Adam and pilgrim are now on the journey to restore the Stone, once again black as it is in its concrete manifestation. Since the Stone is heavy, Adam and the angel take turns carrying it until they arrive at Mecca and the Black Stone is once again embedded in the corner of the Temple. Along with the Secret of the Black Stone is that of the White Pearl, which I discuss on page 24.

The recovery of connection with God is known in all faiths, particularly monotheistic ones. Islam contributes a most poignant reading here, in that it is understood, once more, that God is to accompany us on our path to discover and live what we are uniquely and what we are meant to be. Our foolishness is the belief that we can do so without God. Our initial rebellion, therefore, was undertaken in the erroneous belief that we could achieve selfhood without God.

The symbols of the divine as Stone and Pearl are well-known to modern students of psychology and alchemy. They carry that image of the divine embedded in matter itself, being both the most long-lasting element that we know (stone), linking with eternity, and the most beautifully rounded and fascinating (pearl). So God is both outside the stone and in the stone; a paradox of opposites.

The Fourth Devotional Visitation

Now that Adam and pilgrim are worthy to enter the Temple, the ritual continues. Gabriel, the angel of knowledge or gnosis as well as healing, accompanies Adam to Mecca. Reunited with God, the angel, too, is his companion. On the path to Mecca they pass Mina once again, but this time the symbol of "desire" is touched because Adam has now attained the goal of his very desire, namely reunion with God. Once in the Mina valley, however, an important rite remains. The pilgrim is to make a gesture of defiance at a figure that represents Iblis (Satan), by throwing stones (*jimrah*) at it. This is the last moment in which Iblis-Satan can try to triumph over the pilgrim once again by making him stop at the awareness of being carried away. The pilgrim needs to be annihilated (*fana*) to himself, which means that instead of being absolved of egocentricity, the ego is now in danger of being exalted to the status of the absolute. The pilgrim must even annihilate his annihilation! This means that he must refuse to so consolidate himself to the degree that he might once again fail to keep company with his divine Companion. In other words, he now must maintain the mystery of his bi-unity with God, without becoming either exalted (ego-inflated) or separated again.

Once more we witness a profound realization of the human difficulty of staying united or even connected with the divine, walking on the path of our life and growth, without succumbing to arrogance and pride and thus bringing a parting of the ways. It is notable that the "stone," symbol of the Self, is again involved. This time the pilgrim uses it to defend himself from further blandishments of Satan, the dark side of the divine, which employs ever more subtle ways of telling Adam (human and pilgrim) that he is capable of being quite alone and like God. This was Satan's initial rebellion, was it not?

Then Iblis departs and the angel takes Adam (the pilgrim) to the Temple, where he is ordered to walk around it seven times.[4] This is the culmination of the ritual, known to everyone from those spectacular aerial views of that circumambulation, seen in films. The pilgrims now understand and undertake the journey from God, in the company of God, toward created beings. This completes the journey of repair of the ego's separation from God, in which, as we shall next see, angels invisibly construct the temple in the heart.

The Secret of the White Pearl

The foregoing is the Secret of the White Pearl, the heart and center of the personal Ka'aba, restored to the radiance of its original form after having been the Black Stone embedded in the material temple. Thus the Black Stone is the secret of the Temple and the secret of humankind, which consists in the building up of one's own inner form, the "body of light," as it is called, *malakut* or "Temple of Light." This construction is the spiritual task also found in disciplines such as Kabbalah in Jewish mysticism and in the Kundalini Yoga of Hinduism. We also know it in the alchemical process revealed in psychological work. It is in Islam, however, that we uniquely see this particular construction of the inner Temple of Light as a collective effort, the Divine Among facilitating the Divine Within.

Now, when we have a chance to gaze, once more, on those aerial views of the masses of faithful Muslims circumambulating the Temple of Ka'aba, we can understand this impressive and even frightening vision, in its massiveness and grandeur, more deeply. It is a journey of the soul to reunite with God, taken both individually and collectively. This can, indeed, be something that is no longer so strange and foreign.

Notes

[1] Henry Corbin, *Temple and Contemplation* (London: KPI and Islamic Publications, 1986), pp. 245–253.

[2] Corbin, *Temple and Contemplation*, p. 247.

[3] Corbin, *Temple and Contemplation*, p. 247.

[4] Corbin, *Temple and Contemplation*, p. 251.

CHAPTER 3

Divine Within:
The Zen Oxherding
Pictures

The Divine Within is addressed in most world religions, as well as among shamans in all cultures, in the form of guidelines for individuals on the spiritual path. We shall examine one shaman path in chapter 11, but I want to begin the exploration of the Within with an example from Zen Buddhism. We all—in the East and West—are blessed by having the path to enlightenment demonstrated to us in a series of woodcuts, accompanied by short poems and commentaries, by Kaku-an Shi-en, a spiritual genius who lived in 15th-century China (other versions of this series go back as far as 1278).

I first happened upon these wonderful pictures in 1960. I had been back in America for just a year, following the completion of my analytic training in Zurich, and was suffering doubts and dryness in my native land, arid Southern California. Furthermore, I was not at all sure that I could practice the introverted depth analysis that I had been trained to do in Switzerland in my highly extraverted home country. In my parched spiritual condition, I chanced upon a book by the illustrious Japanese master, Daisetz Suzuki,[1] which described the training of a Zen Buddhist monk, including these centuries-old illustrations and poems. This encounter was like the discovery of a marvelously refreshing well in midst of this desert. I was impressed by the similarities and differences between this group of pictures and those of the medieval German alchemical series (done a century later), the *Rosarium Philosophorum*, which Jung used to shed light on the transference in analysis and the individuation process.[2] I shall discuss the latter work later on, in chapter 6, but here I will occasionally show how these two works help us understand comparisons between the Eastern and Western psyche (see figs. 26, 27, and 29–37).[3]

First of all, we note that there are 10 pictures in both sets, just as there are ten "emanations" or sephiroth in Kabbalah. The number 10 is often seen as a principle of totality or completion, a symbol of unity that is called "God" or "divinity" in the West and "Self" in the East. True enough, there are other numerical sequences representing this process, such as the twelve-step programs in Alcoholics Anonymous and other addiction groups, and the Stations of the Cross for Jesus' spiritual path, but 10 links specifically with both unity (one) and transcendence (zero). This combination seems to go beyond contrasts between East and West, perhaps touching a deeper level in the psyche itself where both attitudes can find common ground. That 10 unites one plus two plus three plus four is a numinous fact in itself, isn't it?

When we look at the structure of the pictures generally, however, we immediately notice a difference between the *Rosarium* and Zen. The Western alchemical pictures have no frame at all, in contrast to the oxherding pictures, which use both an outer square and an inner circle to contain the content and action. It seems to me that this reflects the actual social conditions in relation to the spiritual path that prevailed at the time the pictures were created. In the East, the individual path to enlightenment was not only permitted but encouraged, via the use of meditation, and Suzuki even comments on some of the pictures as illustrating the hazards in this activity. If one pursues this meditative path in the manner given, fully in consonance with the prevailing religion, then the desired result will occur. This is in contrast to alchemical work, which was deemed secret and even dangerous by the Christian culture. The alchemical path was seen as the pursuit of the occult, something that was rejected as purely materialistic (turning base matter into gold, for instance). For many alchemists, however, their aim was nothing less than the transformation of both gross matter and themselves. They wanted to redeem the sparks of the divine that had fallen into the laboratory chemicals and their own souls, as well.

This is further demonstrated in the very first picture of the *Rosarium* (see page 118), where the very problem of the "vessel"—namely that which is to be the containing image for such a process—appears at the outset: a Mercurial fountain is shown into which waters flow and from which they arise, while the"framing"is provided by snakes spitting smoke, along with stars, sun, and moon—all natural powers. No person is shown at the beginning here, in contrast to our oxherder. This immediately hints to us what is afoot: what or whom is to be transformed? In Zen, it is clearly the person who is to undergo change and enlightenment; in alchemy we don't know if it is the divine in matter itself or the soul of the alchemist. This is an important difference and one that we will address once again when we study the Divine Between.

The presence of the person is also a crucial difference between the sets of pictures. A single human being is present throughout the Eastern series, with the notable and important exception of the last three pictures, with meanings that we shall consider. The Western series, on the other hand, after the beginning "vessel" is presented, shows the continuing vicissitudes of the relationship between a king and queen, culminating in their union as a hermaphrodite at the end. In the oxherding series, we are presented with an ordinary mortal, until he temporarily vanishes in picture 8 (page 53), only to reemerge at the end in picture 10 (page 60), transformed, old, but full of the life and vitality of an enlightened man.

We can clearly see the complementary nature of this process as grasped by two worldviews. In the Eastern one, contained and understood by the general religious consciousness of the day, there is the task of the ordinary person to achieve enlightenment and we are shown how this is done. In the other worldview—secret, apart, and not even knowing for

certain what one is about—there gradually emerges a knowledge that the person is a vessel for the union of opposites
in the psyche (as Jung discovered), and that this process of
individuation is one that requires relationship as well as self-
transformation in isolation.

Realizing this difference, we can note how the two sets or
processes end. In the West, there is unity, one androgynous
creature. In the East, the lonely young man, after long work
with himself, finally joins other people in ordinary life (winebibbers, laborers, prostitutes, etc.). At the end, he even meets a
young man looking quite like he did at the beginning!

Such contrasts evoke images. In the East, it seems (at least
in Buddhism; Hinduism has a somewhat different character,
as we shall see later on), the seeker on the spiritual path
meditates, alone. He seeks advice from a master, may even
live in a monastery for a time, but ultimately he meditates
alone. Modern Westerners, seek psychotherapy, for example,
and the process of individuation is very much felt in the
context of the analytic relationship. Indeed the very con
tent of the transformational process in deep therapy reveals
itself—unexpectedly for the founders of this discipline—in
the relationship itself, the transference. So the human being
transforms himself/herself and returns to the world; or the
human being finds herself/himself only in relation to another
and thus heals the fragmentation of the soul. It is striking
that the complementarity of the psyche was revealing itself
in this nascent manner in 15th-century China and Japan and
16th-century Europe. Perhaps this "other" renaissance of the
soul was going on when the outer world was at the same
time being "discovered" and "experimented" with by Western
explorers and scientists. The East, though, continued with
its own age-old, more introverted experimentation with the
psyche. Now, four and five hundred years later, in addition
to experimenting, are we not working on a world unity that
will encompass both East and West, spirit and matter, divine
and mortal, inner and outer, Self and God?

Another distinction between the oxherding sequence and
the *Rosarium* further addresses the issue of "persons." In the

East, there is no female in the pictures; in the West, the feminine has equal importance. How many women meditated, visited gurus, and sought enlightenment in 15th-century Asia? Women were religious, to be sure, in the sense of pursuing the Divine Among, and there were always some Zen priestesses, for example, but mostly this was a man's work. But was alchemy so different? There were surely some female alchemists, and Jung intuits—rightly, I think—that there was often some form of woman companion to match the image of the *soror mystica*, but we do not know for certain. In the pictures, the feminine principle itself is assumed in the East (in the various images of circle, nature, moon, etc.) but is not personified, whereas in the West the feminine is present both symbolically and actually as queen. Perhaps it has been and remains part of the West's gift to ultimately relate to the feminine principle by having a woman as an equal, participatory partner. We do know, however, that the pictures do not portray merely the man's spiritual path, East or West, but reveal the soul in both its masculine and feminine characteristics. Whether a future "series" is devised, by spiritual Buddhist women and men, with more differentiated male/female images, may be the work of the new millennium. Until then, it behooves us all, men and women, East and West, to make use of and integrate what has already been achieved by all those laboring, loving individuals in both world hemispheres who persisted on the spiritual paths despite frustration and failure.

Searching for the Ox

The beast has never gone astray, and what is the use of searching for him? The reason why the oxherd is not on intimate terms with him is because the oxherd himself has violated his own inmost nature. The beast is lost, for the oxherd has himself been led out of the way through his deluding senses. His home is receding farther away from him, and byways and crossways are ever confused. Desire for gain and fear of loss burn like fire: ideas of right and wrong spring up like a phalanx.

Figure 6. Oxherding picture 1. All of the Oxherding pictures are from Suzuki, Manual of Zen Buddhism, *plates II-XI.*

Alone in the wilderness, lost in the jungle, the boy is
    searching, searching!
The swelling waters, the far-away mountains, and the
    unending path;
Exhausted and in despair, he knows not where to go,
He only hears the evening cicadas singing in the maple-
    woods.[4]

These 500-year-old words of Kaku-an sound very modern,
indeed, don't they? The complaint of this Asian youth is very

much like that of a modern person who, not believing in anything, has "lost his soul," as Jung expressed it, and is searching
for it here, there, and everywhere. But what is it exactly that he
is searching for? The Zen master Suzuki tells us that it is the
Self, which is the center and higher authority within, or the
totality of his being, which is here portrayed as an animal. He
also tells us that the word for "ox" in Chinese, *niu*, designates
the bovine family generally—cow, ox, and bull—of no specific
gender. We know that such an animal is also sacred in India
and compared to the Self or, as we in the West might say,
the Divine Within. We also know that such a reference to the
divine as animal is to be found in many traditions, such as
the Lamb in Christianity.

How can it be that the young man (ourselves) is estranged
from the Self, himself? "The beast has never gone astray,"
says the text, and Suzuki, agreeing, tells us that, "owing
to our intellectual delusions, we are led to imagine (the
Self) has disappeared from our sight."[5] Jungian psychology
can help us understand this paradox. The original Self, of
course, is always there; it is the "face before we were born,"
or the potential wholeness from which we come at birth
and to which we both return and achieve consciously with
hard work. But it is also something from which we can be
estranged, just as we can be cut off from our animal nature,
as implied in the oxherding pictures. Our modern rational-
ist delusion is the belief that reason and external evidence
provide the only source of truth; such a prejudice separates
us from our animal nature, which reveals its wisdom in our
instincts. We thus endure a kind of deadness, cut off from
vitality and spontaneity, or else we are split and experience
mind and body as separated. So, if our medieval poet tells
us something that is also quite up to date, perhaps we are
seeing the human condition in any epoch, particularly one
in which there is need for renewal. Even better than that,
we are perhaps shown how anyone can begin the spiritual
path at any time.

Kaku-an tells us about the psychic content of such a
soul who is confused and knows he is lost but has no

sense of direction. "Desire for gain and fear of loss burn like fire," he tells us; "ideas of right and wrong spring up like a phalanx." Again, what insight! Desire, competition, and yearning for material gain is our plague. We are wild, undisciplined animals, living in an urban jungle, far from home, our origin in wholeness. Along with that, we are judgmental and rigid, ever evaluating Self and others, finding them wanting, enjoying neither compassion nor rest. Freud saw this as the battle of superego versus id, the source of our neurotic discontent, and was pessimistic about the outcome for civilization. The oxherding pictures, however, are more optimistic, even in this first picture, when the poet tells us that the lost youth hears "the evening cicadas singing in the maple-woods."

What is this cicada if not the voice of Nature Herself, chirping Her age-old tune of joy and happiness, of oneness and harmony with Herself? Our Western version of the cicada, the cricket, "was much esteemed in antiquity,"[6] and brought either good or bad fortune, depending upon our attitude toward it. The cricket was a personification of the spirit of the house, especially the hearth, and is a symbol of healing and order, for oneness or union of animal and man (insect and warming center of the civilized house). Depending on our attitude, we can be in tune or not. Our suffering youth, hearing the cicada, is given an intuition, a promise of future wholeness, in a tiny, hardly-visible form.

Other symbols in the poem speak to us also. "Swollen waters," a symbol of a filled-up unconscious, ready to disgorge its contents, frightening but promising renewal, is a typical image of dreams at the outset of a spiritual journey. The flood awaiting us in our own soul compensates our very barrenness, calling us to attend to it in dream and fantasy. "Far-away mountains" is a well-known symbol of the individuation process, the struggle to climb to a higher vision, to master one's self and to find where the divine lives, on top of the mountain. Where God or the Self lives there is higher consciousness and greater vision. Finally, the "unending path" is an ancient symbol of the "way," the process of moving toward the treasure hard-to-obtain. All this does the poet reveal to us, in the very first picture of this spiritual path.

Seeing the Traces

By the aid of the sutras and by inquiring into the doctrines, he has come to understand something, he has found the traces. He now knows that vessels, however varied, are all of gold, and that the objective world is a reflection of the Self. Yet, he is unable to distinguish what is good from what is not, his mind is still confused as to truth and falsehood. As he has not yet entered the gate, he is provisionally said to have noticed the traces.

By the stream and under the trees, scattered are the traces of the lost;
The sweet-scented grasses are growing thick—did he find the way?
However remote over the hills and far-away the beast may wander,
His nose reaches the heavens and none can conceal it.[7]

Kaku-an now tells us how one can proceed on the path of spiritual growth when confused and tormented: study! Given our ignorance, we must study the sutras and doctrines. We need to read the Bible—Hebrew and Christian—the Koran, the sutras of the East, and the commentaries. We will thereby "understand something," find the traces. Traces of what, you may ask? Well, how the Spirit has presented Itself in various epochs and climes, deposited Its wisdom in the holy texts and commentaries. This way we will glimpse something of the mysteries, even of those "vessels"—the religions and belief systems—in which we can no longer or never have been able to find sustenance or answers to our questions. By studying and comparing, we discover that all vessels, all systems and carriers of the divine are made of gold, are holy and valuable. We may also discover that no one of them is exclusively golden, even though when one is in the midst of the powerful

Figure 7. Oxherding picture 2.

experience formulated by that faith, it may seem so. Yet it is the experience itself that is convincing, and at this point one has only noticed the "traces." We are only at Oxherding Picture Number 2, after all, and this is modern enough!

Yet picture 2 teaches us something else, equally modern, even postmodern, for our now environmentally sensitive psyches: "The objective world is a reflection of the Self." That same world which deceived us is also a representation of the Self we are seeking; the divine is not only within (just as the Rainmaker Model suggested). God's body, so to speak, is "out there" for all to see, and resides also in the confusion and darkness, hatred and division, as well as in the wonder and harmony. We have learned something, it seems, but Kaku-an assures us that we still do not know the truth of thinking or the values of feeling. We are not yet in touch with our own truth, values, and Self, which, after all, is quite personal to us, as well as connecting us to a transcendent and universal dimension.

I am reminded of the journey of a modern Jewish man, one who said the ancient Kaddish each day in honor of his recently deceased father, during which he also noticed that, "A man may see God and still speak only for himself."[8] Perhaps it is peculiarly our syncretistic time that can permit such realizations.

We may have to wander by the stream and under the trees, as the poem says, and lose ourselves in the sweet palm-grasses and the swamps of our desire and fantasy, in order to begin to reach our own "ox." That is what Jung suggested—that one's fantasy and dream life is where our ox is to be found. It may also be that the ox wants to be found and has its own motives. Suzuki says that the Self is everywhere and it is foolish to even begin to search, while Jung thought that the divine needed human companionship for its own development—the divine that resides in our own souls, that is. At this point, however, we, like the oxherd, only speculate, see traces.

Seeing the Ox

The boy finds the way by the sound he hears; he sees thereby into the origin of things, and his senses are in harmonious order. In all his activities, it is manifestly present. It is like the salt in water and the glue in colour. [It is there though not distinguishable as an individual entity.] When the eye is properly directed, he will find that it is no other than himself.

On a yonder branch perches a nightingale cheerfully singing;

Figure 8. Oxherding picture 3.

The sun is warm, and a soothing breeze blows, on the bank
the willows are green;
The ox is there all by himself, nowhere is he to hide himself;
The splendid head decorated with stately horns—what
painter can reproduce him?[9]

Now, having wandered in our unknowingness, after reading
and reflecting, we go with the oxherd beyond seeing the traces
and come to the experience itself—we see the ox. Suzuki says

that is an "awakening to a new consciousness; it is the finding of the precious animal which is no other than the man himself."[10] Yet this finding, we already know—and the commentary tells us—was already present in everything our oxherd did and perceived; it was not distinguishable (the salt in water and glue in color) from the surroundings; it is that quality inherent in all things. Our oxherd knew this from reading but now he knows this directly, by the "sound he hears." What does he hear? Why, it is the Self or God, both personal and universal, and it is to be found within his own psyche. Kaku-an learns that "When the eye is properly directed, he will find that it is no other than himself." And what is it in himself that the ox represents? Is it not his dreams and fantasies, strivings and affects? And was it not the ox itself, the Self, which both summoned him and now reveals itself to him? I think so.

What, in those dreams and fantasies and desires, is actually revealed, we may ask? The poet speaks of the "splendid head decorated with stately horns," and that no painter could reproduce him. Our ox wears the beautiful crown of the divine, the horns of grandeur, and there is no way to show his image. This reminds us of the Torah commandment, enjoining us to produce no graven image of the divine, since this would limit its grandeur and could lead to false idols. Our modern Jewish seeker had another take on this question of images: "If God could be seen, we would do nothing but look. We would squander our lives on the contemplation of God."[11]

But we need to understand this unexpected image of the Self, all the same, and look at the picture itself. What we see there is no grand head, but a homely behind! No kingly, spiritual crown or impressive sound of voice do we see or hear, but the vulnerable place of man and beast, our hind-end. From that source comes our excreta, the parts of us that are rejected or unused, the "back-side" we cannot see, of which we are unconscious. It is our shadow, as Jung says, our own dark side, which is also often the first thing that is revealed when psychoanalysis is our spiritual path.

The rear end we discover, however, is not only our own, which we can apprehend all too painfully and sorrowfully, but that of the Self. The ox, after all, is not only our personal ox, but also the collective ox, the common content of the soul of us all. And now Master Kaku-an intuitively shows us that it is the dark side of the Self (of God, as we would say in the West) that is revealed as well, and this is not so clear to us when we read the sutras and study. It is only in our own struggle and pain, our dry meditation, anger, and discomfort, our bleak dreams and disgusting images that we come to our darkness and, at last, to the darkness of the divine as well. "The dark night of the soul," another seeker has told us, is essential before we can find the light. It is even, paradoxically, the light itself. So suggests this picture, too.

We have at last found the ox, anyway, and once seeing him we know that he arises from our inner search, our reflection and meditation, fantasy and dream. Knowing this, we can also rejoice in the warm sun and soothing breeze, the beauty of nature, for we are now in connection with the divine, found both in Nature and in our own nature. We share with the animals and plants a cleansing process, and we also partake of materiality and unknowingness. This realization, however, a gift to human beings alone, is the source of our spiritual struggle and path. No body, no true spirit; no shadow, no true light; no dark side of God, no real light side, either. With our awareness of these opposites, we can truly join what the artist and poet, in this picture, divergently presents. Together, it is the deeper truth.

Catching the Ox

Long lost in the wilderness, the boy has at last found the ox and his hands are on him. But, owing to the overwhelming pressure of the outside world, the ox is hard to keep under control. He constantly longs for the old sweet-scented field. The wild nature is still unruly, and altogether refuses to be broken. If the oxherd wishes to see the ox completely in harmony with himself, he has surely to use the whip freely.

Figure 9. Oxherding picture 4.

With the energy of his whole being, the boy has at last
   taken hold of the ox;
But how wild his will, how ungovernable his power!
At times he struts up a plateau,
When lo! he is lost again in a misty impenetrable
   mountain-pass.[12]

The hands of the youth are now upon the ox and the task
of training and discipline is upon us. Oh, how our desires
and our laziness are unruly! Our primitive nature refuses to
be broken. Suzuki thinks that pictures 5,6,7 are misleading,

that it is really not the animal that needs to be trained or broken, but our own animal nature.[13] This is surely true, but Jung has also shown us that our animal nature is an essential part of the Self. It, too, needs our ardent and careful attention, collectively, so that one day, perhaps, we shall once again be in harmony, just as we were when we were totally unconscious, long ago. After all, does not Buddhism see this in a similar way? At the beginning of the path, they say, trees are trees and mountains are mountains. Midway through the work, trees are no longer trees and mountains no longer mountains (everything becomes symbolized, we would say). But at the end, trees are once again trees and mountains are mountains, but in a new way. That new way is the happy harmony, but we are far from there right now.

We can say, though, that we face the paradox that the Self, God, is in all Nature, in its beauty and horror. It both transforms us and needs transforming (as will be more apparent when we look at the alchemical path).

Kaku-an tells us that the animal longs for the sweet-scented field, the old unconsciousness. The work is both against Nature, *contra naturam*, as alchemy tells us, and with Nature, which sets us upon this task as well. It is the hidden desire of the ox to be tamed and to tame us, and it is this insight that gives us permission to "use the whip freely," whether it is to maintain our meditative posture and no-mindedness, or restrain our greed and lust. Only this awareness, of commanding and obeying, keeps us from succumbing to the overweening pride, the hubris, of such an "unnatural" act.

Suzuki comments: "Heaven above, heaven below, I alone am the honored one."[14] We Westerners can remark, however, that we are honored, because we are called and addressed, and because we honor that which addresses and calls us. We must engage in our struggle with the energy of our whole being. It must command all of us. Do I seek my totality? Then I must give my totality. Even then, the ox vanishes and I must start again. On the path of individuation, upon the ascent to our largest vision, we lose the divine spark, the source of Nature within and beyond our self, but we continue to seek and civilize those bits of untamed nature that defy us, yet seek us, too. The work is hard, not only because of the ox and ourselves, but, as Kaku-an says, "the overwhelming pressure of the outside world." What a modern, enlightened insight from this 15th-century man! The divine we seek and struggle with inside ourselves also approaches us from outside, with the same demands, prohibitions, and blockages. But now we know that the place to look, even when disturbance comes from without, is within us, our own affects and ignorance, our own propensity to attract or be unable to cope with the demons coming from without.

Herding the Ox

When a thought moves, another follows, and then another—an endless train of thoughts is thus awakened. Through enlightenment, all this turns into truth; but falsehood asserts itself when confusion prevails. Things oppress us not because of an objective world, but because of a self-deceiving mind. Do not let the nose-string loose, hold it tight, and allow no vacillation.

The boy is not to separate himself with his whip and
   tether,
Lest the animal should wander away into a world of defile-
   ments;
When the ox is properly tended to, he will grow pure and
   docile;
Without a chain, nothing binding, he will by himself follow
   the oxherd.[15]

Picture 5 shows the ox, tamed, tempered, and tethered, following the oxherd and indicating success, but the words reveal continuing struggle. Thoughts move, confusion persists, the animal wanders away into defilement. Why, we wonder? Suzuki tells us that the "habit of intellectualization, or conceptualiza-

Figure 10. Oxherding picture 5.

tion, which has been going on ever since his 'loss of innocence,' is extremely difficult to get rid of. . . . The adjustment
will naturally take time."[16] This is helpful and enlightening. It
is intellectualization that has cut us off from our instinctual
nature, has resulted in a loss of innocence. Again, a paradox
emerges: we develop intellectually in order to advance our
consciousness, but to advance further we must return to our
non-thinking nature! This apparent regression is problematical.
Perhaps we could just give up and be an animal again (although
this would be repugnant to our differentiated consciousness),

but it is even harder to both return and advance, to recover our nature and tame it.

The difficulty and complexity of this struggle may be the reason why, in Kaku-an's series, six of the ten pictures, 60 percent of the process, portrays the image of dealing with the animal. Indeed, the name of the series itself, the Oxherding Pictures, tells us that the central problem in both enlightenment and individuation is the recovery and taming of our lost animal nature. Without this we may perhaps have a bodiless and false spirituality, fit only for those who have no stomach (*hara*) for the real thing. Later on, in discussing the final picture, I shall discuss this issue of the belly center and what it means. Here, as we confront the overwhelming importance of the ox, we understand that the main focus of consciousness on the Zen path is at the belly, the hara, where we touch life in its "isness."

We notice something more about this ox, now, that commands our attention: it has undergone a whitening. From its dark initial condition, it is now in a lightened state. That this is not just an accident of printing is shown by the fact that a related series of pictures (see Suzuki's *Manual of Zen Buddhism*, pp. 135–144) clearly expresses the process of the whitening of the ox. In that series, the whole process ends with an empty circle (an image which Kaku-an found insufficient to describe enlightenment). It is from this fact that we can clearly and unequivocally link the Zen enlightenment process with alchemical work. The alchemical transformation of the *nigredo* (darkening, unconsciousness) to *albedo* (whitening, cleansing) is described in detail in Jung's work,[17] showing us once more how a deep underlying need of advancing consciousness was going on at the outset of the modern era (since the 15th to 17th century) in both the East and the West.

We also see here a direct reference to the sitting (*zazen*) austerity of Buddhist discipline:"when a thought moves, another follows. . . ." Our associative mind takes us away from the necessary concentration on the moments of nothingness and stillness, the transcendence of enlightenment that we seek. How different is sitting and its aim of enlightenment, from our modern psychotherapy! Overcome free-association, says our Zen master. Go with free-association, says our Freudian analyst. Ignore the fantasies that arise and let them go by, says the Buddhist teacher. Focus on the fantasies and ultimately dialogue with them, says the Jungian analyst.

Does such instruction produce different results? It seems to. For the Freudian path (arduous daily sessions on the couch for years), we find the face after we were born, the childhood desires and terrors that are parent to where we are now. Our consciousness aims to overcome these traumas, to arrive at a full capacity to love and to work, to know the world and psyche without illusion. For the Buddhist (years of daily sitting), it is the face before we were born that we seek, to discover our unity with Nature and our seamless oneness with all life. For the Jungian (a lifelong path), it is both of these, ideally, the link with the collective psyche, outer and inner, and the discovery and relationship to our Self, the center and authority of the soul. Each of these paths is truly spiritual and valuable, "a treasure hard to attain," but only the latter two acknowledge it as such, as something more than overcoming neurosis.

Let us further consider Kaku-an's words. He tells us that the endless stream of associations "turns into truth" when enlightenment prevails, but this is not so when we are confused, uncentered, unknowing. So, it is not the content or the flow that deludes us, he informs us, but how we relate to it. When we are centered, all is in harmony; when we are not, confusion makes it all mere falsehood. Kaku-an is a great psychologist here. He is a combination cognitive behavioral psychologist, a Jungian, and, of course, a Buddhist. Would that we could achieve now what he saw five hundred years ago!

He also tells us that we are oppressed not by the outside world, but because of our own self-deceiving mind. Again, it is our attitude that is the source from which the confusion and trouble arise. These are hard words and wrong from an extraverted point-of-view (which sees the social order, capitalism, communism, the environment, etc. as the problem), but right for the introvert. Either way, Kaku-an shows us how we can independently deal with our own attitude, our own contribution to the oppression that falls upon us. If we can center ourselves, find the right relationship to "it," then we are all right. Sounds like the Rainmaker of our Taoist example, doesn't it? The medicine of "holding tight," allowing no vacillation, is not only an instruction in how to meditate effectively but also a statement of the psychological condition: hold tight to the Self as it manifests, within and without, and do not let go until resolution. This reminds us of Western images, such as Jacob wrestling all night with the angel of God or the Greek image of holding fast to the wildly changing manifestations of the demon until there is transformation.

This is the theme expressed beautifully in the poem: Do not separate from the Self, lest the animal wander away into defilement. When properly attended, the ox grows pure and docile, and finally, "without a chain, nothing binding, he will by himself follow the oxherd." What a promise this is, and what a task: struggle and relax, hold tight and let go! No wonder we drive ourselves crazy in the search for enlightenment and wholeness! But a hint is presented: the ox will come along by itself when the time is right. Ultimately, he needs no chain, only a relationship, and will join us this way because he wants to do this himself, for his own needs, and not only because of our efforts. Is this not also what Jung was hinting at when he suggested that the unconscious archetypes (the gods) need humankind too?

Coming Home on the Ox's Back

The struggle is over; the man is no more concerned with gain and loss. He hums a rustic tune of the woodman, he sings simple songs of the village-boy. Saddling himself on the ox's back, his eyes are fixed on things not of the earth, earthy. Even if he is called, he will not turn his head; however enticed, he will no more be kept back.

Riding on the animal, he leisurely wends his way home:
Enveloped in the evening mist, how tunefully the flute
   vanishes away!

Figure 11. Oxherding picture 6.

Singing a ditty, beating time, his heart is filled with a joy
   indescribable!
That he is now one of those who know, need it be told?[18]

Suddenly, we find that the boy has become a man. It is as if
one is a youth when beginning the struggle with the instincts
and becomes a man when one has satisfactorily adjusted to
them and to the world. This is certainly how it is to grow up
in society, but here we see that it is similar on the spiritual
path. For initiation into enlightenment, maturity of the soul
requires an inner struggle with our animal nature as a way to

selfhood. This is concluded only when harmony is achieved. Is this similar for women? Is one a girl until one has related fully to the instincts? It seems so; in most cultures, however, it is marriage and motherhood that brings maturity for women. Yet it is also apparent that relationship itself is one means of the larger spiritual path for women, in particular, and we shall see this more clearly when we address the Divine Between. But we can also note that even in Roman times, as Linda Fierz-David has shown,[19] women's mysteries included a similar struggle with passion and the inner animal world in order to come to maturity of soul (see chapter 10 on women's initiation).

Here we see the struggle has reached an apparent finality. The seeker is no longer concerned with gain and loss. What an achievement of mastery this is! In the West, are we ever freed from endless striving for this and that, our bottomless pit of desire, which Native Americans see as our "mad mind?" Here we can see the resolution as becoming in tune with our heart, maintaining a feeling for life and nature, singing the song of the village boy without being identified with it, namely not just being a boy but a man. Now we are simple again (a tree is once more a tree).

The man is saddled on the ox's back, in contact with his instinctual life and the divine itself, in harmony. His eyes are not fixed on the earth, however, he is free to follow heaven or earth, no longer enticed. The poem tells us that he finds his way home and it is clear that the animal leads the way. This is a special wonder for us Westerners. Our tradition of dealing with the animal can be seen in the bullfight. True enough, this is a spectacle and a ritual, not a sport. Also true is the fact that the matador's passion includes self-discipline and relationship to the bull. And finally, it is true that the ritual's depth implies that human and animal are one; when one kills the other, one is also sacrificing oneself, a last historical remnant of the great Mediterranean practice of such service to the Goddess. We are also reminded of the Mithraic mysteries of two thousand years ago, in which the hero sacrifices the bull of his own nature and carries it as a cornucopia of riches on his back.[20] The Mithraic religion rivaled early Christianity and was particularly popular among many Roman soldiers. Like us, they surely needed such discipline for their further development.

Perhaps this difference between East and West, however, riding the bull rather than sacrificing it, is an enlightening one for us. Until the modern age, China, Korea, and Japan turned within, sought perfection and differentiation in their own culture and time, and valued the taming of their own nature. We in the West, with our predatory birds (eagles) as national symbols, our sacrificing of animals to gods or God, turned our captured energy into conquest, victory over others, and subduing Nature, Itself. In the modern day, this, too, has changed. There is an increasingly intense plea to end bull sacrifice in the ring, to embrace vegetarianism, to give up the Western aim of missionizing and colonizing, to abjure our lust for endless domination, and finally, to end the drive toward conquest and to turn toward Self-transformation. In the East, there has been a dying of the tradition of Self-mastery and a turning toward outer achievement and the "isms" that the West has successfully pursued—often at the expense of Asians. Some say that Buddhism may be dying in the Orient but is alive and well in California, Colorado, and Europe. In the end, we learn from each other and perhaps a synthesis is now building.

Let us return to the words: the heart of the man is filled with a joy indescribable and even the ox seems to wear a smile, head tilted upward as if listening to his rider's song. Their mutual joy is great and harmony is achieved. Yet even this rapturous condition is not the end, as we shall now see.

The Ox Forgotten, Leaving the Man Alone

The dharmas are one and the ox is symbolic. When you know that what you need is not the snare or set-net but the hare or fish, it is like gold separated from the dross, it is like the moon rising out of the clouds. The one ray of light serene and penetrating shines even before days of creation.

Figure 12. Oxherding picture 7.

Riding on the animal, he is at last back in his home.
Where lo! the ox is no more; the man alone sits serenely.
Though the red sun is high up in the sky, he is still quietly
  dreaming.
Under a straw-thatched roof are his whip and rope idly
  lying.[21]

The poem both carries us onward and links us back to picture
6 (fig. 11 on page 47), whereas poems of the earlier pictures
only took us beyond the image at hand. After the fulfillment
of "coming home on the ox's back," we now see where the

oxherd's higher "home" lies, atop the mountain. This high point is a symbol of his achievement of enlightenment; he has "attained," as the Hindus are fond of saying. The poem tells us that now "the ox is no more." Does this mean that he is dead, vanished, or gone out of sight, as in the earlier picture? No, the ox is now integrated into our oxherd, or is perhaps transformed into the red sun or moon rising out of the clouds. It is "forgotten." Kaku-an's words tell us that the ox is symbolic (and this modern kind of consciousness is already known in the 15th century!) and that the *dharmas* (justice, law, and practice) are one, unified. We thus learn that our struggle with instinct, desire, and passion, with gain and loss, was all a vehicle, a method, perhaps even a "snare" or "set-net" (a way to trap the desired content). All this was real enough when we were struggling, but now it is just illusion, as we sit quite serenely atop this mountain. We now know that theories, techniques, even images, are but vehicles and what we want is the "hare" or "fish," the reality of the experience in its definiteness and concreteness. When we know this, it is like separating gold from dross, an alchemical transformation of the valued part from all the surrounding detritus. East meets West in transformation imagery.

Our man sits in meditation, even in prayer perhaps, with his clasped hands before him, as he gazes up at the "moon rising out of the clouds." He has not only "come home," as in the previous picture, but now is "at home," at one with that "lesser light" (the moon) which can even be the greater. He has forgotten the ox, his struggle, and even what he was searching for. Here it is. He now has it—or even is it.

But the red sun is high up in the sky; consciousness shines brightly around him. He is still quietly dreaming, at one with the inner world as a friend, not a foe. His consciousness is now like "one ray of light serene and penetrating"; it is the consciousness that was there always, "even before creation." He is once more connected with the Self-potential, the face before he was born, now known as the Self-actual, as a presence. The Self is no longer experienced at the animal level, something that we shall also find when we examine the Hindu kundalini series later on (chapter 4). This level of consciousness does not require a bodily basis, it is psyche transcending. Sun and moon, those polar twins known in the alchemical series, are also present, but the process is still not over.

The Ox and Man Both Gone out of Sight

All confusion is set aside, and serenity alone prevails; even the idea of holiness does not obtain. He does not linger about where the Buddha is, and as to where there is no Buddha he speedily passes by. When there exists no form of dualism, even a thousand-eyed one fails to detect a loophole. A holiness before which birds offer flowers is but a farce.

All is empty—the whip, the rope, the man, and the ox;
Who can ever survey the vastness of heaven?
Over the furnace burning ablaze, not a flake of snow can fall;
When this state of things obtains, manifest is the spirit of the ancient master.[22]

What more might we in the West expect from such a process? In picture 6, we found serenity and oneness with our animal nature along with union with the longed-for God-image itself. In picture 7, we went even beyond instinct and found serenity in stillness. But now, "serenity alone prevails; even the idea of holiness does not obtain." This is a truly Eastern notion: a development beyond the holy. It is a condition in which there is no longer any worship or seeking at all, not even after the divine! We no longer seek the Buddha and we quickly move away from places or conditions where there is no Buddha. A true selflessness is to be found here.

Suzuki quotes for us, in connection with this picture, a Western mystic, Meister Eckhart, in which the latter says, "He alone hath true spiritual poverty who wills nothing, knows nothing, desires nothing."[23] Even the desire to fulfill the will of God is an obstacle here. Now we understand the statement,

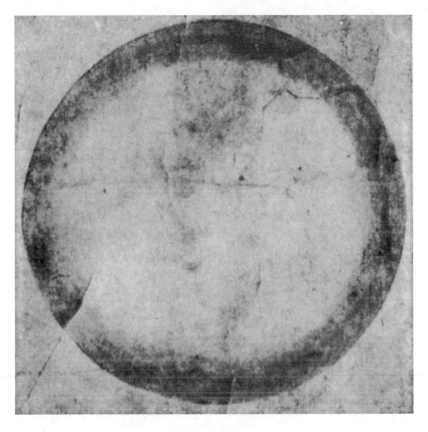

Figure 13. Oxherding picture 8.

"serenity alone prevails;" it is when the ego is gone. Not only the ox, but now the man, too, has "gone out of sight."

This is Suzuki's "second awakening" and is symbolized by the circle, which is empty and has no limits because it is not circumscribed, has no boundaries, even no actual center. He says: "In spite of its eternally being empty (*sunya*) [it is] in possession of infinite values. It never exhausts itself."[24] For us in the West, that definition is the mystic understanding of God: God is a circle whose center is everywhere and circumference nowhere. So here, East and West meet, not in the definition of the divine, but in the experience of it. All numbers meet in the number beyond number: zero, the circle.

How are we to understand this psychologically? The Jung of the 1930s commented that the Eastern way of saying that the ego is totally obliterated made no sense to him.[25] Who was it, he asked, that experienced this divine, if not the ego? If Jung seems to be correct here, how can we reply to the statement that when there is no form of dualism, no one, not even a thousand-eyed one, can find a loophole? Don't we need some observing consciousness to report the experience? The resolution of this paradox, I think, comes from the poem.

"All is empty," says the poet, "the whip, the rope, the man and the ox." All partake of *sunya*, emptiness, and none is more or less important than the other is. All, in short, are part of a whole, which itself is nothing and everything, an ever-replenishing source yet empty in itself. Without all the parts, the whole is nothing; without the whole, the part is nothing. Together, they are mutually dependent, are both everything and nothing. Translated into psychological language, we can say that the symbol of wholeness, the Self, is the mandala, the circle. It contains the ego and therefore the distinction between them vanishes. I am both aware of myself as an entity, yet realize myself as part of a larger whole within, around, and encompassing me. This is the "second awakening."

"Who can ever survey the vastness of heaven?" asks the poet. Who, indeed, except heaven itself? Psychologically we would say that heaven, or the Self, is doing the surveying and that the ego is its vehicle ("God sees through my eyes," says the Sufi). The blazing furnace melts any possibility of separation and when the ego is in service of that wholeness, "manifest is the spirit of the ancient master." Ego and Self are now one.

Returning to the Origin, Back to the Source

From the very beginning, pure and immaculate, the man has never been affected by defilement. He watches the growth of things, while himself abiding in the immovable serenity of nonassertion. He does not identify himself with the maya-like transformations [that are going on around him] nor has he any use of himself [which is artificiality]. The waters are blue, the mountains are green; sitting alone, he observes things undergoing changes.

To return to the Origin, to be back at the Source—already
  a false step this!
Far better is it to stay at home, blind and deaf, and without
  much ado;
Sitting in the hut, he takes no cognisance of things outside,
Behold the streams flowing—whither nobody knows; and
  the flowers vividly red—for whom are they?[26]

How can one go beyond the mandala, the condition where ego and Self are one? Indeed, there are oxherding series where the process ends in just such a condition, *sunyata* prevails; emptiness and fullness in the circle is the end of all. Yet Kaku-an takes us further, there is more to this process. What do we see in the next stage? An image of Nature, Itself, a blossoming tree with a twisted trunk, two circles embedded in it. We are shown, I think, that Nature is beyond the abstraction of the circle. The fullness of life in the blossoms and the deadness and emptiness of the circles show us the opposites united in the very ongoing life of the tree.

The symbol of the tree is also one that transcends differences between East and West. For us in the West, the image of the Tree of Life in the Hebrew Bible reminds us that we were cut off from knowledge of our immortality "in the beginning," when we fell out of Paradise by eating of that other Tree. A sword of fire separated us from it. But Jewish mysticism tells us, in the Kabbalah, that we can come once again to that precious tree when we discover, as Jesus also told us in the New Testament, "ye are Gods," that God and person are one.

The tree is also a world tree: in Hinduism it is quite central and among the Norse Pagans it is known as Ygdrassil. That tree, with its roots going deeply into the earth and ascending into heaven, is a symbol for our own

Figure 14. Oxherding picture 9.

individuation. It is wholeness taking on organic life at a level even deeper than the animal. Heroes are born from that tree; gods die on it; we all live in it. So, the tree appears to be an even higher form than the circle: we rise in consciousness, attain to the circles of sun and moon, yet fall to earth in the play of life in that seamless whole of the tree. Blossoms and dead wood, beauty and emptiness, it is a living symbol of wholeness.

Suzuki does not see it this way, however. Once again, he thinks that we get a distorted idea from the view of Origin or Source, leading us into dualism, with the man unattached and watching maya-like transformations going on around him. He says:

> For the man will never be found "sitting in his hut." Not only does he take cognizance of things going on outside, but he is the things, he is the outside and the inside. Nor is he deaf and blind. He sees perfectly well even into the interior of an atom and explodes with it wherever it may fall regardless of its effects. But at the same time he sheds tears over human ignorance, over human follies and infirmities; he hastens to repair all the damage he produced, he contrives every possible method to prevent the recurrence. He is forever kept busy doing this, undoing that.[27]

What a heartfelt commitment to human action! Even the enlightened one endlessly makes blunders, causes damage, and must spend half of his time repairing the evil he has done personally, as well as mourning and having compassion for human folly. One thinks of when and where Suzuki said these words. It was in Switzerland in 1954, not so long after the terrible events at Hiroshima and Nagasaki. Could not this have been in the back of his mind when he spoke of not being deaf and blind, seeing perfectly well "even into the interior of an atom"? I think that Suzuki was quite aware of the paradox of human good and evil in a personal way, when he added that the enlightened one "explodes with it wherever it may fall, regardless of its effects." That he can rise above the horror done to his people (perhaps also not forgetting the horrors they permitted and performed), yet not be blind to mankind's follies in general, is great enough; to take on his own charge of repairing the damage he, himself, has done puts him into a deep brotherly relationship with the best that the West has to offer. I am thinking, in particular, of Jung's vision, after the Holocaust and World War II, of humanity's deepening awareness of the problem of good and evil in the divine itself, along with the necessity of individual consciousness in this struggle.[28] Perhaps Suzuki's passion is really less connected with this picture than with picture 10 (fig. 15, page 60), where, as we shall see, the man who is "forever kept busy doing this, undoing that" is just what the symbol of the old one who is "daubed with mud and ashes" means.

Kaku-an tells us that the man has never been affected by defilement and that even the process itself may be an illusion, that we never left "home." Not only is it better to be blind and deaf, to stay home and not complain, but even to have the audacity to start on the spiritual path to enlightenment is presumptive or foolish. What does this mean? Have we not, on this path, struggled with the sutras, found the ox, disciplined him, given him up, sacrificed our ego, done all those important things that have shown us the truth? Apparently not. The waters are blue, the mountains are green, and "things undergo change." Maybe that is the point: changes are just happening, even those effects we think we are accomplishing. It is Nature, Itself, shown here as the tree, that is doing them. Nature, including our nature, is expressing itself and we are foolish enough to think that we did it, our ego lays claim to special achievement. The poet says that the whole process is that of Nature, Itself. Alchemy strikes at the same wisdom when it says that nature battles nature, nature overcomes nature. Then, we ourselves are part of that natural process of life finding itself, becoming conscious of itself. We glimpse a deep hint, here, of the vast unfolding of evolution in every way, including the most recent realization that consciousness itself evolves.

Picture 8 (page 53) told us that in the circle, "manifest is the spirit of the ancient master." Here, in picture 9, perhaps we can say, "manifest is the spirit of Nature, Herself." This is an appreciation of the feminine at a deeper level: only when the circle is felt in Nature, when wholeness goes from abstract to concrete, does the process approach completion. For whom are the flowers red, the Koan asks? Why, for Nature, Herself!

One more thing needs to be addressed. It is the puzzling statement that follows the understandable, "He does not identify himself with the maya-like transformations (that are going on around him). . ." After this comes, "nor has he any use for himself (which is artificiality)." What does this mean, to have no use of one's self? Is it a repeat of the notion that the ego is valueless in itself, is only a part of the whole, or is something else intended?

A possible answer may be found in the Zen story of the tree that remained in a forest when all others were cut down. When queried as to how it survived when the rest were cut down, it replied that it "had no use for itself." All the other trees were beautiful, had good wood in them, were needed for houses, etc., but this tree was neither beautiful nor valuable. It was "unworthy," the tale says. It was of no value to anyone, so it survived. The deeper meaning may be that the tree was only of value to itself. So, does the man who has no use of himself know that he is only of value to himself, or better to his Self? This reminds me of the statement, "What others think of me is none of my business," a variation of the paradox that being of no use and of full value can occur at the same time. Such truths are relative to time and person: balm or poison depending on the moment. Yet we are of use only for Nature . . . or God. Thus, at the highest level, East and West meet.

Entering the City with Bliss-Bestowing Hands

His thatched cottage gate is closed, and even the wisest know him not. No glimpses of his inner life are to be caught; for he goes on his own way without following the steps of the ancient sages. Carrying a gourd he goes out into the market, leaning against a staff he comes home. He is found in company with wine-bibbers and butchers, he and they are all converted into Buddhas.

Bare-chested and bare-footed, he comes out into the
   market place;
Daubed with mud and ashes, how broadly he smiles!
There is no need for the miraculous power of the gods;
For he touches, and lo! the dead trees are in full bloom.[29]

Figure 15. Oxherding picture 10.

We come now, as Suzuki says, to "the final stage of the drama."
For Suzuki, the final stage is that the cottage is not only shut,
but cottage and gate are gone. No one can locate where the
enlightened one is. "Yet he is ubiquitous; he is seen in the
marketplace, he is seen on farms, he is seen with the children,
with men and women, he is seen with the birds and animals,
among the rocks and mountains. Anything he touches grows
into full bloom, even the dead are awakened."[30]

In short, the final stage for Suzuki is one in which the
enlightened one returns to the world as an ordinary man,
but he has bliss-bestowing hands. He contrasts this bare-

chested and barefooted figure in our picture with the painting by Michelangelo in the Sistine Chapel of Christ in the
Last Judgment. The latter, says Suzuki, "is almost impossible
to approach, much less touch, for he is majestically and vig-
orously passing out judgments. If you come near him, you
would surely be torn to pieces and thrown into eternal fire."[31]
This is quite different from the bodhisattva in picture 10, who
is so genial. What a difference between these two images of
the Enlightened One in the world! Perhaps Suzuki does not
understand (or perhaps understands too well?) our Western
struggle with duality, since that same Christ, full of judgment
in the Apocalypse of John (like his Father in the Hebrew Bible),
is also the Lamb. The West has its own variety of images of
enlightenment, but we can also understand how an Easterner
can contrast a Zen image with one of ours, in which our version comes out second best.

The difference, perhaps, is in the degree and quality of
humanity that emerges. Our usual Western image of the God-
Man may be all too kind, redemptive, and far from ordinary
man, not subject to the passions that plague the rest of us.
He longs to be with ordinary people, but we have the feeling
that even though he also seeks the company of "wine-bibbers
and butchers," like the Eastern Buddha-Man, he is unlikely to
get drunk or enjoy women in a carnal way. The center for the
Eastern enlightened one, as Suzuki tells us, is in the belly, he
is a belly-man. Jesus, on the other hand, centers in the heart;
He is a God-Man of love. Belly-centeredness is quite instinctive, grounded in earth and life, while Christ-centeredness looks
toward heaven, transcending life and death. Both images have
"bliss-bestowing" and healing hands, but the Zen figure is almost
fat, whereas Jesus is usually portrayed as lean, even gaunt. No
cross of the suffering of the opposites prevails in the bodhisattva. Instead he carries a cornucopia on his back, an unending
source of bliss. In this, he somewhat resembles that early rival
of Jesus, Mithras, who carried the sacrificed bull on his own
back, equally laden with riches. Both Jesus and the bodhisattva
are compassionate, but the great contrast lies with the issue of
godliness: our Zen hero has "no need for the miraculous power

of the gods," but Jesus has to unite within himself the extreme opposites of being both God and man.

Another difference is apparent in the carrying of the gourd, a symbol of *sunyata*, emptiness, in contrast to the cross. Yet Suzuki again quotes the great Christian mystic, Meister Eckhart, saying:

> A man shall become truly poor and free from his creature will as he was when he was born. And I say to you, by the eternal truth, that as long as ye desire to fulfill the will of God, and have any desire after eternity and God, so long are ye not truly poor. He alone hath true spiritual poverty who wills nothing, knows nothing, desires nothing.[32]

Eckhart's enlightened man is close to the Zen image in this image of emptiness. The oxherding bodhisattva carries only a staff that reveals, says Suzuki, that he is free from all extra property, since he "knows that the desire to possess is the curse of human life."[33] Our two figures, therefore, are alike and different, just as is the experience of East and West.

From the psychological point of view, we see two ways of viewing and experiencing the Self. In the West, we have much to learn from the Eastern presentation. When we are with our smallness, we can see ourselves serving the Self-within as our larger totality, like Christ, the God-within. When we are with our "bigness" (or "smallness," in another way), we can see ourselves in the undivided totality of the Buddha-Man here represented. Luckily, we need not choose, only experience.

If we examine another aspect of this tenth picture, we note that the figure shown here is no longer the "youth" of the early pictures, nor the "man" transformed spiritually by the time of picture 6. We now see an old man and realize that this ten-picture process is a lifetime path, not a single event or brief period. To finally arrive at this destination (and we need not have even started out, as we are reminded in picture 9) apparently requires not only meditation, study, and life-experience, but it also just takes a long time! Why should it take so long? A Zen answer might be that it just does. But another answer comes in the realization that the resolution of such profound opposites requires work not only on the complex nature of a human being, but as we said before, on the paradoxical nature of the divine principle itself. It is this principle—as we experience it in image, thought, and deed—that is itself undergoing evolution and slow change. As if to underscore this fact, our final picture once more gives us a symbol of the tree, as in picture 9. Now the tree frames the enlightened one, and its blossoms also go forward to the other person, a youth.

Much can be said about this new appearance. Throughout these pictures we have seen either one youth or man, or nobody at all. Now we suddenly find two figures, the enlightened one of age and the youth greeting him. Is it not close to the truth to conjecture that this young man is another version of our original seeker, as he looked in the first picture? And that the function of our enlightened one is to help just such creatures as he was in the beginning to advance on their way? Student becomes master and instructs new students; thus is the process carried onward.

The Tree of Life covers both seeker and teacher and the long path is like Nature, Itself, slowly growing with concentric rings of development, showing hardness and softness, resistance and flexibility, sweetness and decay. Both master and student carry emblems of that same Tree: the one with his wooden staff of chosen poverty of spirit; the other his ordinary stick carrying his few possessions, symbol of his material poverty. A happy meeting and a happy union. "He and they are all converted into Buddhas," promises the commentary, but clearly only after a long time!

In Jung's *Rosarium* series, the tenth picture (Fig. 36, p. 132) presents a hermaphrodite, representing the union of king and queen, a single figure combining all that has been achieved in the work. In the beginning there was only a vessel, the fountain and the well. All through the middle there was the pair of king and queen, opening, uniting, struggling, dying, in the fountain become bath become tomb. At the end there is a union of male and female, with the accent on the feminine. In the oxherding series, we began with a person. This person was joined by relationship with the animal, in which there was struggle and resolution. Then the animal was gone, the person was gone, and only Nature remained. At the end there is achievement (the enlightened one) and relationship results (master, student, and others). It seems to me that again we discover the contrast of methods, East and West. In the East, aloneness is the way, meditation the method, and, in the end, relationship with others. In the West, the vessel is relationship itself and the capacity to stand alone is the achievement. There is a useful complementarity between the two, I think. The same aloneness, however, ultimately adheres to both: "He goes on his way without following the steps of the ancient sages," is said of our Eastern master, and so can it be said of the Western master. As Jung put it so eloquently: "[E]ven the enlightened person remains what he is and is never more than his own limited ego before the One who dwells within him, whose form has no knowable boundaries, who encompasses him on all sides, fathomless as the abysms of the earth and vast as the sky."[34] Easy to proclaim, hard to attain. All the same, when the "end" comes, the "dead trees are in full bloom" and we experience relationship again, with "bliss-bestowing hands." What is not stated here, but what Suzuki tells us, is that the enlightened one still does damage and still tries to repair the damage done, his own or that of others, "he is forever kept busy doing this, undoing that." So, then, we are in the right company when we are with winebibbers and butchers, for such are we, too.

Notes

[1] Daisetz Suzuki, *Manual of Zen Buddhism* (New York: Grove Press, 1960).

[2] C. G. Jung, "The Psychology of the Transference," *CW* 16.

[3] See also J. Marvin Spiegelman and Mokusen Miyuki, *Buddhism and Jungian Psychology* (Tempe, AZ: New Falcon, 1985) for more about the Zen oxherding pictures.

[4] Suzuki, *Manual of Zen Buddhism*, p. 129.

[5] Daisetz T. Suzuki, "Awakening of a New Consciousness in Zen" (1954), in *Man and Transformation*, Eranos Yearbooks, vol. 5 (London: Routledge, 1964), p. 198.

[6] *Funk & Wagnall's Standard Dictionary of Folklore*, Maria Leach, ed. (New York: Funk & Wagnall's, 1949), p. 260.

[7] Suzuki, *Manual of Zen Buddhism*, p. 130.

[8] Leon Wieseltier, *Kaddish* (New York: Alfred Knopf, 1998), p. 441.

[9] Suzuki, *Manual of Zen Buddhism*, p. 130. Brackets are in the original text.

[10] Suzuki, "Awakening of a New Consciousness," p. 199.

[11] Wieseltier, *Kaddish*, p. 420.

[12] Suzuki, *Manual of Zen Buddhism*, p. 131.

[13] Suzuki, "Awakening of a New Consciousness," pp. 198, 199.

[14] Suzuki, "Awakening of a New Consciousness," p. 199.

[15] Suzuki, *Manual of Zen Buddhism*, p. 131.

[16] Suzuki, "Awakening of a New Consciousness," p. 200.

[17] For example, C. G. Jung, *Psychology and Alchemy*, CW 12.

[18] Suzuki, *Manual of Zen Buddhism*, p. 132.

[19] Linda Fierz-David, *Psychological Reflections on the Fresco Series of the Villa of Mysteries in Pompeii*, MS (Zurich: Jung Institute, 1957).

[20] See Franz Cumont, *The Mysteries of Mithra*, originally published in French, 1902, Thomas J. McCormack, trans. (New York: Dover, 1956).

[21] Suzuki, *Manual of Zen Buddhism*, p. 132.

[22] Suzuki, *Manual of Zen Buddhism*, p. 133.

[23] Ibid., note 1.

[24] Suzuki, "Awakening of a New Consciousness," p. 200.

[25] C. G. Jung, "Psychological Commentary on Kundalini Yoga" (1932), in *Spring* (1976): 1–31.

[26] Suzuki, *Manual of Zen Buddhism*, pp. 133–134. Brackets are in the original text.

[27] Suzuki, "Awakening of a New Consciousness," p. 200.

[28] See C. G. Jung, *Answer to Job*, CW 11.

[29] Suzuki, *Manual of Zen Buddhism*, p. 134.

[30] Suzuki, "Awakening of a New Consciousness," p. 201

[31] Ibid.

[32] Suzuki, "Awakening of a New Consciousness," p. 202.

[33] Ibid.

[34] Jung, CW 11, ¶ 758.

CHAPTER 4

Divine Within: The Kundalini Path in Hinduism

To enter into the world of Indian spirituality, particularly the Tantric tradition of which Kundalini is a part, is to find yourself luxuriating in riches of imagery and concept, in words and sounds and movements, the effect of which is trance-inducing and ecstatic. If you listen for several hours to Indian religious music, for example, chant the Sanskrit language, or watch the magical performance of dance or ritual, you know that here is an ancient and wise culture, alive with the opposites and paradoxes. In this tradition, there is simultaneous awareness of the all-embracing One and the endless variety of the Many, whether of gods and goddesses or conditions of the soul. Along with this comes the realization that the ultimate truth lies within—it is there in potential from the beginning but we must achieve it by dint of hard work. There are words and god-names for every imaginable condition of consciousness, each subtly different from the other. Like Inuit, with their 29 names for varieties of snow, Hindus have many words for awareness.

We can hardly plunge into the riches of the *Upanishads* or the thousands of years of India's development here, but we can surely get a significant taste of one of its spiritual paths—as we did for Buddhism—by exploring Kundalini Yoga and its chakra symbolism. Just a brief glance (see figs. 17–22 and Table 1) shows us that these god-filled images of the path to enlightenment are quite different from the austerity of the Buddhist oxherding series. No gods or goddesses are present in the latter, nor is there an aim of ultimate liberation (*mukti*) from the world. Yet the spirit of meditation, concentrating within, with the goal of transformation and enlightenment, of ego being encompassed by the Self, is the same for both paths.

My own exploration of the Kundalini path actually began in the third year of my first analysis, 1952. I dreamed I was in India and a powerful guru was angrily shouting at me, trying to get me to pay attention, but I, in my suspicion of gurus, turned away. In actuality, I had spent a month in Calcutta as a sailor in the Merchant Marine during World War II. I was deeply moved by all that I saw there, including many hours spent at the Temple of Kali, where I was "enchanted" by the chanting of the *Mahabharata* and *Ramayana*. Yet the suspicion of gurus that my dream self showed was also true for me consciously. Over the years, however, I had read at least a little on Hinduism and I was deeply impressed with a lecture about Kundalini that my analyst in Zurich, Dr. C.A. Meier, gave in 1956. It was only when I started to write my own fictional account of a Hindu woman's individuation process (the story of Maya the Yogini in *The Tree of Life*, pages 202–248) in 1967 that this material came alive. Curiously, years later, in 1986, when I was stuck in my attempt to write a serious essay on Kundalini,[1] I suddenly felt the presence of the guru of my dream of 34 years earlier. He now announced that he would help me since I had done the work that he was going to suggest long ago! I meditated with this inner guru as an image and saw him sitting in the classic meditative lotus position, shaped rather triangularly, focused on a large eye in the middle of his forehead (the *ajna* chakra). Above his head appeared a larger eye as a circle. This image calmed me and accompanied me through that particular work. I tell this story to illustrate how contents in the unconscious can maintain an ongoing, unchanging life—while consciousness goes about its merry way—only to emerge, perhaps, when conditions are favorable, long afterwards.

The triangularity, or "threeness" of this guru, I think, suggests the importance this symbol has in Hinduism (as well as in Christianity). This "threeness" is shown not only in the classic Hindu understanding of divinity as Brahma, Vishnu, and Shiva, but also in the effort of the *yogin* or *yogini* (male or female Kundalini practitioner), to unite Shakti, the divine feminine, with Shiva, the divine masculine. The divine pair of Kundalini, Shiva and Shakti are respectively representative of form and power, structure and energy, underlying everything in the universe. They are both separate and united (as when power takes shape) in the One, which is conceived of as a trinity, or *satchitananda* (*sat*, meaning "being," *chit*, meaning "consciousness" and *ananda*, meaning "bliss"). The ultimate Oneness, like the great eye above my inner guru, is untouched and untouchable, yet manifests in the masculine-feminine polarity of all that exists. The human being also combines both Shiva, or consciousness, and Shakti, or energy. We mortals are expressions of this power of the universe. The yogin's aim is to worship (*sadhana*) and to bring this power of Shakti to its perfect expression by raising the energy from the lowest level of existence in gross matter to the highest spiritual level. In so doing, he helps Shakti to mate with Shiva, yet also discovers that they were never separated in the first place. This paradox, like that which we saw in the Buddhist oxherding series, is central to grasping this doctrine. It is the paradox that the Self is present from the beginning but is realized, made manifest, only in the course of the work.

The yogin accomplishes this work by focusing, purifying, and moving energy through the three primary channels, or *nadis* (nerves), and centers, or *chakras*, of the body. When the energies of the two *nadis*—the *ida* (moon) and *pingala* (sun)—are purified, they join in the central column, the *sushumna nadi*, where this kundalini energy then moves from the base of the spine up through each chakra, like a subtle body undergoing stages of transformation.

While Hinduism has a grand vision of the meaning and functioning of the universe, in connection with Kundalini Yoga it is the task of our lonely seeker (*saddhaka*) to work on and reconcile the union of the divine opposites within him. Whereas the yogin is everything because there is nothing in the universe that is not in the human body or soul, his aim is to bring this power into full expression and dissolve himself (his ego). Contrast this aim with the Kabbalistic work of bringing the divine into manifestation and the Buddhist path which denies the gods altogether! Yet the goal of the connection with the divine opposites is the same. This similarity and difference is amazing, but only when we forget that the world psyche, at bottom, is the same everywhere, taking different forms in time and condition and culture, yet remaining one, just as our human anatomy and physiology are the same.

In considering the chakras, we can understand them as "subtle centers" of consciousness. These connect with physiological activity, as both antecedent to it and finding expression in it, hence the various yogic *asanas* or bodily practices, even though so much of the work has to do with the psyche or imagination. *Pranayama*, or breathing meditation, is an instance of this, since the diastole of inhalation-exhalation, rhythmically and consciously practiced, mirrors the spiritual cleansing process.

The chakras (also called *padma*, or "lotuses") have different mandalas, numbers of petals, animal symbols, and tattvas, or principles, and organs. Table 1 on page 70 summarizes these qualities. I have adapted this summary from Arthur Avalon's *The Serpent Power*, but have also added—from Jung and from my own reflections—what might be considered the psychological significance of each of them.

How are we to understand these chakras psychologically? Jung said that each one is a whole world. That is to say, each of them expresses a different type of consciousness, worldview, or religious attitude, since they are replete with imagery, elements, mandalas, types of instinctive expression (animals), as well as gods and goddesses. Is it little wonder, then, that this system has been so long-lasting and has influenced other religions as well? With the help of Purnananda, Avalon, and Jung, we shall now visit the symbolism of this chakra system.[2]

Table 1. Chakras: Qualities, Symbols, and Meaning.

Chakra	Location (Plexus)	Petals	Mandala	Animal	Tattva (sense-act)	Shiva	Shakti	Element
Muladhara, "root support"	Perineum: between anus and genitals	4	Square	Elephant	Cohesion; smell; feet	Brahma child	Dakini	Earth
Psychological Significance: Everyday reality; grown into; family, work, etc. Elephant, domesticated libido.								
Svadhisthana, "proper place"	Hypogastric: bladder, above genitals	6	Crescent	Makara crocodile	Contraction; taste; hand	Hari-Vishnu youth	Rakini	Water
Psychological Significance: Unconscious, devouring, dangerous, negative fish-monster. Moon.								
Manipura, "plenitude of jewels"	Solar plexus: navel/ diaphragm	10	Triangle	Ram	Expansion; heat; sight & color; anus	Rudra old	Lakini	Fire
Psychological Significance: Handles of crucible-triangle form of swastika. Emotion, passions; Rudra is destroyer; affects; belly is action-reaction; no reflection.								
Anahata, "unattackable"	Heart	12	Hexagon	Antelope/gazelle	Movement; touch; feel; penis	Isha	Kakini	Air
Psychological Significance: Conscious. Union of opposites, *atman* (self) appears. Small flame in castle; heart in lungs. Here is reflection, discrimination, judgment. Come to impersonal aspect of oneself.								
Vishuddha, "purification"	Throat: pharyngeal plexus	16	Circle	White Elephant	*Akasha* (space-giving); hearing; mouth	Sada-Shiva	Shakini	Ether
Psychological Significance: Pure concepts, reality of psyche. World is inner drama, has to do with Hindu idea that word and speech beyond tangible reality (compare John: "In the beginning was the word…")								
Ajna, "place of command"	Between the eyes	2	—	No animal	*Manas* (mental faculties)	Shambhu	Hakini	None
Psychological Significance: Command, no animal means psychic reality does not require animal, bodily reality. Yogin is a psychic content of God.								
Sahasrara	Above crown of head	1000	Lotus	None	None	None	None	None
Psychological Significance: *Shunyata*, the void. All being is no longer being. Union of opposites. Union of opposites. *Advaita* (non-two); *Nirdvandva* (free of opposites), objectless subject. Total union of Shiva-Shakti.								

Muladhara Chakra: "Root Support"

Jung's interpretation of the psychological meaning of this center is that the Self, the divine center within, is asleep and the ego is conscious. We can see what he means: the Kundalini Herself, the divine energy, is wrapped as a snake around the central lingam, but is slumbering, needing to be awakened. Our ego, however, is conscious insofar as we are living our everyday lives. We are "rooted" in the earth, the element of this chakra, and safely seated on the elephant, which, in India, is a symbol of strength, firmness, and solidity. The elephant is the equivalent of what the horse used to be in the West and what the ox is in both East and West: energy for the tasks of everyday life and our biological existence.

Not only are we rooted and supported by the earth, we are under the principle (*tattva*) of cohesion, hanging together and connected with that earth reality by our feet, and also, like the animals, by our sense of smell. Our mandala is foursquare and solid, our connection with life is through the institutions into which we are born, our family, temple, place, and nation.

The divine images are not asleep, however. The deeply red, four-armed goddess, Shakti-Dakini, holds a sacrificial spear, a sword, a skull-staff and a drinking cup. She is powerful yet shows that her energies bespeak the sacrifice and conflict of everyday life, limited by ultimate death. Her energies are contained in the vessel of institutional worship and addressed as such by everyone. Her consort, Shiva, is presented as a Child-Brahma, also with four hands (another symbol of totality), holding a staff, gourd, and *mala* beads (rosary). He makes the fear-dispelling hand gesture (*mudra*). The spirit here, Shiva, is yet a child, but holds the community symbols of containment and prayer, evoking a healthy fear of the gods. So it is that the "banality" of everyday life contains the powerful forces of the universe, but we are conscious of them only in a projected or external fashion, revealed in our rituals and unexamined beliefs.

Purnananda tells us, however, that the sleeping Kundalini is a "world-bewilderer . . . Her sweet murmur is like the

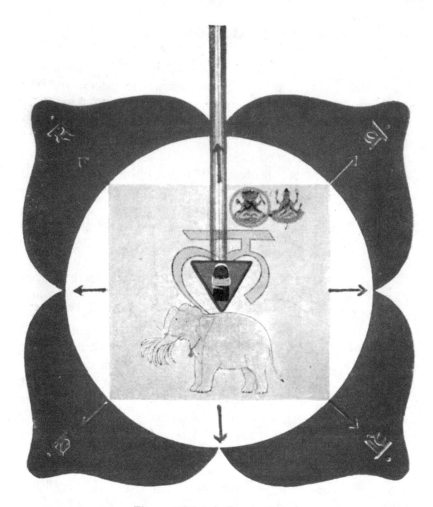

Figure 16. Muladhara *chakra.*

indistinct hum of swarms of love-mad bees. She produces melodious poetry and all other compositions. . . . It is She who maintains all the beings of the world by means of inspiration and expiration, and shines in the cavity of the root Lotus like a chain of brilliant lights."[3] We are also told that the yogin who meditates upon Her will become "a king of speech, lord among men, an adept in all kinds of learning."[4]

In short, one who meditates and thus awakens the sleeping Kundalini is already in touch with the power of love and creation. Knowledge, we find, as with the first oxherding picture, is our initial task of awakening to the Self, and our means is that of inner focus.

Svadhisthana Chakra: "Proper Place"

Just as the muladhara is the "root support," the beginning of a process of spiritual growth, rooted or having its foundation in the culture into which we are born, the next phase of development—after meditation and raising the energy—is to the "proper place," the region of water. We have risen from the earthly condition of the perineum between anus and genitals, to the "root" of the genitals in the hypogastric region, the bladder. After earth comes water; after awakening from ordinary life comes "baptism," or immersion in the spirit.

It was Jung's genius to understand this second step of spiritual growth as a conscious immersion into the sea of the unconscious. In all initiation rites and mystery cults there is a kind of baptism or descent into water, the way to higher development leads through an immersion into our own depths. And what is it that we find in our depths? Why it is the *makara* fish, a kind of devouring crocodile like the leviathan of the Bible. Here we meet our primitive, infantile, and never-ending desires (*klesas*).

The god-images in the *svadhisthana* chakra are notably changed. The Shiva image now takes the form of Vishnu, in his youth. The spirit-form has grown up from the child-like condition in which it began and the principle under which he/it now operates is one of contraction. There is a narrowing of consciousness, from one point of view (descent into the unconscious), but this is done in order to gain a higher or deeper perspective. The hand is now necessary; one not only stands on common ground but also is actively engaged in the struggle with the psychic conditions of lust (*kama*), anger (*krodha*), and egoism. The youthful deity, who is also a symbol for the time when our lusts are consciously activated,

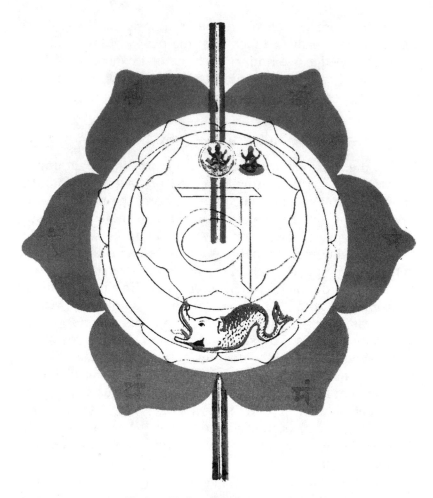

Figure 17. Svadhisthana *chakra.*

is called upon as Hari (remember the young Hari Krishna chanters in the 1960s?) to protect us. We might think that he would shield us from our greed and demands, but no, this is not the case. We need him to protect us from the Goddess Rakini, who is indeed very beautiful but is "of furious aspect. Her three eyes are red, and her teeth show fiercely. She, the Shining Devi of Devas, is seated on a double lotus and from one of her nostrils there flows a streak of blood. She is fond of white rice and grants the wished-for boon."[5]

Avalon and Purananda tell us that Rakini cleanses us from our greedy faults, such as egoism, but she is terrible to behold and it is from her that we need the protection provided by youthful Hari-Vishnu. Jung would say that the divinities of the unconscious, the archetypes, also have a dark and fierce aspect that both challenges us and carries us onward on our path of spiritual development. If we succeed in mastering them, then they do indeed "grant us boons."

But it is no mean task to engage all the inner evil incli-nations and demons I mentioned earlier, along with delusion (*moha*), pride (*mada*), envy (*matsarya*), all subsumed under the condition of "mineness" (*ahamkara*). When overcome, the dark-ness of ignorance is replaced by the Sun of knowledge, says Kalicharna.[6] Could it be, according to Jung and to alchemy, that the darkness of the fierce divinity is itself also transformed?

Manipura Chakra: "Plenitude of Jewels"

Manipura is so named, Avalon tells us, because the principle of fiery *Tejas* (heat) at this level produces a lustrous gem (*mani*),[7] which Jung's study of alchemy reveals as a symbol of the Self. The mandala here is ten-petaled, in contrast to the four of muladhara and the six of svadhisthana, which leads us to conclude that there is more development, complexity, and differentiation here, as well as more intense movement. This is also suggested by both its fiery element (see table 1) and the triangle, which the tradition of the symbolism of the number 3 interprets as dynamic, in contrast to the passive, even, numbers. On each side of the triangle, furthermore, are three swastika marks. Originally, the swastika was not invested with the horror we have come to associate with it, yet it is not by chance that this chakra is connected with destruction, as we shall shortly see.

First, however, we need an overview of the various condi-tions of the lotus. The animal, here, is a ram, symbol of battle and power, and Shiva takes the form of Rudra seated upon a

Figure 18. Manipura *chakra.*

bull, yet another carrier of that instinctive energy that we know from the oxherding pictures. Furthermore, the *tattva* (principle) condition is that of expansion, in contrast to the cohesion of muladhara and the contraction of svadhisthana. This expansion must indicate the enhancement of energy and power as well as the consciousness of dealing with it. The qualities of heat, sight, and the "organ" of the anus confirm this paradox of conditions that add energy and vision (consciousness) yet produce detritus and destruction.

The *bija*, or meditative point, is that of fire, called Ram. This is a seed mantra (a chant) which is seated on a ram, carrier of Agni, Lord of Fire. Shiva is here called Red Rudra, who is smeared with white ashes, while his Shakti is Lakini, who is "fond of animal food." This is a digestive center, Avalon tells us, in which the *saddhaka* (seeker) is expected to satisfy the appetites of this *devata*, Lakini.[8] We are still in the region of desire and we continue to eat meat, something given up in the higher chakras.

The verses of Purnananda tell us that power and destruction are the issues to be dealt with at this chakra. For one thing, we are faced with the fire of the passions, which analytic work has shown to be truly a source of "fullness of jewels" (energy and vitality), but also an inferno of suffering. If we can cope with these passions, being neither possessed by them nor avoiding them, we can rise above the ordinary situation of automatic action and reaction, achieving objectivity and a calm perspective; otherwise we roast others or ourselves in the hell of our own affects.

But here, too, says Jung, is where the sun rises, where consciousness can appear. If we transcend, we can recognize eternity; if not, we remain a creature of the abdomen, we think with our intestines, dominated by fear and aggression. When we ask what it is that we are afraid of, we note that we no longer deal with the immature forms of a boy or youth but with a more ambivalent adult Shiva, who is both a granter of boons and a "destroyer of creation." Shakti is somewhat less fearsome now, but her power (remember that she represents the energy of the universe) is still awesome. Purnananda tells us that Lakini is the benefactress of all, exalted with the drinking of ambrosia, but in her right hand she holds a thunderbolt and in the left she makes the gesture of dispelling fear and granting boons. Ambivalent, is she not? Not only is she "fond of meat," her "breast is ruddy with the blood and fat that drop from her mouth."[9]

This is not a pretty picture but presents a potent one: the opposites (dispelling fear while she also scares us to death!) come into play. Clearly this chakra is a representation of the power principle, when viewed psychologically. One might even think that the spiritual orientation suggested by this chakra is the province of Adlerian psychology, whereas svadhisthana, with its sexuality, would belong more to Freudian psychology and the next chakra, *anahata*, which brings the Self into play, that of Jung. In any case, these lower chakras confront us with instinctive conditions and passions, through which we must move in meditation and confrontation, in order to achieve the promised bliss and consciousness of the higher chakras. Yet we must remember that the flow of the Kundalini, at last, is circular and that the energy that rises also returns—it is meant to "circulate."

Avalon's interpretation of the "fond of animal food" condition of Shakti Lakini is that the appetites of this *devata* are meant to be satisfied. This brings up the question as to how the various instincts are to be dealt with in the meditation of the saddhaka, or seeker. On the one hand, it is expected that the yogin controls and sublimates these desires; on the other hand, there is the tacit indication that they are to be fulfilled. This paradoxical injunction is certainly something commonly found in analytic work; the proper direction to take for each specific event is something to be closely monitored. In general, the analyst tries to relate to the total needs of the soul (rather than indulge in partial or split fulfillment). We wonder how the saddhaka approached this. Some Tantric texts tell us that there was a sequence of beginning with denial and devotion, followed by service and fulfillment, culminating, finally, with indifference.

Anahata Chakra: "Unattackable"

For Jung, the *anahata* chakra is where individuation, as a conscious awareness of the Self, truly begins. Until this point, we are immersed in desire, passion and the thousand-and-one things of existence. Above all, there is no detachment. Reason begins here, not in the cut-off, intellectualizing manner of the modern neurotic condition, but in the sense that we have the capacity to rise above the emotions objectively, without repress-

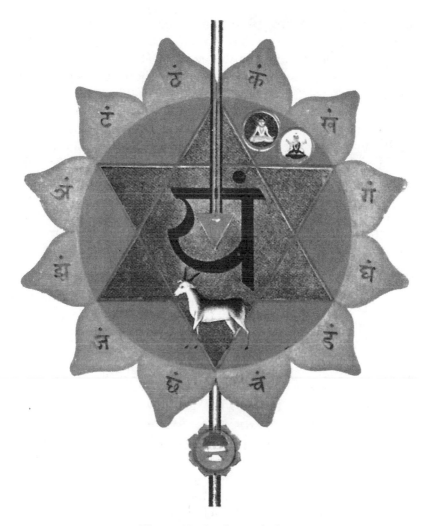

Figure 19: Anahata *chakra.*

ing or succumbing to them. This means we get a glimpse of *purusha*, the "thumbling" condition of the Self. But we must remember, says Jung, that we can become quite inflated by thinking that we have "arrived" at anahata when our egos remain at muladhara, for the most part, yet we can behold and experience—at times—purusha from below.[10] For this, we truly need the sacred words (mantras) because our capacity for true civilization, for our spiritualization, is quite weak.

We can see, as Jung suggests, that there is a significant development at this point, beyond the first three chakras. The mandala is now a hexagon (combining masculine and feminine triangles), the number of lotus petals has increased to 12, the animal is a less demanding and aggressive one (antelope or gazelle), and the *tattva*, or principle, is significantly changed. In contrast with the previous cohesion, contraction, and expansion—all of which keeps us contained in a single place—we now have the aspect of movement, which allows us to proceed outside of the previous condition. Furthermore, there are other tattvas of touch, feeling, and the organ of the penis, all of which imply relationship, connection to another. This suits the heart center, which evokes feeling, compassion, and relationship with others in a manner quite different from the exploitation and dominance that characterize the dark side of the lower chakras.

Avalon and Purnananda tell us that this lotus is "charming," beguiling in its color, red as the *bandhuka* flower.[11] We can also see that the mandala is a Star of David, uniting male and female triangles, having a smoky color that contrasts nicely with the warm-hearted reds. Can we guess that here we find the "smoke" from the manipura fires below, that here the flame becomes gentle and refined as the flower that charms us? Peace is encountered here; the wars below are overcome. For example, anahata is called "unattackable" because the sound which is heard here (says Kalicharana) is "that which issues without the striking of any two things together."[12] We are reminded of the Buddhist "sound of one hand clapping." We are given a glimpse of the condition in which there is a "steady tapering flame of a lamp in a windless place."[13]

Furthermore, we are told that the element here is air, that the animal is the fleet-of-foot gazelle, which is truly gentle and light in comparison with the previous elephant, crocodile, and ram. Even the Goddess is less violent here, for her "heart is softened with the drinking of nectar."[14] The saddhaka who meditates on this heart lotus, Purnananda tells us, "becomes (like) the Lord of Speech and (like) Ishvara he is able to protect and destroy worlds."[15] Translated psychologically, we would say that he is no longer subject to the waves of creation and destruction in the universe of his own passions. Now, by the grace of the Word, he can protect the gentle fire of the spirit and guard against destructive attacks from both within and outside himself. He is "illumined by the solar region" and is full of "charm." Indeed, Kalicharana tells us that such a yogi is "dearer than the dearest to women," because he is so skilled in pleasing them.[16] Would a yogini be equally attractive to men? One would surely think so, but at that stage in Eastern civilization, this gender awareness was not stated.

God and Goddess are transformed here also, the latter having three eyes (far-seeing) and clad delicately in silken raiment. Shiva-Ishi wears gems on his neck and bells on his toes, possessing the "soft radiance of ten million moons."[17] Shakti-Kakini becomes "exhilarated and auspicious, . . . benefactress of all." Despite the fact that she still carries a noose and skull, she "makes the sign of blessing and the sign that dispels fear." Her heart (as we have seen) "is softened with the drinking of nectar," an ambrosial fluid dropping from the chakras above.[18] She wears a skin of the black antelope: does this not suggest that she, too, has been civilized?

Finally, we are told that the yogi who attains here not only has his senses completely under control but also can concentrate intensely and is "able to enter another's body." Kalicharana tells us that this means that he can enter the enemy's fort or citadel, even though guarded.[19] We can understand this psychologically to mean that such a person is highly sensitive, can intuitively penetrate people's defenses and can also, best of all, protect him from their darkness ("he may render himself invisible").[20] Yet we cannot discount the statement that *siddhis* (parapsychological powers) are achieved and that such a person can "fly across the sky." Is this astral travel? Out–of–the body experience? At this point, we can only conclude that the yogin here goes beyond the ordinary events of life and the psychology of the first three chakras. With Jung we can conclude that what was started below and at the beginning in muladhara is now achieved in anahata. It is notable that this capacity to come to the impersonal aspect of the Self is located at the "heart" region. To think with the heart, as the Pueblo Indians also know, is to truly have consciousness. This is no mere mental activity, as we shall later see.

Vishuddha Chakra: "Purification"

For Jung, the attainment of the *vishuddha* chakra is to reach the level of psychic reality.[21] The element of this chakra—ether—is a substance that is no substance; it is a conception of substance. It is at a level of abstraction that goes beyond the empirical world. The evolution of the yogin's work has moved him up from the gross matter and earth of muladhara, all the way through the five elements, now including that of ether. The ancient idea of transformation is also found in alchemy, says Jung, and hinges on a kind of cooking process. Manipura, with its "handles," resembles a pot, which is like the cooking process found in the "kitchen" of the stomach, the region where that chakra is located. If manipura is the center of transformation, via the fire of the emotions, then anahata, which is the place of transformation and is invisible, provides the psychic foundation that is fully realized, at last, in vishuddha, the region of psychic reality.

Jung thinks that civilization as a whole has reached anahata—our center is no longer in the diaphragm as it was with the Greeks.[22] Despite this growth, however, we have not yet reached vishuddha, with its conception of the world as psychic reality. Only here can we grasp the Self as purusha, dimly felt in anahata, in which our essence is seen as a subjective condition. Jung thinks that when the abstract ideas of modern physics (quantum uncertainty and relativity) and analytical psychology (the archetypal level of the collective unconscious) are generally comprehended, then civilization will have reached this level of understanding.

I think that Jung is overly generous in this evaluation of our general condition. It seems to me that relatively few

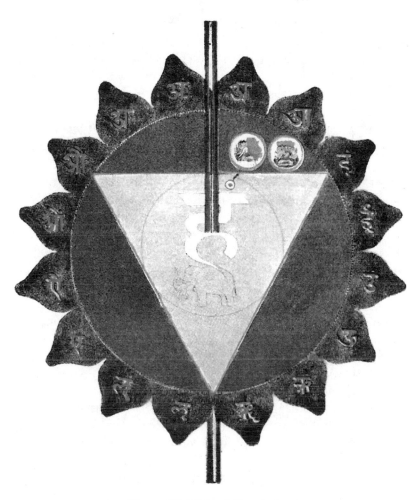

Figure 20. Vishuddha *chakra.*

people really grasp the Self, the divine, as an inner center of their own personality, and that we human beings are largely spread out in all the lower chakras. Indeed, I think it is even more accurate to say that most of us have parts of our psyche at all the different chakras, even the highest. Our evolutionary task may be to continually encounter and struggle with this dilemma, raise ourselves up and also circulate what we have achieved in spirituality back into our lower chakras and into the general world condition. Be that as it may, dwelling in vishuddha means being with the subjective level of existence: everything that happens to us, inside and outside, is actually our self or is an encounter with the Self. Seen in another way, the world is a reflection of the psyche.

This progression of the development of psychic reality, says Jung, can be seen by the changes in the animals that belong to each chakra. The elephant, like the horse at muladhara, is both the instinctual urge that supports general consciousness and contains the possibility of the will to enlarge it. Makara, the crocodile at svadhisthana, is the strongest animal in the water, just as the elephant is on the land. As we continue up the scale, we come to the ram at manipura, the animal of fire and passion. Here sacrifice is central; we give up being mere slaves to our passions and desires. The result is to be found in the animal at anahata, the gazelle or antelope. This animal is neither domesticated nor sacrificed. It is fleet and shy, light as air, and has lost the heaviness of the earth. Only here is the psychic factor realized. It is like the unicorn in alchemy (the Holy Ghost) and bespeaks a psychic factor not even vouchsafed in Freud's understanding of the instincts.

When we come to vishuddha, at last, we arrive at a level of instinct that transcends all of the foregoing, for now we experience a purified condition of instinct (white elephant) in which instinctual power supports human thought. As in Platonic philosophy, where reason is meant to be a servant of the passions, there is an appreciation of the subjectivity of the mind, but not just as intellect. The latter requires physical evidence for its conceptions, while the psyche, itself, does not. Consider, for example, the image of God! Finally, in the next chakra (*ajna*), there is an absence of the animal itself—there is only psychic reality. Here, however, in vishuddha, we are in the realm of pure concepts, and the world itself is an inner drama.

This is commensurate with the Hindu idea that word and speech are beyond tangible reality, something we noted about mantra. This is hinted at by the presence of the Sanskrit letters on the petals of all the mandalas. Particularly noteworthy is the fact that the largest number of petals (except for *sahasrara*), sixteen, is found here, and that the chakra itself is located at the throat, the pharyngeal plexus, without which speech would be impossible. Furthermore, the tattva is *akasha,* the space-giving principle, in which hearing and mouth are its senses and act-capacities. In Western tradition we have known this understanding in our sacred texts in the words, "And God said, Let there be light," as well as, "In the beginning was the Word. . . ."

There is more to be said about *akasha.* The word refers to a kind of region or condition known in magical and mystical circles as the "place" in which all the psychic "records" of humankind are kept. To tune in to this region is to be able to read all of one's previous incarnations and even anticipate potentialities of future lives. To translate this idea psychologically: we could say that when we are so deeply connected with the unconscious as to be in touch with the Self, then psychic reality transcends our usual conscious ideas of time and space. We are in the web of existence in which all things are connected and synchronistic events take place. It is quite right, then, that the mandala of this center is a circle—no more angles or corners. "God is a circle whose center is everywhere and circumference is nowhere" is our Western version of this.

If we now look at the images of god and goddess at this chakra, we discover that the male principle has grown significantly in power and presence and that the female principle, already "softened" in *anahata,* has become—like "light itself"—white.[23] The god Sadha-Shiva is seated on a great lion-seat, holds a trident, battle-axe, sword, thunderbolt, great snake, bell, goad, noose, and makes mudras (hand gestures) dispelling fear. In short, he contains all the powers of the previous chakras, but is now in a condition of purification, in which all is subjective; mind is the only reality. Indeed, he is now united with the female principle, is an androgyne (as in alchemy) and is known as the "ever-beneficent one." Similarly, the Goddess—here the Shakti-Shakini—is white, carries a bow, arrow, noose, and goad. No longer frightening, she still conveys the power, like her consort, to urge the seeker onward to continue in meditation and attain the akashic level of consciousness. The saddhaka will thus become free of the bonds of illusion (maya) and open the gate of liberation (*moksha*) as the next step.

Ajna Chakra: "Place of Command"

At this level, after a long development and differentiation during which the petals of the lotus increased, they are now reduced to two in number. There is no mandala, no animal, nor element. For Jung, when there is no animal, there is no bodily reality; only psychic reality exists. In short, the yogin now realizes himself as a psychic content of God.

In the beginning, at *muladhara*, God, or Atman, was dormant and the yogin (ego) was aware. Now that God is fully awake, the ego realizes itself as a mere fragment, focused on what is known in Western mysticism as the *unio mystica*. This is symbolized by the original lingam appearing again, but now white in color. In vishuddha, says Jung, psychic reality was opposed to physical reality; here, in ajna, there is no longer any physical reality at all, only psyche exists.[24] Here are echoes of the empty circle in the oxherding series!

This chakra is also the seat of the tattva of *manas*, or the mental faculties. Avalon tells us that ajna is called "command" because the saddhaka receives commands directly from the inner guru, from above.[25] All else recedes and loses significance. Only two petals remain and all the previous letters are exhausted. The mantra now is Om, the ultimate, and fire, sun, and moon converge. The *Atma* (Self) shines lustrously like a flame and the yogin gains the final *siddhis* (powers) that permit him, at his death, to voluntarily put his *prana* at this spot and enter purusha directly, needing to reincarnate no longer.

The goddess at ajna is the Shakti-Hakini with six faces (moons) and six arms, in one of which she holds a book. The others are lifted up in gestures of dispelling fear, granting boons, and holding a skull, a small drum, and a rosary (*mala*). "Her mind is pure."[26] The holding of a book is interpreted as a gesture conveying learning or knowledge. The yogin is now connected with wisdom as well as purity. Shiva is described

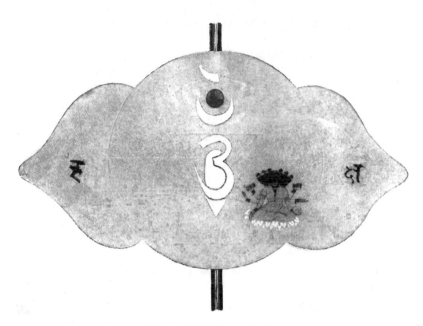

Figure 21. Ajna *chakra.*

as Itara in phallic form which "shines like a chain of lightning flashes."[27] Is this not a further purification of the earlier phallic energy into intuitive insight of the divine? Reference is also made to the subtlest of energies, what one understands in alchemy and elsewhere as the "subtle body." Here the sad-dhaka realizes that his "Atma is nothing but a meditation on this Lotus," which is to say that he himself is only a content of the Self.[28] Recall Jung's late dream, in which he comes upon himself as a meditating guru. He awakens wondering, is he the guru or the dream ego? The answer is that his ego is now a content of the Self.

Sahasrara: "Lotus of a Thousand Petals"

When we come to the ultimate goal of the Kundalini Yoga endeavor, the place of fulfillment at *sahasrara,* Jung is surpris-ingly laconic:

To speak about the lotus of the thousand petals, the Sahasrara center, is quite superfluous because that is merely a philosophical concept with no substance whatever for us; it is beyond any possible experience. In Ajna there is still the experience of the self that is apparently different from the object, the God. But in Sahasrara it is not different. So the next conclusion would be that there is no object, no God, there is nothing but Brahman. There is no experience because it is one; it is without a second. It is dormant, it is not, and therefore it is nirvana. This is an entirely philosophical concept, a mere logical conclusion from the premises above. It is without practical value for us.[29]

Thus speaks the Jung of 1932, consistent with his long-held theory that without an ego it is pointless and ridiculous to speak of experience. Self without ego is a mere "concept." How would the Jung of almost 30 years later (he died in 1961) have described this? Would his dream of discovering himself as a yogin meditating in a temple, with his ego as an object of the yogin's dream, have changed his view? Probably. But in his 1932 seminar, he was trying mightily to remain empirical and scientific.

Purnananda, on the other hand, and his commentator, Kalicharana, engage in many paragraphs of distinction of names, concepts, this and that, just as if they were giving us a specific recipe that can be fulfilled only in the prescribed manner. The remainder of Purnananda's treatise, furthermore, is given over to the specific directions for doing the work. So much for "symbolism" or mere cogitation!

The sahasrara surely constitutes a mandala, but this vastly differentiated totality is both symbol and concreteness, is no longer located "inside" the body but floats on top of the head. All the letters are gathered here and there is supreme bliss and void, supreme light and formlessness. The bliss is a consequence of Atma realized. Once here, the yogin has no further need of rebirth. Bliss pours down to the lower chakras, the filaments of the lotus are multitudinous conditions, names, and qualities about which much is

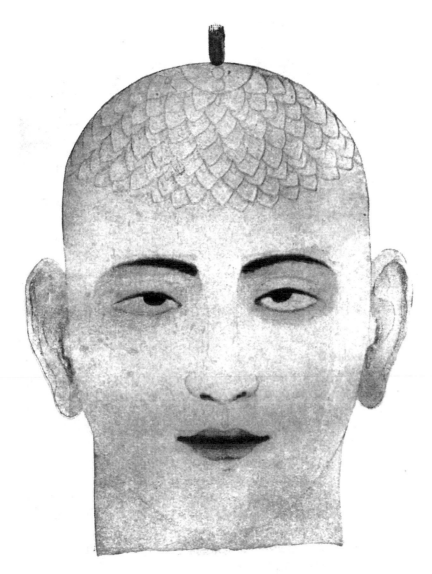

Figure 22. Sahasrara *chakra.*

written. The letters are luminous, there is wisdom and gladness. The saddhaka is now increasingly separate and private upon approaching his or her goal, free from bondage. The yogin who has gone through these experiences "dances at the feet of Ishta-devata,"[30] is beyond words and deeds, even beyond experiences, and celebrates joy and fulfillment in ecstatic dance. This is especially poignant since, at this point in Avalon's book, he gives us a series of photographs of a yogin demonstrating the various postures and procedures to be undertaken in this yoga. The simultaneous power and fragility of the gaunt and somewhat wild-eyed saddhaka makes all this intensely human, in his—and our—search for the divine.

What are we to make of this long hymn to the sacred, along with its recipes and enjoinders? Are we to haughtily turn up our Western noses at this primitive, nonscientific presentation? Assert that it is not practical, as the early Jung did? Or, more honestly, shall we admit that this goes beyond our understanding? I think that the latter is the best response, but we can expand our comprehension by seeing the parallels in alchemy. There, too, we are given vast numbers of words, procedures, and enjoinders, along with descriptions of bliss and knowledge. There, too, as Jung showed us many years later in his life, human beings attempted to both produce and explain the experience of a Self that is nonproducible and unexplainable. In each generation or era, there are those who have undergone such ordeals and they haltingly try to convey these experiences and help us come to something similar. Our own experiences, for the most part, are partial and we are both led and lead others astray. We generalize too much or impose structure where there is none. Yet that same overwhelming content is being approached by all seekers and, if we are modest enough, it seems to me, we can glimpse that which is being described and asserted.

The particularity of the Hindu Kundalini experience is that it combines the concrete and abstract simultaneously. It prescribes precise exercises, breathing techniques, and meditations. Like alchemy, the experience is clearly "inner." It is deeply Asian, yet the final condition is miles apart from the equally Asian Buddhist oxherding pictures where the adept is finally back in the world, in the marketplace, among ordinary people.

Comparisons

Looking at the Kundalini process from a comparative perspective, beginning with the alchemical series, several similarities leap out. The opposites (king and queen) are central in the latter, just as they are in the Tantric work, but true to the Western embrace of monotheism, these are royalty, not gods. The East understands that Oneness, or monotheism, is something to be achieved and is no more valid than polytheism. In both cases, there is a gradual development of a "divine" or "royal" pair, representing the fundamental opposites and their effect upon each other within the psyche itself. The pair also affects the poor human being or beings doing the work. In both Kundalini and alchemy, this divine pair ultimately becomes a oneness at the end. The feminine principle is powerfully at work in both systems so that, in alchemy, the final androgyne is more heavily female than male and, in Kundalini, the final condition itself, nirvana, is also seen as feminine. This is not so in Zen; there the story is told of a single male with feminine symbols all around him, in structure and picture and particularly in nature. He achieves via negation, by simplifying, in contrast to the richness of imagery and prescription in the Hindu and alchemical versions. Buddhism was clearly a revolt against the "excess"—if one can legitimately call it that without disrespect—of the Hindu tradition. And alchemy was compensation, as Jung showed, for the Christian negation of nature.

The Buddhist and Hindu works are similar in that they seek enlightenment, arise in the context of meditation, and are clearly introverted methods. Alchemy, on the other hand, had a strong mixture of experimentation, of uncertainty as to whether the "stone" or "gold" was truly "philosophical," residing within the soul, or also had a material, outer basis.

We have only recently understood that it was both, since the alchemical work with the divine can be found in relationship, itself.

All three works are replete with fantasy, with symbols of searching and prescriptions for self-improvement. All stress the need for discipline and study, necessitating the abandonment of preconceived ideas. Finally, all call for fully opening one's self to the divine. It is remarkable that all these works were completed around the same time in history, roughly during what the West refers to as the Renaissance. Perhaps there was truly a worldwide renewal of spirit, expressing a similar psychological content but in the context of different traditions. The Jewish mystical tradition of Kabbalah was astonishingly enriched during this same period by the Lurianic school of Safed with some students making use of the tarot images, as well. These instances provide strong evidence of what Jung calls synchronicity, a meaningful coincidence of religious renewal in different parts of the world.

This worldwide renewal, perhaps, constitutes a background or prefiguration to our presentday global meeting of spiritual paths. Experimentation is rife, much of the older beliefs and dogmas in all the religions have lost power or have died. Yet sometimes these systems find renewal, from both without and within. Syncretism is richly apparent in cults and sects. In the 1960s, we saw a veritable revolution of the spirit, whereas in the subsequent quarter century we have seen (depending on our perspective) a regression, or renewal of conservatism. In any event, there is a clear increase in fundamentalism and an intense longing to hold on to values and beliefs under threat from an apparent danger of chaos at the end of one millennium and beginning of another. Yet Eastern cults and religions have taken root in the West and continue to develop.

Nowadays, of course, we have tremendously facilitated communication among the nations and peoples, in contrast to the Renaissance period, when such interchange, if it happened at all, was slow and rare. Indeed, it's easy to see the current World Wide Web or Internet, provided by computers, as a concrete realization of the rich Hindu image of Indra's Web. The latter symbol, however, tells us that people and events are connected by significance and emotion in meaningful moments (like synchronicity), rather than the causal, intentional means provided by our increasingly powerful Western science and engineering.

It's interesting to note that wine, women, and materialism have corrupted many gurus coming to the West from the East. Rather, I should say, it was not our wine, etc. that corrupted them, but the inability to cope with the availability of these things outside the cultural prohibitions in which these gurus would normally be "safe" from such temptation. This, in my opinion, does not vitiate the messages they brought, nor does it even cast a particularly negative light on the masters so "corrupted." It might even be expected, not only because of human weakness, but also because there is much more work we all need to do. The task of integrating the spirit (wine), the feminine (women), and the body (materialism and nature), in a manner adequate to a coming world civilization is daunting. All of our traditions, East and West, are indeed wonderful, yet they are also all lacking in the face of the present necessity of going beyond the patriarchy in all traditions, as well as beyond revealed knowledge, beyond, even, individuality. The psyche is in "continual travail" and movement at this time (think of the "feminine" in the Apocalypse of John). We might speculate that all humankind are indeed individual experiments of the "soul of the world," in which that same *anima mundi* is trying to build up a new image of the Self, of God, that is sufficiently inclusive or representative of our larger and growing capacity for totality. In order to do our part toward the gradual emergence of a sufficient worldview, it is useful to integrate what has already been revealed in the rich spiritual paths we are exploring. It is essential that any worldview that ultimately results (in several hundred years, thought Jung)[31] should continue to honor diversity in all the religions and spiritual paths as well as in individuals themselves, while revealing the common ground of humanity and all life.

Notes

[1] J. Marvin Spiegelman and Arwind U. Vasavada, *Hinduism and Jungian Psychology* (Tempe: New Falcon, 1987).

[2] The illustrations and some of the quotes in this chapter come from the classic *The Serpent Power*, written by Sir Arthur Avalon (Madras, India: Ganesh & Co., 1953), which in addition to an extensive introduction by Avalon includes a translation of the *Shatchakra Nirupana*, a Kundalini treatise written in 1577 by the yogin Purnananda, with commentary by Kalicharna as well as Avalon. The Serpent Power is essential reading for anyone who wants to delve into a serious study of Kundalini Yoga.

[3] Avalon, *Serpent Power*, p. 347.

[4] Avalon, *Serpent Power*, p. 355.

[5] Avalon, *Serpent Power*, p. 363.

[6] Avalon, *Serpent Power*, p. 364.

[7] Avalon, *Serpent Power*, p. 119.

[8] Ibid.

[9] Avalon, *Serpent Power*, p. 369.

[10] C. G. Jung, "Psychological Commentary on Kundalini Yoga, Lectures One and Two" (1932), *Spring* (1975): 31.

[11] Avalon, *Serpent Power*, pp. 120, 371.

[12] Avalon, *Serpent Power*, pp. 371–372.

[13] Avalon, *Serpent Power*, p. 379.

[14] Avalon, *Serpent Power*, p. 375.

[15] Avalon, *Serpent Power*, p. 379.

[16] Avalon, *Serpent Power*, p. 380.

[17] Avalon, *Serpent Power*, p. 374.

[18] Avalon, *Serpent Power*, p. 375.

[19] Avalon, *Serpent Power*, p. 382.

[20] Ibid.

[21] C. G. Jung, "Psychological Commentary on Kundalini Yoga, Lectures Three and Four" (1932), *Spring* (1976): 1–2.

[22] Jung, "Psychological Commentary on Kundalini Yoga, Lectures Three and Four," p. 5.

[23] Avalon, *Serpent Power*, p. 388.

[24] Jung, "Psychological Commentary on Kundalini Yoga, Lectures Three and Four," p. 17.

[25] Avalon, *Serpent Power*, p. 126.

[26] Avalon, *Serpent Power*, p. 395.

[27] Avalon, *Serpent Power*, p. 398.

[28] Avalon, *Serpent Power*, p. 401.

[29] Jung, "Psychological Commentary on Kundalini Yoga, Lectures Three and Four," p. 17.

[30] Avalon, *Serpent Power*, p. 488.

[31] See Max Zeller, *The Dream: The Vision of the Night* (Los Angeles: Analytical Psychology Club of Los Angeles, 1978), p. 2.

CHAPTER 5

Divine Within: The Tree of Life in Jewish Mysticism

Kabbalah, the inner and mystical aspect of Judaism, has a long history, dating back at least as far as the vision of Ezekiel in biblical times (from which arose a branch called "Merkabah" or "Chariot mysticism"), and continuing through the early centuries of the current era. It enjoyed a renewed flourishing in southern France and Spain (the Zohar) in the 11th to the 13th centuries and again in 17th-century Palestine and 18th-century Eastern Europe. The study of the Kabbalah suffered decline in 19th-century Europe as a consequence of the emancipation of European Jewry and of rationalism (also called the Age of Enlightenment, interestingly), but it has enjoyed a tremendous resurgence once again in the latter half of the 20th century in both Israel and the United States.

The central symbol in this long meditative and mystical history has been the Tree of Life, that longed-for image of immortality barred to our first parents in the Garden of Eden. This tree is actually a complex diagram (see fig. 24, page 104), in accordance with the biblical injunction against graven images. Its roots arise in heaven above, unlike most divine Trees in other spiritual traditions. It then grows downward to the earth, gradually coming into increasing degrees of manifestation. This potent image serves as a focus for the meditative and reflective efforts of its practitioners. According to tradition, to begin such work, one should be at least 40 years old, and well-established in the everyday world and in Torah study, lest one lose one's way. Tradition also has it that of the four who embarked on this path in the early years of our now-ended 2,000-year aeon, one died, another went mad, a third lost his faith, with only the sainted Rabbi Akiba achieving the goal, despite the fire blocking the way. That fire was placed there as a flaming sword, the divine informs us in Genesis, lest humans become immortal like the angels, as well as knowing good and evil. Despite the dangers and difficulties, the pursuit has persisted and flowered for well over 20 centuries.

There are many books and specialty monographs on the Kabbalah, but two good introductions are those of Z'ev ben Shimon Halevi and Gershom Scholem.[1] The classic original text is the Zohar.[2] This far-reaching compilation attains the status of the holy books among practitioners. Presumably, Moses De Leon wrote it in the 13th century, but is has largely been attributed to Rabbi Simeon ben Yohai, who flourished in the second century C.E. (thus the venerable tradition of Jewish mysticism). This honored text is an imaginative and reflective work, bathed in the soul.

I first came upon the Zohar in 1950, during the first few months of my first analysis. I had performed my first active imagination (a dialogue with the unconscious) and came to my analytic session armed with a written fantasy conversation with a dream figure and with a painting I called "Purple in the Blue." While waiting for my session, I saw on the waiting room table a five-volume edition of the Zohar, which had apparently just arrived in the mail but was already unpacked. I opened a volume at random and started to read a fantasy that was written there. This fantasy proved to be very much like the one I had committed to paper, including the color use, and I began shaking when I realized that this was an ancient Jewish text. As I went upstairs for my analytic session, I continued to tremble. This synchronistic meeting with an ancestral soul was enough to frighten me away from the Kabbalah for 15 years! Instead, I explored many other mystical traditions. Only when I was 40 did I take up this potent text and only then did I learn that one is not supposed to undertake such study until one has attained that very age! With this preliminary taste of the numinous effect of this text, we can now discuss the concepts and imagery belonging to this spiritual path.

In Judaism, God is God, beyond any comparison. In Kabbalah, this transcendent God is called *Ayin*, a Hebrew word that translates into "No Thing." In this conception, God is beyond existence, movement, or stillness, is neither above nor below, and is represented by a circle or zero. This utter transcendence is followed, in sequence, by the second name of God, *Ayin Sof*, meaning, "Without End." This is the title of God Who, a totality of that which is everywhere, what is and what is not. This image is that of the Immanent God, the One, in contrast to the Zero of Ayin. The Immanent God is still without attributes because the latter can manifest only within existence and existence is finite. "Who" also implies agency.

The oral tradition tells us that the reason for existence is that "God wished to behold God." This is very much in line with what Jung concluded, psychologically, about the Self, arrived at by empirically examining the depths of the unconscious. The image of God, the Self, had everything except a partner with whom to engage in dialogue in order to develop consciousness. Hence the creation of the tiny, but evolving, self-consciousness of humans, who could then bring such consciousness back to God, ultimately attaining co-creator status with Him. This is the meaning of man being created in God's image. Before creation of ego-consciousness, says Kabbalah, "Face did not gaze upon Face." This is another pungent phrase expressing the same loneliness of consciousness in the divine Being. God longs for Man, is even "in search of man,"[3] as the Jewish (and Sufi) mystics have proclaimed.

In an act of total free will, God withdrew the Absolute All, *Ayin Sof*, from one place in order to allow a void to appear. This made it possible for a mirror of existence (Face gazing upon Face) to manifest in an infinitesimal "point." This act of contraction (note the similarity to the initial conditions of con-traction in Hindu Kundalini), was called Tzimtzum. From this infinitesimal "point," creation ultimately began, an image that is remarkably similar to conceptions in present-day physics, in which the creation of the universe is conceived of as having taken place via the "Big Bang." We can also now note that the longing of God for self-awareness was the background and condition for the creation of human consciousness, something that Jung has noted in his master-work, *Answer to Job*.[4] From the psychological point of view, naturally, we are speaking here of the human image of God needing development and realization and not something which utterly transcends our conscious-ness (Ayin Sof), since we are not capable of conceiving that in actuality. In short, our images of God change as we develop. This may or may not affect God-in-Itself, but we may never be able to know this for certain. It is quite enough that we cope with and are increasingly aware of how God manifests to us and in us, enabling us to engage in a relationship that can affect this image, as well as change ourselves.

The initial divine creation which preceded biblical creation entailed an emanation of a beam of light from the Endless Light, *Ayin Sof Or*, which surrounded the void, penetrating from outside toward the center. This beam, or *Kav*, was also the Divine Will manifesting itself in ten stages of Emanation. These stages are called "Sephirot" (singular is Sephira), which has no equivalent meaning in any other language but is roughly related at its root to "cipher" or "sapphire," words known to us also from alchemy as the circle and the precious jewel. These Sephirot constitute the Tree of Life and each is a vessel of divine power, manifesting attributes of God, all held in complex relationship from the beginning of creation until God wills them to vanish into the Void again. The relationships among the ten Sephirot are ordered by three principles, the "Hidden Splendours" (*Zahzahot*) which are conceived, as we gaze upon it, as a left pillar (feminine), a right pillar (masculine) and a middle pillar, balancing these opposites. Each Sephira has its own names and meanings. Justice and Severity are on the left, for example, while Mercy and Love are opposite on the right, with Will and Equilibrium balancing them both from the center. All the Sephirot manifest under the influence of the three pillars, going from opposite to opposite, and reconcile in the center. They flow in a zigzag lightning pattern from the Crown downward, finally manifesting on the earth. The worker in Kabbalah, in contrast, makes his/her way back up this Tree of development in a snake-like path. Figure 23 on page 101 represents these images of descent and ascent.

The first Sephira, Keter, or "Crown," is the initial emanation and therefore contains all that exists, has existed, and will exist (as potential) until the end of time when all returns to the Source. Its divine attribute is found in its name, *Ehyeh Asher Ehyeh* (I Am That I Am). The beam of light now descends to the second Sephira, under the Pillar of Mercy, Hokhmah (Wisdom), representing active, inner intellect, experienced as both human and divine inspiration or revelation. The movement then goes to its balanced opposite on the Pillar of Severity, to Binah (Understanding), which is intellect in its receptive and reflective capacity, thus human reason and tradition. The Light now heads toward the third Sephira on the Pillar of Mercy but touches, at the Middle Pillar of Equilibrium, a "non-Sephira" that is the place of Ruach ha Kodesh, the Holy Spirit, which hovers below the "supernal Sefirot" above it. It is itself unmanifest but has a place on the Tree marked by the "non-Sephira" of Daat (Knowledge). At this point, the Absolute may enter directly into existence (known in Christianity as the Holy Spirit). Daat is knowledge which emerges out of nowhere, directly from God. Daat is a "child" of the previous Sephira, but is more than revelation or pondering, combining these, yet something "other."

Below Daat, the Lightning movement passes on to another pair of opposites, on their respective Pillars, which have to do with emotion, as contrasted with the intellect above. On the side of the Mercy Pillar, there is Hesed, translated as the active, inner emotion of Mercy or Love, whereas its opposite of Gevurah, on the Severity Pillar, is the passive and outer emotion of Justice. These centers also have other names that describe the Attributes more fully. We would call them symbols, in the sense that Jung uses the term, referring to something like a diamond, having multiple facets of meaning, but surrounding a

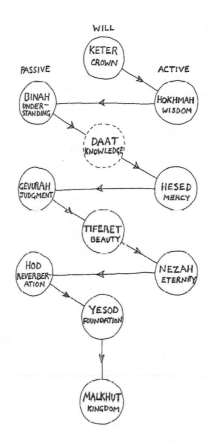

Figure 23. Lightning flash downward and snake-like ascent.
From *Halevi*, Kabbalah.

core that escapes total description (like the archetype). At the human level, Hesed represents qualities such as love, tolerance and generosity, whereas Gevurah carries the qualities of discipline, rigor and discrimination. These opposite processes underlie all human experience. One definition of evil is that it results when these Sephira are out of balance, e.g., there is too much judgment unbalanced by mercy or vice versa.

Following this pair of opposites, the Lightning Flash passes on to the Middle Pillar and arrives at the central Sephira of

Tifereth, Beauty. Here we are at the heart and essence of the Tree. Along with the emotional Sefirot, it forms a triad of the Divine soul; with the higher Sephirot of Hokhma and Binah, it constitutes the triad of the Divine spirit, in the midst of which the Holy Spirit hovers. It is the core of the individual, the Self, which stands over the human ego like an observer. Even in old Kabbalistic tradition, it is understood that the processes above this Sephira are "unconscious" to the human being and are mediated and focused via Tipheret, itself, just as Jung has independently discovered.

As the Lightning Flash continues, it reveals itself in another pair of opposites traditionally called Victory and Splendor, but also Eternity and Reverberation. These are the Hosts of God sent out to perform the Will of God but are revealed, at the human level, as psychobiological processes, such as the instinctive and impulsive functions (Nezah) and their control through cognition (Hod). How psychologically profound, one might innocently exclaim! Depth psychology has clearly confirmed this ancient mystical truth that the human condition of struggle with the instincts is our task, but the religious jewel of understanding adds that these functions, both desire and control, are divinely inspired and, therefore, are our human reflection of the divine nature (the Self).

This lowest pair of opposites on the two Pillars is joined together by Yesod (Foundation), which is phallic and generative. It itself generates new trees; it is also reflective, in that it is an "image of the image" or mirror within the Mirror. These two complementary functions, active and passive, are thus a foundation at the human level, and are therefore representative of the ego, reflecting our own consciousness, how we see and are seen in the world (mirror), and how we relate to the Sephirot above, particularly Tipheret. The divine reflection in our own ego is beautifully completed, thereby, including both creativity and reflection.

Finally, at the base of our diagram, complementing Keter the Crown, is Malkhut (Kingdom). Here the Lightning Flash is earthed, the Crown greets its Kingdom, constituting the *Shekhina*, the feminine presence of God in matter and the world. Its nature is fourfold, encapsulating the four levels of the Tree—root, trunk, branch, and fruit (as I shall describe next)—as it comes into existence. The four fold nature of the diagram is manifested as the four elements (earth, air, fire and water), and as solids, liquids, gases and radiations, which dynamically combine and interact in our lives. It is the human home, psyche on earth, in which both the divine and mortal drama takes place.

In addition to the Sephirot, the Tree of Life constitutes four Worlds also, as seen in figure 24 on page 104.

The first World, as the Tree comes into existence, is Emanation (*Azilut*). This represents a latent totality: everything here is only in potential, nothing has yet happened, since this is the stage of pure Will. What is required is for the Divine Will to unfold Creation in a series of cosmic cycles (*Shemittot*), in which the Presence manifests from the highest and most complex to the smallest particle, from eternity to now and to the End of Days, when all will be complete.

This powerful development begins with Azilut, whose image is the part of the Tree called "Root" and contains the letter Y of the sacred tetragrammaton name of God, YHVH (Yehovah). This first level, closest to the Crown, is associated with fire, Will, and divine calling. Unlike trees of life in other traditions, as we have noted earlier, the Kabbalistic tree has its roots in heaven and grows toward the earth.

The second World, associated with air, represents Intellect at the Divine level of *Beriah* (Creation). As you can see in the diagram, there is an overlap of this level onto the one above, Emanation. Creation extends upward beyond even potential manifestation, reaching its highest point in the region of Keter, Crown. It focuses upon Wisdom and Understanding and is modulated by the Holy Spirit. Potential, therefore, begins to manifest only when the creative act begins. In Rabbinical tradition, it was understood that God had a blueprint in his mind (first World of Emanation) which was revealed to human beings in the form of the Torah, the Hebrew Bible. God, therefore, consulted this blueprint when He created the Universe, which plan is revealed in Genesis.

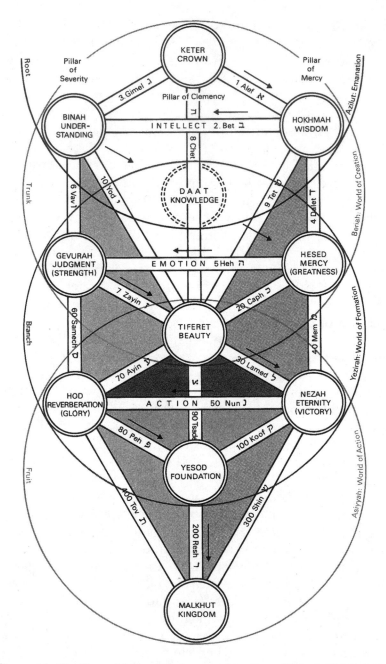

Figure 24: The Tree of Life with four worlds. From Halevi, Kabbalah.

The third level is associated with water, being an expression of emotion. In consonance with the nature of the volatility of emotion, the ever-changing becomes the region of the Divine World of *Yezirah* (Formation). Here the world of forms originates, as the unmanifested takes on specificity. From a Jungian perspective, we might understand this level as one in which archetypal images are manifested; the variety and multiplicity of expressions of a particular archetype, such as the Mother, appear. The latter basic form, in its pure abstractness and not-yet-formed quality, can be found at the level of Beriah, Creation, or what Jungian psychology would call the "archetype itself." Above that, at the World of Emanation, we would encounter a realm beyond the archetype, a region which is unknowable to us, except by our very fantasy of the unknown itself.

The fourth and last level, associated with earth, is that of *Assiyah* (Action). This is where all that has developed above comes into worldly concreteness. It is the consequence of Divine "making." Each level, as we descend, contains the qualities of all that has been included above or preceding, becomes more complex and further from the Source. Our Tree reveals a pattern of four stages: Conception takes place (in fire), followed by Creation in Manifestation as a principle (air), but not yet in an image. This continues as a third stage of a specific yet fluid World of Formation (water) where images abound, after which the solid World of Action in the material plane comes into existence. Yet each level, each of the worlds, also has its own complete Tree which can emerge from it.

These Worlds and Sephirot constitute the mind of God, so to speak, imagined as a dynamic structure, as well as the mind and behavior of man and the universe. Hence the Tree is a blueprint for almost everything in life, from the most abstract or spiritual to the most concrete and physical. As an example of this in the sister religion of Islam, we might remember how it was for the Muslim psyche, when conceiving of the great temple, the Ka'aba. There was a blueprint in heaven, long before the actual temple was built. But the latter got its value and numinosity from the divine plan. So it is here also.

The fact that both divine and human dynamics are thus revealed is further shown by the fact that each of the Worlds is related to the next one by the biblical blueprint. God, for example, has multiple Names that reveal the essence of each Sephira. At Keter, the Crown, the revealed name is *Ehyeh Asher Ehyeh,* meaning "I Am That I Am," signifying the beginning and end of existence; God is Being. Wisdom and Understanding, the next Sephirot, have the names of YHVH and Elohim, respectively. This means that both the merciful and just aspects of divinity are displayed and this is exactly how the names of God show up in the right context in the biblical narrative. God the Creator, at the center of the Tree, in Tipheret, is known by the composite name of YHVH Elohim, while the rest of the Sephirot are also under Elohim, which, interestingly, is a plural noun with a singular pronoun. Does this not stand for the multiplicity of creation arising from a single source? In tradition, this is also to be understood as revealing and manifesting all the divine attributes, which are also found in both the human condition and in matter.

The four Worlds, as has been suggested, permeate all existence. They may be seen as a Jacob's Ladder of Ascension (for human beings) and of Descension (for the divine), in which the angels, as told in Torah, move up and down. This is certainly grand and impressively positive, but the Kabbalists also speak of *Kelippot,* or shells, which recognize the presence of the demonic or destructive aspect in the created universe. This quality of destructiveness occurred as the result of residual elements from previous Worlds created and rejected by the Creator. Parts of these rejected worlds still exist at all levels. These demonic forces, a consequence of divine experimentation, are not entirely evil but function as powers to test the goodness of all that exists. They thus "prove" the soundness of each creation. This difficulty is in addition to the other source of evil in the world which results from the imbalance of the Sephirot, of which I spoke earlier. Demonic forces are also sons of God, surprisingly. They appear as such in the Book of Job but are unlike the condition of Satan in Christianity. These demonic forces are products of the initial Chaos, seeking disruption, and are opponents of humankind but, usefully, testing them as well. Human beings, however, like Adam, have the image of God within them (revealed by the same Tree which guides the Divine) and have the same free will and choice to create and destroy, just as God did, thus effecting their given internal divinity. Is this not precisely what the Hebrew Bible is suggesting in the statement that a sword of fire stands in the way of humans approaching the Tree of Life, lest they become god-like? If one does undertake such a Kabbalistic path, the dangers, as I mentioned earlier, are apparent: death, madness, and heresy, with only a 25 percent chance of success! Yet some risk it and the numbers grow larger, if not the odds.

The details of how this work is to be done, apart from the routine meditation and reflection performed also on the spiritual paths of Zen and Kundalini, is to be found in another aspect of the diagram of the Tree, namely the interconnections among the various Sephirot. Interestingly, these are called Paths. They constitute the way that a searcher proceeds "up the Tree" toward its summit and Root. Each path, as one can see, has both a letter name, from the Hebrew alphabet, and a number, based on the arithmetical significance of this name. Each path, constituting as it does the properties of both ends with which it connects, has its particular significance and reflection, denoting tasks that the person will need to do. It is also especially notable that ever since the tarot cards were invented and put into use, a particular branch of Kabbalists has used the greater trumps, or major arcana, as significators for the Sephirot and for the Paths. Indeed, it is part of the tarot tradition that the cards were devised for the specific purpose of carrying on the occult path of this Jewish mystical tradition.[5] Such images supply additional material for reflection and thought as one refines one's soul on the way to apprehension of the Divine.

Finally, we must consider the significance of Adam Kadmon, the image of Adam (man) before the actual person was created. He is an initial reflection of God made manifest in the successive creative events and is similar to the image and idea of the *anthropos* in Gnostic speculation. For all practical purposes, the initiate seeker, in effect, "incarnates" this primordial image when he or she does Kabbalistic meditation. The various Sephirot then become connected with various parts of the body and meditation brings these into psychic reality. This is made visible in figure 25 on page 109.

One meditation in this tradition, with which I am particularly familiar, can serve as an example: It is called the Middle Pillar. You, as the meditator, focus upon an imagined ball of light, beginning at the Crown of the head (Keter). You then bring this ball of light down through the mid-line of your body, sequentially touching the various centers, circulating around each of them, in turn, while chanting various names of God belonging to each center. At the top, you chant *Ehyeh Asher Ehyeh* (I Am That I Am) and at the next center on this Middle Pillar, the throat, you chant *Yehovah Eloah ve D'aath*, linking the Holy Spirit with the two upper Sephirot. You then continue downward to the heart/chest region, chanting *Yehovah Elohim*, once again uniting the opposites of Gevurah and Hesed at Tifereth. Then you move downward to the genital region, Yesod, and chant *Shadai El Chai*, which refers to the divine as Lord of Life. Finally, you come to the feet, Malkhut, and chant *Adonai Haaretz*, Lord of the Earth. Following this dwelling in, circling, and chanting at each center, you imagine a rotation of the light/energy. First, there is a circulation around the sides of the body, beginning at the crown and going down on the right side to the feet and than back up the left side to the crown, performed several times. This is followed by another rotation, from the top of the head down the back to the feet and then upward on the front side of the body. A final energy movement, called the Fountain, entails gradually raising the energy from your feet to your head and then visualizing it shooting up into the air and falling to your feet once more, like a fountain. A closing prayer gives thanks for this divine contact. A further description and discussion, in the context of the ancient work with "magick," can be found in Israel Regardie's book, *The Middle Pillar*.[6] Famed secretary to Aleister Crowley, Regardie was also a noted occultist, an accomplished Reichian therapist, and one of my revered teachers. But I must warn you

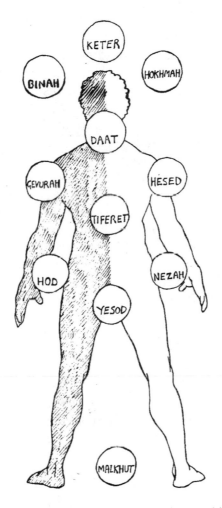

Figure 25: Adam Kadmon. From Halevi, Kabbalah.

that the magical tradition includes intentionally presenting at least one error in such teachings, so that the adept can discover this on his or her own, while "treading the path." This error is also found in Regardie's meditation, I believe, but I have corrected it, above, since I do not regard this devious instruction as useful in the present age, which tends to be more democratic, less elitist, and centrally seeking of maximum enlightenment.

It remains for us to consider how this ancient and developing mystical system is similar to and different from the other inner and relational paths we have investigated thus far. First and foremost, like Kundalini and the oxherding series, we are faced with a sequence of encounters/experiences that begin with one's aloneness, an awareness of the ego and its limits. This is soon eclipsed by the tremendous problem of coping with the psychophysiological instincts, especially raising questions of expression and control. Reconciliation of these opposites—after long effort—results in the experience of the Self, the center where one finally is at home with one's body and soul, connected to an inner authority. This is similar to the heart chakra of Kundalini and the coming home on the ox's back in Buddhism. The Kabbalistic path, presenting a gendered manifestation of the divine (feminine on the left, masculine on the right), with neutral or conjoined expression on the Middle Pillar, seems more in harmony with the Hindu experience. Both also recognize that God is present in each place and movement. The Kabbalistic focus is also on the inner work, however, rather than on the relational experience of the alchemical process. Just as in the Buddhist and Hindu paths, a teacher or guru is presumed to be in the background, but is not as central in this system as in the Eastern versions. Certainly, the further development of Kabbalah after the Middle Ages was influenced by Kundalini (perhaps the reverse was also true), and this mystical system also garnered special continuing development outside of Jewish circles (e.g., tarot specialization), particularly in Christian mysticism. Its flavor, however, as in each of the sister religions, is unique.

Beyond the experience of the Self as is found in the oxherding pictures, and somewhat differently but essentially the same as in Kundalini, the subsequent process of development revealed in the pictures focuses on the relativization of the ego. This process then leads to its possible dissolution (Hinduism) or being contained in a unified whole, either by living apart or active in life. For the Jewish system, the remaining development certainly means ever more profound contact with aspects of the divine, but the ego's continuing relation to the Self and immersion in everyday life is assumed. Connection and devotion is the goal (as in alchemy), not dissolution. Hence, what Jung would call questions of the animus and anima are then dealt with (Judgment/Power and Mercy/Love), followed by Understanding and Wisdom (coping with the Holy Spirit), leading to final unity with the simultaneously transcendent and immanent at Keter.

It is remarkable that the various systems are so similar, really, in dealing with the inner opposites: with expression versus control of instincts, with inner masculine and feminine qualities, with soul and spirit, with ego and Self. It is equally remarkable that the particular taste of each system is profoundly revealed in its imagery, such as the One God with the Many manifestations, particularity of culture as well as individuality. Each system, at any rate, reveals special aspects of the spiritual path that can be useful to everyone on such a quest at the beginning of the new millennium. We shall later have occasion to question whether and how an ecumenical union of these images can take place, but now we will leave this sojourn into one way of the attending to the Divine Within.

Notes

[1] Z'ev ben Shimon Halevi, *Kabbalah: Tradition of Hidden Knowledge* (New York: Thames and Hudson, 1979), and Gershom Scholem, *On the Kabbalah and Its Symbolism* (London: Routledge, 1965).

[2] The Zohar, five volumes, Harry Sperling and Maurice Simon, trans. (London: Soncino, 1933).

[3] Abraham Joshua Heschel, *God in Search of Man: A Philosophy of Judaism* (New York: Noonday Press, 1997).

[4] C. G. Jung, *Answer to Job,* in *CW* 11.

[5] See, for example, Paul Foster Case, *The Tarot* (Richmond, VA: Macoy Publishing, 1947).

[6] Israel Regardie, *The Middle Pillar: A Co-relation of the Principles of Analytical Psychology and the Elementary Techniques of Magic* (St. Paul, MN: Llewellyn, 1970). Currently in print in a revised edition under the title *The Middle Pillar: The Balance Between Mind and Magic.*

CHAPTER 6

Divine Between: Alchemical Relationship and Jungian Analysis

In one sense, it has always been known that the divine can be encountered "between" two people, namely in the experience of love itself. Eros was a "mighty daimon," said Plato, and one Greek creation myth tells us that it was that god who was the originator of the universe. This centrality of love in relationship is found in other cultures' stories also, particularly in Christianity ("God so loved the world that he gave His only son . . ."), although here it is generally seen as agape, in the form of connectedness and tenderness, rather than the Eros passion of sexual union. Yet the passion of the self-sacrifice of the divine Son is equally powerful.

In another sense, however, the divine "between" is not only a fairly recent emergence in the development of consciousness (e.g., since the Age of the Romantics in 19th-century Europe); it is also a kind of cutting-edge of our current and prospective spiritual situation.

First, however, I want to mention two areas in traditional religions that do mark the significance of particular relationships as a hallmark of spiritual fulfillment, if not as a path itself. One area that will leap to mind for many is that of Tantra, which is found in both Hinduism and Buddhism. We saw, when examining Kundalini Yoga, how the images of divine union, male and female, are central to each chakra, even though the yogin practices his art alone. There are traditions, however, in which the yogin goes through certain phases of development in relating to the divine feminine. The first phase begins with the yogin serving a selected woman for six months. Following this, he may enter her bed, but may not be sexually intimate with her for another six months. Only after he has proved himself, in this way of service and restraint, can he then engage her in the long, slow, Tantric lovemaking which serves as both a union and as spiritual development.

On the Buddhist side, the Vajrayana Tantrics (9th century C.E.) reinterpreted Shakyamuni Buddha's biography to render it more compatible with their doctrines, so that the ascetic phase that was typical of Buddha's life (and thus that of the monks), was only temporary. They realized that a repressed desire is not a desire mastered, and thus was only partly "on the way" to Enlightenment. According to *Candamaharoshanatantra*, Buddha experienced divine bliss with his wife, Gopa, thus attaining highest Enlightenment:

> Along with Gopa, he experienced bliss,
> By uniting the diamond scepter and lotus,
> He attained the fruit of bliss.
> Buddhahood is obtained from bliss, and
>
> Apart from women there will not be bliss.[1]

Tantric iconographers portrayed female buddhas as red, uniting with male buddhas who were blue in color. They participated in dance and in nakedness to achieve such union. In this sense, they continued the Hindu tradition of Shiva-Shakti conjunction, now in somewhat different "coloration."

Islam, too, itself a religion of passion, presents the story of the great mystic and poet, Rumi, who had such great love for the wandering Sufi saint, Shams of Tabriz, that it caused jealousy among his disciples. This was so serious that Shams left the region of Konya and was later murdered. Rumi turned his anguish into volumes of poetry in which passion for his companion provides the central metaphor for union with the divine. Yet Rumi was also a mystic who, when asking for a blessing from the "wall of divine," receiving none, blessed himself!

Such religious genius, totally at home with the divine "within" and "between" at the same time, is rare. Yet there is the well-known story of the medieval monk and nun, Abelard and Eloïse, whose great love could not be successfully consummated, despite their intense spirituality and mutual engagement on the Christian path. And the biblical Song of Songs, a marvelously erotic piece of mystical poetry, has touched almost everyone. It is simultaneously a paean of love to a most human woman, on the part of the great King Solomon for the Shulamite, but is also a metaphor for the love of God.

Yet the idea of a mutual pursuit of a spiritual path to the divine (in contrast to "within" or "among"), is a relatively recent development, at least in the West. It is alchemy that has provided both imagery and ideas along this line, which only gradually has been realized in recent years. Surprisingly, this realization arose in the study of the relationship between analyst and analysand, called "transference." Here Jung paved the way to the deeper understanding of this relationship as potentially something more than the parent-child connection. We shall examine the series of woodcuts from that medieval book of the alchemists, the *Rosarium Philosophorum*, from the 16th century, along with Jung's commentary, to guide us for this deeper understanding.[2] It is useful, however, to look again at the woodcut which I presented in the Introduction to this book (see fig. 4 on page 11) This art work, from the 18th-century text, the *Mutus Liber*, was created only at the "end" of alchemy (that is, when chemistry replaced alchemy's laboratory function and its psychological aspect went underground until Jung excavated it in the middle of the 20th century).

Is it not remarkable that at the very climax of the "art," some of the practitioners realized that it was not only aspects of themselves that were meant to be transformed, namely their base instincts of greed, lust, violence and so on, but that their great work was to redeem and transform the divine that had fallen into matter? Most important for the "divine between," some of them realized that this work both could and needed to be done in pairs, the alchemist and his mystical sister, his *soror mystica*. It dawned on them that mutuality would arise in their work on themselves and each other. Thus they would find themselves in a joint effort, a "mutual process" as I have called it,[3] and that the "third" between them, the divine dark figure of Mercurius, was to be experienced as a "fourth" as well, in the form of the divine pair above them. The larger Oneness, both in its source and origin and in its goal as fulfillment, looked down on the work, as a Sun, from above.

It has only been in the last half century that some psychotherapists, mostly Jungian, have realized the "intersubjectivity" of the transference, have recognized that there is indeed a "field" in which these processes from the unconscious are manifested both between and around the participants. Indeed, the very attention to the unconscious by both parties ultimately awakens or activates this deeper or archetypal layer. Their attention to this field constitutes much of the work done by them, in raising consciousness of their own unconscious, that of their analytic partner and what arises between them. The great preponderance of psychotherapeutic work enterprise limits itself to the parent-child archetype and myth suggests that it is not only in childhood that we are deeply affected by our parents. More importantly, it is in that very same childhood that the great archetypes that underlie our myths, our religions and our very nature, are also activated. These powerful images and affects are initially experienced largely with parents, and this is why psychoanalysis continues to emphasize early life.

Ultimately, however, these primordial stories, arising from beyond our personal unconscious, become the basic material of our own spiritual path of transformation. The alchemists called this area of the psyche the *prima materia*, saying that it was to be found in the *rejecta* of life, e.g., in urine and feces. Jung, from his extensive experience of dreams and fantasies, realized that these *rejecta* should be translated as the imagination itself, also generally rejected as "mere fantasy." Imagination, which for William Blake was even the region of

God, is commonly seen as "just fantasy," namely meaningless or illusory. How we deal with fantasy is the issue, of course, which I will discuss later on when I explore more directly Jung's stages of individuation.

If we look briefly at the alchemical series from the *Rosarium*, we can see how the process manifests itself, in dreams, in the analytic relationship, and fundamentally, in the psyche itself. Naturally, what we present here is a limited generalization; particular analytic cases or processes will not be so orderly. But, like Jung's stages of individuation, this provides a kind of useful classification of what is generally experienced.

The first picture of this series (see fig. 26 on page 117), like numbers 8 and 9 of the Zen oxherding series, shows no people but scenes of Nature and Culture, both concrete and abstracted. We see a square mandala (in contrast to the achieved circle of wholeness in the oxherding pictures), made up of four stars, with a double snake's head (the *Binarius* or devil-image) spitting its toxic cloud as a frame. The alchemists and we see this as wholeness in matter (the square as its symbol) that needs to be transformed into a perfected circle. Mercurius, the hidden or absent God who is present in matter, is hereby shown as an initial condition. The alchemists understood that it is this aspect of the divine, or its sparks left over from the initial act of creation, that is portrayed in every aspect in all the pictures. The central fountain in the picture complements the "four" of the stars, along with the "two" of the snake. This fountain has a circular form, in which the "three" of the spigots (animal, vegetable, and mineral, referring to different aspects of this rejected divine content in the soul), circulate in an endless flow. All of this is witnessed from above by the two opposite male and female principles of sun and moon (a more benevolent "Binarius") and the One, quintessential (meaning both "five" and "one") star as well. This, in a nutshell, portrays the famous "Axiom of Maria Prophetissa." The latter was a famous woman alchemist who presented the principle that the process involves going from one (an initial but undifferentiated whole) to two (the opposites separated and in conflict), to three (the reconciling "third" but still incomplete as

Figure 26. The mercurial fountain. From Jung, CW 16, p. 205.

a union), out of which comes the "fourth" as the One. This is a statement that says much about how we develop individually, psychologically, and how things manifest in therapeutic work. This is not to say that we often discuss this numerical understanding in the work, but examination of dream series reveals this development very well.

We begin analysis with a general conception of who and what we are, get a rude awakening as we examine the unconscious as it is revealed to us in our dreams, discovering that we are really divided, "two." The warring of internal opposites takes a long time to deal with—instinct versus spirit, light versus dark, masculine traits versus feminine, etc.—until a reconciling "third" emerges. But even this, in the long run, is not enough, and we ultimately find a balancing "fourth," in which our Self, and a relationship with the divine within us, is made psychologically real.

In the second picture of the series (see fig. 27 on page 119), we are presented with two apparently human figures, a king and a queen. These are not ordinary human beings, however, they are royalty and they are clearly meant to be imaginal rather than literal, sitting, as they do, upon a sun and moon, respectively. Mercurius has now divided himself into the opposites of the masculine and feminine principles. They meet formally, in regal garb, and this contact is made via the touching of left hands, "sinister" (left-hand) or atypical, suggesting that the connection is not ordinary or usual, and may even be taboo. This *sub rosa* meeting, however, is balanced by the presence of orderly flowers in their other hand, which cross each other as a mandala (the Self or one symbol of totality) and join together with the dove from above (the Holy Spirit or Aphrodite's bird of Love) which brings its own flower to the union. Above all is the single quintessential star of the first picture, clearly showing this as a spiritual union, titled *philosophorum*.

Jungian psychology understands this as a symbol of all the opposites that arise when one addresses the unconscious carefully. We also see this as how things begin in analysis: the partners in this confrontation of soul to soul are initially quite formal and circumspect (with a left-handed *sous entendu* of readiness to address painful, rejected, difficult, yet also wonderful qualities of the soul). Yet it is really Mercurius himself/herself who is being so addressed and is differentiating itself in the psyche of the analysand and in the relationship. Jung goes to considerable length to understand these

Figure 27. King and queen. From Jung, CW 16, p. 213.

figures as the inner masculine of the female participant and the inner feminine of the male participant in the process. During those earlier days of depth psychology, most analysts

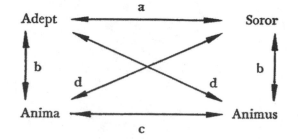

Figure 28: Diagram of the opposites. Adapted from Jung CW 16.

were male and most analysands female! He understood that this archetypal pair is meeting in the unconscious while a conscious relation exists between the therapeutic couple. Yet this holds true, these days, for same sex relations, since we are dealing with the principle of the opposites here, and not actual people. Initial dark wholeness, in this process, differentiates into opposites, ultimately leading to a new, differentiated wholeness over time.

Jung's diagram (see fig. 28, above), modified to include all opposites, shows us in a nutshell all the varieties of connection that can and do happen in this work.[4] A particular content of Mercurius—say the coldness of a Bluebeard with his female victim—constellates itself and hops about, now experienced in the one partner or the other. Each thinks that the other is "doing this" to him/her and therefore enacts or becomes conscious of this dynamic. In actuality, both are being "done unto" by the archetype itself. "It" is present, dividing itself and affecting both parties. When consciousness of this dynamic is achieved, there is the "third" above to which both relate (perhaps the dove or the star). This "third," in turn, might also be experienced as an actual pair, so that the participants can recognize both the cold Bluebeard and the female victim in themselves, in the partner, and as the archetypal energy between them. At times, the flow can become the "fourth," a pair itself experienced by the partners as such. This dynamic is better expressed in the next picture.

In figure 29 (page 122), the king and queen are now unclothed: the "naked truth" of the psyche in all the grandeur and horror of its opposites is revealed. The crowns remain, signifying the "royal" nature of these opposites, and the connection is still mediated by both a simplified union of flowers and the bird of the Holy Spirit. There is no more subterfuge (left hand), however, and the quintessential star vanishes. Thus confusion arises: Which content belongs to whom? Is it projection? Projective identification, as the Kleinian psychoanalysts prefer to call one way that this can happen (where the unconscious content of the analysand is pushed into the analyst for communication, or safe-keeping or to be gotten rid of), or truth? Or is it both?

Actually, I think, the divine in matter is being expressed in both partners and in the relationship itself. In classical Freudian psychoanalysis, it is the patient who is exposed while the analyst tries mightily to keep his/her objectivity. In Kleinian analysis, the analyst uses his counter-transference reaction (as it is called) to the patient as an indication of what the latter is unconsciously trying to "put in" to him or her, or to serve as a communication of his/her condition (called the aforementioned "projective identification"). In advanced Jungian "mutual process" understanding, however, the situation is symmetrical; the archetype is manifesting within both parties simultaneously and in the relationship itself. It is this shared awareness that truly advances consciousness and brings about the possibility of deeper union, both within and between.

In truth, figure 30 (page 123) shows a picture which more clearly depicts what is happening in the psyche of the participants, since the "vessel" (fountain) of the first picture returns and is now the container for the work. Analysts like to think that the process of analysis, with its regularity of meeting, intentionally addressing the unconscious, formal engagement as a psychological work, is the "vessel." Here, however, we can see that the "quintessential" star, present at the beginning and then vanishing in the previous picture, becomes the "bath," the vessel itself. So we can say that it is the God-image within the psyche, both "above" and

Figure 29: The naked truth. From Jung, CW 16, p. 239.

"below," spiritual and material, that contains the opposites, the therapeutic participants, and the process. This important realization, hard-won in the still largely atheistic psychoanalytic field, brings a truly "religious" attitude to the work. One

Figure 30. Immersion in the bath. From Jung, CW 16, p. 241.

realizes that a "higher power" is at work and requires the best efforts of those engaging in this process. Doesn't this remind us of that woodcut presented in the Introduction to this book, of the alchemist and his mystical sister working on their transformation while the angels and the Divine participate from above? There is deep truth in this: the participants work on transformation and are worked upon, while the divine in the soul undergoes the same process.

The joining together in the bath leads to union of the king and queen, taking place in the water. There are two pictures for this event, one in which the figures are sexually conjoined as humans (fig. 31, top, page 125) and another in which the figures are also in coitus, but they are winged creatures. Now the medieval alchemists certainly intended no pornography here; the union of opposites was wonderful and alarming enough for them and the sexual metaphor for this was natural. That this was not meant to be a literal union is emphasized by the fact that in both cases the act takes place in the water, namely in the vessel in which the chemicals are worked with—the unconscious, from our point of view. One of the illustrations emphasizes that these are winged, hence spiritual creatures, whereas the other does not. Is this not the same ambivalence that the powerful sexual instinct arouses in us? We experience a strong need to simultaneously concretize and sublimate or spiritualize. No wonder that the driving force for such tabooed consummation in the therapeutic process sometimes overcomes the equally powerful pressure to keep this union at a spiritual, non-literal level!

My analyst in Zurich, Dr. C. A. Meier, was of the opinion that the power of the sexual instinct was really based on a deep inner sense of the need for the union of the opposites in the soul. The evidence for this, he believed, was that the biological necessity of coitus for reproduction could have been fulfilled with far less propulsion. Think of our animal cousins, for example, who need to mate only once a year. Is it not true that creative people tend to be more sexually driven than the average person, suggesting that the creative urge itself has at least an equal power in the spiritual realm? Just the same, the taboo against concretization (upon which the legal and ethical injunction is unconsciously based) arises from that same negation, which has its origin in the incest taboo, found in all cultures. Jung understood this as the need of the soul to fulfill its need for both consciousness and wholeness, as powerful as the reproductive drive itself. Here the central image is of a king and queen, as equals or as brother and sister, also taboo biologically, but less taboo than the union between parent and child. Now that this has taken place all the same, but in the psyche, not concretely what could happen next?

CONIVNCTIO SIVE
Coitus.

FERMENTATIO.

*Figure 31. The conjunction. Illustrations from
Jung, CW 16, top: p. 247; bottom: p. 249.*

CONCEPTIO SEV PVTRE
factio

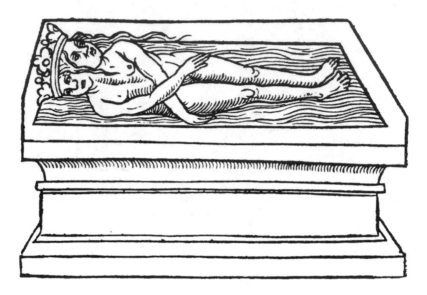

Figure 32. Death. From Jung, CW 16, p. 257.

The figures, having united, become a bisexual individual, portrayed as dead (see fig. 32 above). They are contained, once more, in the vessel that vanished in the previous picture, but now returns as a coffin. What does this death mean? First of all, the glory of *coniunctio*, the joy of union, is followed by the *nigredo* (darkness). Every union in the psyche, alas, follows this pattern, as do many unions in ordinary life. Hence the need, in analytic work, to undergo the suffering of the clashing of opposites in one's soul and in relationship, followed by a sense of achievement and peace, and followed again by the darkness of depression, no action.

This suffering of the soul seems to be a necessity when the spiritual path is pursued, no matter what form it might take. Union here means a death of the power of the opposites and an enduring of uncertainty, even chaos, for a time. Translated psychologically, this means that the union of the conscious mind or ego personality with the unconscious produces a new personality, which is compounded of both and therefore is also neither one. It is truly a birth of the Self, a transcendent experience when this union takes place at the level of the ultimate opposites, but this is also easily recognizable when less profound opposites are conjoined.

Out of this death, there is born the *filius philosophorum*, the divine child of the soul, which now ascends (with the smoke and cloud of Mercurius returning from the very first picture) to the heavens above (see fig. 33, page 128). What does this mean? The suffering of the opposites and their union gives birth to—that is, produces—a new condition of spiritualization that arises from that same suffering of the divine element in matter and is now brought to the divine in Heaven. This is a powerful image. We do the work of God within ourselves and within a spiritual relationship, and the fruits of this work ascend to our most differentiated image of the Divine itself. Thus, we are the honored vessel of divine transformation and so, too, we perform a kind of *imitatio Christi*, a model of a chief image of Western civilization, the crucifixion of Jesus Christ. Jesus, carrying the symbol of the union of the most extreme opposites, being both God and human, suffers this condition, sacrifices himself, and then also ascends to his Father in Heaven. In alchemy, as we shall see later on, pagan imagery combines with Christian imagery in surprising ways, true to the psyche but perhaps shocking to some members of a particular faith. The psyche itself is ecumenical, however, as we have seen; it both leads and includes whatever consciousness has produced at a particular place and time, going on in its evolution Godward.

Our next picture signals relief. The depression and chaos that accompanies such a struggle with both human nature and God's nature—namely the archetypes as they manifest in our psyches and analytic work—produce a "whitening." This is a purification of the darkness, symbolized by the moisture of love and forgiveness which comes from above (remember the

ANIMÆ EXTRACTIO VEL
imprægnatio.

Figure 33. The ascent of the soul. From Jung, CW 16, p. 267.

"quintessential" star). It is also called "Gideon's Dew," reminding us of the biblical story (Judges 6:36 *ff.*) of a man who was told by God to undertake very dangerous and important activity yet doubted whether it was truly asked of him. When he asked

ABLVTIO VEL
Mundificatio

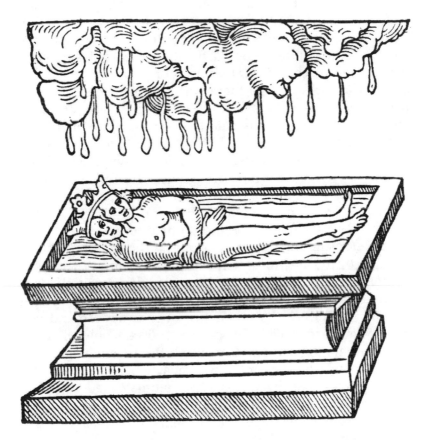

Figure 34. Purification. From Jung, CW 16, p. 273.

for proof or confirmation that the message came from God, he was granted an experience of dew falling upon a particular place on the ground when all around continued to be dry.

Don't we all ultimately doubt even our most profound religious experiences? Doesn't our inner skeptic, who has become even demonic since the Age of Enlightenment, gradually demolish all faith and conviction in goodness and legitimate spiritual achievement, requiring continual renewal? Yet the moisture occurs. I am reminded of a three-year period in my life when I feared disaster and catastrophe, needing to endure this fear as an ever-present dark companion. The biblical injunction to "fear God" became quite real to me. When this fear lifted, due to positive events, I surely felt purified and redeemed. As I wrote to a respected senior colleague, I understood why there was a whole group of angels in heaven whose only task was to sing the praise of God. I had never understood this before: was God something like a Mafia chieftain, I asked, needing to be told He is wonderful when there is manifest darkness and destruction around Him? It became clear to me that these angels are residents of the psyche; they are automatically grateful, without request, and sing God's praise, not only in propitiation (as every primitive culture knows also), but also in gratitude for redemption. My ego did not sing these praises, it did not have to; my unconscious did it for me, to my redounding benefit!

In figure 35 (page 131), the reconciler, the soul, itself, dives down from heaven to bring life back to the dead body. This is the fruit of renewal, the experience of revivification and new life in a new personality. This condition occurs only when the most extreme opposites are endured; the fragmentation and unification which occur in the workaday world of day-by-day, week-by-week, year-by-year analysis ultimately add up to an ever-larger wholeness when such redemption can occur. It also suggests the possible impending termination of this particular period of analytic work.

Such achievement is balanced, in our picture, by the appearance in the lower segment of a partly buried bird and one attending it. Doesn't this suggest that the spirit (bird) in the unconscious itself, does remain as a witness and is indicative of still further work (redemption of that earth-spirit) to be done? All of our strenuous efforts on the spiritual path, as long as we are alive, are the last but one, aren't they? This picture reminds us of this fact.

ANIMÆ IVBILATIO SEV
Ortus seu Sublimatio.

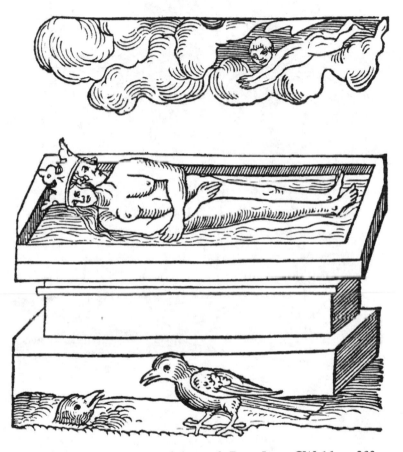

Figure 35. The return of the soul. From Jung, CW 16, p. 283.

The last picture in the series which Jung uses, the tenth, is seen by him as the *denarius,* a perfect number (adding together Maria Prophetissa's 4+3 + 2+1), and therefore is another symbol for wholeness (see fig. 36 on page 132). We see clearly the reborn Self as a triumphant union of

Figure 36. The new birth. From Jung, CW 16, p. 305.

male and female, holding the vessel for the original snake
energies and sharing another symbol of wholeness (as
development), the Tree of Life. This new Self combines
our conscious and unconscious, our maleness and femaleness and, therefore, is triumphantly whole. Interestingly, this
figure rests on the Moon, omitting the Sun. Jung thought

that this was because the alchemists tended to be mostly male and the unconscious compensated by emphasizing the feminine. But can't we also add to this understanding that the birth of the Self from below, from matter and the Earth, will perforce have a more markedly feminine quality? And that the alchemists were, in effect, anticipating the emergence, several hundred years later, of the necessity of elevating the feminine principle, once more, into the Godhead? Jung recognized this profound event (in his 1950 book, *Answer to Job*), when he interpreted the *Assumptio Mariae* (the papal pronouncement of Mary's bodily ascension into heaven as a principle of faith) as a statement revealing what was going on in the collective unconscious. The incomplete Trinity in the conscious collective divine image needed the addition of the feminine principle, as Mary, and this meant that matter, body and humanity—all belonging to the image of Mary—would also ascend into a renewed image of God, as well. We also note that one bird in this picture remains on earth, perhaps telling us that the spirit in nature cannot be forgotten even after we and the rejected divine spark ascend.

Jung felt that the relative primitivity of the alchemical vision in the production of just such a bisexual creature was, in fact, somewhat monstrous. He rightly noted that contemporary dreams sometimes show a bisexual creature, particularly at the outset of an individuation process. This denotes a beginning of a process of differentiation, ultimately leading to other symbols of wholeness. Yet perhaps we can look at some other *Rosarium* pictures, which Jung chose not to discuss, to see if further light can be shown. Let's look at the last two (of twenty) which follow similar images of suffering, redemption, and sacrifice.

In figure 37 on page 134, we get some validation of our earlier speculation regarding both the human soul and the feminine principle. The soul is now clearly represented as a human, feminine being, being crowned by two holy male representatives of the spirit. This implies the deification of the soul in its most human form, here emphasizing the

Figure 37: Soul and spirit united in heaven. From Johannes Fabricius, Alchemy: The Medieval Alchemists and Their Ritual Art *(London: Diamond Books, 1994), p. 230.*

feminine as its representative. Doesn't this indicate that the feminine has indeed ascended into heaven and is crowned as equal? This was portended as far back as the middle of the 16th century, when these woodcuts were drawn and assembled. We are now witnessing the realization of that intuition as a fact, all over the world, at the dawning of the new millennium. This is seen in the demands of women everywhere for equality, in the treasuring of nature and the environment, in the turn toward relationship and mutuality as a focus of meaning, rather than in hierarchy and competition alone.

The woodcut in figure 38 on page 136 is both reconciling to the conscious image of the divine, in the form of Christ, and profoundly original. The figure who ultimately emerges out of the coffin (tomb) is surely Christ, but we can certainly not forget that this whole process had to do with the work within the psyches of the alchemist and his *soror mystica* to achieve their own divinity. Secondly, this resurrection in a glorified body is seen, in Christianity, to occur only at "the End of Days." Here it is presented as a legitimate outcome of the alchemical work done by mortals.

To understand this, we can look further into the alchemical procedure. Alchemists understood, as do we, that the work with the base matter to be transformed—all of our instinctual nature—had a first result in what they called the *unio mentalis*, a spiritualization, or what Freud initially called "sublimation." But this was not enough. The spiritualized soul needed to reunite with the body, with matter, in order to attain a true and present resurrection. That is to say that the work of the Self is continually that of spiritualization, but that task includes our embodying and living that wholeness in the world. Only then does the process of individuation truly take place. This is the personal and cultural task of the present and the future. We can now intuit that the work begun by the alchemists is continuing in some analytic processes. The fact that this whole effort is brought back into the psyche bespeaks an achievement of the highest order.

Yet, paradoxically, it's no wonder that such work is relatively rare, largely misunderstood, and often not achieved even when undertaken. But Jung was not far wrong when he suggested that the spiritual work performed in deep analyses consti-

Figure 38. Resurrection in a glorified body.
From Fabricius, Alchemy, *p. 230.*

tuted a kind of Western yoga, something just beginning in
our culture and thus not having the grandeur of that Eastern
thousand-year-old practice.

My understanding is even more optimistic than Jung's is. Having been privileged to have as analysands people from Asian countries, as well as Europeans and Americans, I see this path as worldwide in its ecumenism, as I mentioned at the outset. My recently deceased friend and colleague, Dr. Arwind Vasavada, from India, had the impression that the West (Jung) added more of the personal and individual work to the spiritual process generally and that this, ultimately, would be embraced in the East. It is the experience of numerous Jungian analysts from all over the world, however small and shaky such a source may be (there are fewer than three thousand analysts, worldwide), which suggests that what the alchemists began is continuing as a global phenomenon. After all, alchemy belonged to Arabia, China, and Africa as well as to Europe, and we may be seeing here the path of the collective soul of us all to find both union and individuality.

I do not want to leave the impression that the *coniunctio* or marriage of the opposites, realizing the "divine between," is limited to male and female individuals. There is the powerful image of the marriage of God with the people of Israel, for example, and of Jesus with his Church. At the purely human level, I have already mentioned the power of Tantra and that of the Romantics, as well as the male-male union of Rumi and Shams. This latter relationship, that of the divine in friendship, is also compelling and I would like to dwell a bit longer on that story as well.

It is told that when Rumi was 37, he was a noted theologian, a scholar, artist and lover of the beautiful. One day, he was riding on his donkey and came upon Shams, a wandering dervish monk who mingled with laborers and camel drivers (as did the enlightened one in the last oxherding picture). Shams was enlightened, but shunned fame and only wanted to find one person vast enough in spirit to be his companion. As Rumi rode by, Shams shouted out to him: "Who is greater, Muhammad or Bestami?" (Bestami was a Sufi master who, when merging ecstatically with God, cried out that he and the Godhead were one. Muhammad's greatness, as founder of the tradition, came only as a messenger of God; hence the question).

Rumi answered "Muhammad," as was expected, to which Shams countered: "But Bestami said, 'I am the Glory!' Muhammad said, 'I can not praise you enough!'" This was so powerful a challenge to Rumi, realizing that he had directly encountered one who knew the Mystery, that he fainted and fell off his camel.[5]

When Rumi revived, he answered anew, that "Bestami took one swallow of knowledge and thought that that was all, but for Muhammad the majesty was continually unfolding."

This was enough for Shams to realize that he had found his partner and the two men took long retreats together in which they experienced a deep communion of words and silence called *sobbet*.

Their spiritual friendship proved to bring on jealousy from Rumi's students and they forced Shams to leave Konya. Rumi sent his son to bring Shams back and found him playing cards in a tavern with a young wastrel from the West who was later to become St. Francis of Assisi. The young man was cheating, but when the entourage clearly bowed to Shams as a spiritual giant, Francis confessed and tried to give the money back. Shams, however, declined and told him to take this value to the West.

Shams came back several times, but ultimately fanatics took his life, on December 5, 1247, and his body disappeared. Rumi wandered for months, desolate in the loss, but one day, in Damascus, he realized that he no longer had a need to search for Shams, since he was within Rumi, embodying Friendship. With this illumination, Rumi began singing the poetry, now increasingly revered around the world as a true revelation of the divine spirit.

It is notable that this Friendship, spiritual brothers meeting with the "divine between," was attacked and destroyed, remaining only in its psychic interiorization for Rumi. Is it now possible, 800 years later, that the divine might also express itself in friendship once more (same or opposite sex), without being destroyed by envy and misunderstanding? In any case, it seems to me that the Divine Between is destined to spread and become enhanced in this new millennium.

Notes

[1] Miranda Shaw, "Delight in this World: Tantric Buddhism as a Path of Bliss," *Parabola* 23, no. 2 (1998):42.

[2] C. G. Jung, "The Psychology of the Transference" (1946), in *CW* 16.

[3] J. Marvin Spiegelman, *Psychotherapy as a Mutual Process* (Tempe, AZ: New Falcon, 1996).

[4] Jung, *CW* 16, ¶ 423.

[5] Coleman Barks, *The Illuminated Rumi*, illustrated by Michael Green (New York: Broadway Books, 1997), p. 6.

CHAPTER 7

Divine Around: Nature, Art, and Synchronicity

We now come to the final category of our WABA classification system, namely, the Divine Around. With that term, I am referring to the experience of the *numinosum* that we encounter not within, among, or between us, but outside of us and penetrating us in a profound way. These experiences generally occur in Nature, in participating in art and in the kinds of meaningful coincidences that Jung has called "synchronicity." We begin with the experience of the divine in Nature, making use of a story about Ramakrishna, the renowned 19th-century avatar of India. He described his first experience of ecstasy (enlightenment) at the age of six, as follows:

> One morning I took some parched rice in a small basket and was eating it while I walked along the narrow ridges of the rice fields. In one part of the sky a beautiful black cloud appeared, heavy with rain. I was watching it and eating the rice. Very soon, the cloud covered almost the whole sky, and then a flock of cranes came flying. They were as white as milk against that black cloud. It was so beautiful that I became absorbed in the sight. Then I lost consciousness of everything outward. I fell down, and the rice was scattered over the earth. Some people saw this, and carried me home.[1]

Few of us have been so overwhelmed by the divine in Nature as the young Ramakrishna was, to faint away, but most people will resonate at some level with this experience. The modern urban person longs to "return to Nature," to hike, fish, meditate, to find some connection with the "untamed" or wildness in the wilderness. It is Mother Nature who heals us, gives us respite from the stresses of city life, of responsibilities and duties, of endless extraversion, by just accepting us into Her precincts. She nourishes us with Her prodigiously multiple kinds of water (oceans, lakes, rivers, and streams), as well as displaying a gorgeous variety of flowers, trees, and animals. Perhaps only a few of the experiences that we have in such environs might be called religious, however, even though the mark of such *religio* is surely our sense of transcendence. We encounter something larger than we are, impacting and trans-porting us, perhaps not so powerfully as it did Ramakrishna, but effectively all the same.

It has not always been this way. Many country folk do not seek such relief, they live in it! For them, Nature may be just their surroundings, as the city is for urbanites and water is for fish. It may also be the source of unexpressed divinity, not to be spoken of, especially the way that city people do this. Furthermore, Nature has been a place to seek and find the divine only within the last few hundred years. For the ancient Greeks, for example, the mountains (e.g., Olympus) were where the gods dwelt and it would be sacrilege to invade those sacred regions. For most folk and primitive cultures, the divine is all around all the time. The stories and religious myths of the Bushman of Africa are pregnant with the divine in flora and fauna; they would see our urban lives of separation from Nature as madness. And they may be right, at least in their recognition that the modern person is split off and lacking in harmony with the "around."

The early Christians were also enjoined not to seek the divine in Nature. St. Augustine was especially firm about this. To do so would be to fall back into pagan ways, he feared, and it was essential to transcend that way of worship of the divine. It has been largely since the Enlightenment of the

18th century that the return to Nature has carried a numinous quality in itself. This began, perhaps, with the idealized fantasy of Rousseau, but gradually affected most of the people whom Jung could speak of as "in search of Soul."

This quest for relief and renewal, however, is often not seen as a spiritual quest but as one of aesthetics or simply mental hygiene. This attitude is in consonance with those modern persons who reject religion altogether as outgrown or superstition or worse. Somewhere I heard the claim that "people need religion like fish need a bicycle!" Many say, as we know, that it is just "organized religion" that they reject, having undergone various forms of toxic institutional dogmatism or emptiness in that regard. All the same, the religious instinct, if we may call it that, does creep back in as the longing to be in Nature. I understand this, from a psychological point of view, as a need to reconnect with the feminine principle of the divine (e.g., Mother Nature), which includes body, "being," and soul, in contrast to mind, "becoming," and spirit. We are witnessing a continuing and increasing movement of the Western psyche to include that same feminine principle in the divine image, as I have noted earlier on.

This attitude of reverence for Nature has taken form, in recent days, in the attempt to save wilderness from human predation. Many religious leaders have come out to support the idea expressed, for example, in the words of Paul Gorman, director of the National Religious Partnership for the Environment: "Caring for Creation is a fundamentally religious imperative that transcends denominational differences."[2] Evangelicals and traditional religious leaders speaking on behalf of endangered cougars and other species echo this modern affirmation. Greek patriarch Bartholomew, for example, said, "To commit a crime against the natural world is a sin."[3] Pope John Paul II declared: "The dramatic threat of ecological breakdown is teaching us the extent to which greed and selfishness . . . are contrary to the order of creation."[4] This affirmation has a somewhat older foundation, as well. Moses Maimonides, the medieval Jewish philosopher said, "It should not be believed that all beings exist for humanity. On the contrary, all the other beings too have been intended for their own sakes, and not for the sake of something else."[5] And, finally, Black Elk, the Native American spiritual leader, affirmed, "You walk upon the Earth; for the Earth is your Grandmother and Mother, and She is sacred. Every step that is taken upon Her should be as a prayer."[6]

The Divine in Music

It is not usually a search for meaning that drives either the artist or the consumer of art but the formulation and expression of that "something" that moves us or transports us. I remember, at this moment, the quotation from Jean Paul Richter that my high school teacher of music appreciation had on her wall: "Music, thou speakest to me of things in all my endless life I have not found nor shall not find." It is an excitement, an awakening that we seek, ranging from the aesthetic all the way to the divine itself.

If we continue with the example of music, as I described in chapter one with the Krishna-possessed singer, all of us have been moved sometime by religious music. This may be experienced in community ritual or performed outside of the sacred precincts, such as spirituals among African-Americans, the chanting of Buddhist or Gregorian monks, and the "davening" of religious Jews. The Masses and sacred music of Bach move even the nonreligious. You might say that most of Bach's music is an expression of the Self, in its mandala form, and reaches some of us in that way also. Most of Mozart's work, although more secular in its joyfulness than Bach's, still can be seen as one great paean to and expressive of the religious impulse in himself. Brahms saw all his work as mystical, using the poetry of the Sufi mystic, Hafiz, as a basis for some of his work. These outstanding musical "priests" of the divine, including Beethoven, of course, were surely deeply aware of that spirit moving within themselves and it is our good fortune to be also so moved, at least sometimes, by such performance. As Jung noted, music, when archetypally based, overcomes all our defenses and reaches us in our depths.

I now remember another experience at high school age that is relevant in this regard. I had been forced to come home toward the end of the last of my seven summers as a camper and counselor with a demeaning case (for a sixteen-year-old!) of chicken pox. World War II was on and, knowing that I would no longer be able to enjoy those great summer times in the future, I longed to return to camp for the last weeks. Feverish and itchy, I listened to the New York Philharmonic Sunday concert on the radio. They played Bach's *Italian Concerto*, followed by Mendelssohn's *Italian Symphony*. Somehow, the sequence of these very different pieces transported me into a dimension that was timeless and ecstatic, leading not to fainting, but to a blessed sleep. Awakening, perhaps an hour later, I was not only completely fever-free but the pox had reduced in size and inflammation to the point where I could say that I was cured. I then knew that music heals as well as inspires. I was able to return to camp the very next day.

To continue with the distinction made in our story about the Krishna musician, between the divinely inspired and expressive artist versus the merely competent and aesthetic, we can turn to another example from Asia. In China, a very ancient stringed instrument (going back 5,000 years), the *ku-ch'in*, is steeped in tradition and myth. But in that same tradition a contrast is made between the Confucian player, concerned with harmonizing the differences between things, and the Taoist player, having more of a flavor of spontaneity and wholeness. Furthermore, Confucian players can be divided into three groups, based on the intention of the player. The first group, also called the Confucian school, comprises mainly literati or scholars. This is sometimes called "court music," which is very refined and sophisticated. Its distinctive qualities are the use of strict discipline and control; its tones are stately and solemn and mild. Very elegant. The other major school is the Shan-lin (literally "Mountain Forest") school, whose adherents are Buddhist monks, Taoist hermits, people who live in seclusion—lofty characters dwelling outside of the ordinary world. Their specific characteristics are nobility and antique tranquility, serving a creative purpose and intention. The final group includes common players who vie for novelty, modify the ancient techniques to suit popular taste, and generally are clever but fall far from the ideal. This subtle and refined consciousness of the differences I am talking about arises from such ancient civilizations. The poet Li Po (699-762) said:

> The monk from Shu with his ch'in wrapped in green silk
> Walking west down O-Mei mountain,
> Has brought me by one touch of the strings
> The breath of pines in a thousand valleys.
> I hear him in the cleansing brook,
> I hear him in the icy bells;
> And I feel no change though the mountain darkens
> And cloudy Autumn heaps the sky.[7]

In a stunning way, this Asian consciousness bridges the gap between aesthetics and divinity with a seamless appreciation, in which nothing need be said about the differences between the two; they are, or become, one.

Lastly, we remember King David, who healed Saul with his divine playing of the lyre, and who dared to dance before God in His ark. Only in this total expression of his being, thought King David, could the Lord be adequately addressed.

The Divine in Dance

The step from the divine in music to the divine in dance is a short one. Now the active body is included in expression and we once more find a border region between the Divine Among and the Divine Within or Around. For an example of the former, let us consider the innovation brought about by that great Islamic religious genius, Rumi, who is said to be the founder of Dervish dancing.

Muhammad's model of Divine Law was *sunnah*, including ritual prayer, remembrance, fasting, and development of virtues (*ahklâk*), whereas Rumi, who was called Mevlana, brought about the Mevlevi tradition, including community service, study of sacred literature, and cultivation of the arts (calligraphy, design, music, poetry, recitation of Koran). This led to the practice of *sama*, which included music and movement, culminating in ecstasy. Whirling, chanting, and spontaneous poetry developed into the ritual of the dervishes, which are symbolic actions balancing losing oneself in ecstasy and the containment of ecstasy. The ceremony is punctuated by "stops," in which the participants come to stillness, hands upon their shoulders, forming the letter *alif*, the number one. Instead of pursuing ecstasy, they are called back from the brink to testify to the oneness of God, recalling their own "nonexistence." God is everything; they bear witness to their utter humility and abandonment of self. Near the end of the ceremony the shaikh, or leader, turns slowly and majestically in the center of the floor, holding his robe slightly open, which gesture reminds one of the early days when people uncontrollably tore their robes in a state of abandonment. Here we see the divine clearly manifesting from within, expressing itself among, but also around, both for the participants and observers.

This wonderfully special use of dance and movement was not limited, of course, to such specific Islamic religious genius. In all folk cultures, dance is used as an expression of communal celebration and joy, reconnecting with the gods, and everyone participates. Yet there have always been especially "called" or gifted people, such as shamans, whose specific function is to bring an individual sick person back into harmony with community, the cosmos, and the gods. He or she did this via what we now call "holistic" methods, including, most importantly, dancing. Modern dance therapy attempts to do the same thing.[8] In this effort, they follow the customary differentiation of institutions into various professional groups that has happened historically, as we shall see in chapter 11.

The Divine in the Visual Arts

So many people live in a prison of daily life with no one to tell them to look out or look up. If you don't know about God, art is the only thing that can set you free.

It satisfies and challenges the human spirit to accept a deeper reality.[9]

When we turn to the divine in the visual arts, we are met with a plethora of images—in two-dimensional art, sculpture, and architecture—among which are many that celebrate the divine stories or make room for such experience. The sacred dwellings of churches, mosques, temples, and synagogues are clearly the "around" in which we can enter into the divine, as are the holy icons of paintings and statues. Before the modern era in the West, when individuality and a growing secular consciousness came into being, such art was itself an expression of the Divine Within, Among, and Around.

An example of such wholeness, and expressive of a borderline historical situation in the culture, is the famous altarpiece by Duccio, the *Maestà*, painted in 1311. This freestanding work, the largest ever painted in Italy, shows the Passion of Christ on one side and the Virgin Enthroned on the other. Many paintings, before and after this work, had such religious imagery as subject matter, of course, but many critics have noted that subject matter is not the same as content and apparently religious pieces can be seen in a different light, hardly spiritual at all. In this case, however, Duccio inscribed a prayer at the base of the Virgin's throne: "Holy Mother of God, be thou the cause of peace for Sienna and, because he painted thee thus, of life for Duccio." As Jungian analyst Mary Dougherty tells us, a chronicler from that era wrote, "On the day on which [the *Maestà*] was carried to the Duomo, the shops were locked up and . . . all the populace and all the most worthy were . . . next to the said panel with lights lit in their hands; and then behind were the women and children with much devotion; and they accompanied it right to the Duomo making procession round the Campo . . . sounding all the bells in glory, out of devotion for such a noble panel as was this."[10]

Dougherty reports that when she saw this work, she was deeply moved. It was in her subsequent analytic work with artists, however, that she realized that Duccio's prayer had "come to represent to me the symbolic attitude of an artist in relationship to his creative work—a work that is not only an ego possession, but is also a mediatory product connecting to a source of meaning towards which both artist and community can turn."[11] We can now understand this source as the Divine itself. It is linked with the Divine Within (Duccio's inspiration and painting), the Divine Around (the community enjoying and participating in this celebration, in which Duccio both embraced his fellow citizens and himself) and the Divine Among (in which there was an actual religious ritual connected with the event).

It is notable that Duccio signed this painting, probably the first or one of the first artists to do so, which signaled the gradual change in the culture: ego was both present and as important as community. In the centuries since that time, the collective religious participation has lessened, almost to the vanishing point, but inspired art—in museums, collections, films—still has that capacity to produce religious experience and exists "around" us. A high point for the artistic recognition of the value and wonder of the individual as a spiritual expression in itself can be found in the comment of the inspired Vincent van Gogh who wrote, in 1888, that, "Portraiture is the only thing in painting that moves me to the depths, and it makes me feel closer to infinity than anything else."[12]

Almost everyone who has seen van Gogh's art is aware of the artist's divinely-inspired character. My life-long friend, the painter Martin Mondrus, and I were certainly so aware, from the days of our youth, beginning more than 60 years ago when we read that artist's letters, thus participating in his life story. Most importantly, we were overwhelmed by his images. This was life-sustaining for these two adolescents who were looking toward a future of creativity for themselves. Mondrus also wrote some years ago for a publication and exhibition of his work, the following about how art was for him:

> Through art, I respond to the mystery, energy and animation of all things in nature that capture my attention. I become more aware of the relatedness of all life, of the underlying unity in nature. In my paintings, etch-

ings, and drawings of people, animals, landscapes and
the more obviously symbolic works, I find a vehicle for
my emotions and respond to what I am seeing, feeling
and living. The transformation from life to art is achieved
by the relatedness and vitality of colors, the intensity of
mood, the liveliness of the line, and the overall balance
of forces in the work. Each work is a discovery and an
unveiling of forces, attitudes and qualities that I perceive
as being in me and outside of me, and which I try to
unify as one in the work of art.[13]

For my friend Martin, this is his religious work, his spiritual
path. Surely this is also true for many others whose "divine
calling" is similarly expressed. Even many modern artists who
no longer feel connected to a specific religion have a sense
of the sacred in what they do. Philip Pearlstein, for example,
explicitly wants his nudes to be completely objective, psychologically inaccessible. By eliminating narrative and expressive pathos, however, such figurative formalists (including
Wayne Thiebaud, Richard Diebenkorn, and Edward Hopper),
have made their work more meditative, which, according to
Webster, is "solemn reflection on sacred matters as a devotional act." It is understood that their nudes are symbols of
the ultimate in aesthetics. For even these artists, therefore,
making art becomes a devotional act.[14]

I will take only a moment to speak about the divine
in writing and literature, since this category is so vast
and overwhelming that there's not enough room for it
here. The very writing of this book is itself my tribute to
the category of the divine in writing: if the divine is not
expressed, described, and amplified therein, it is not worth
doing! Almost everything written here, when not personal
experience alone, is derived from books and other printed
material.

All literate civilizations have their holy books, records, and
teachings. All spiritual paths have their written guides and
helps, even when they have a history as an oral tradition. To
demonstrate the point, it may be enough to say, "In the beginning God. . . ." and "In the beginning was the Word . . ."

Divine Synchronicity

A final category of the divine "around" can be discovered in what Jung described as "synchronicity." This term refers to the experience that everyone has had, at least once, of a meaningful coincidence between an inner condition, such as a dream or fantasy, and its connecting event or image in the outer world. Such connections are not causal or mechanical, but are discovered to be meaningful and fulfilling, usually in relation to one's own spiritual path. I will give some examples from my own path to illustrate this.

Early in 1956, when I had begun studying to become an analyst at the C. G. Jung Institute in Zurich, Switzerland, I settled into my analysis and had a kind of "initial dream." I had had some other dreams before this, as well as several powerful ones before I arrived, but this dream really set the stage for my serious work. In this dream, I had a vision of a large ant colony, arranged as a great rectangle. I was amazed at the intensity of activity of these ants, engrossed in watching their various tasks and activities—carrying, saving, defending, transforming. All of this was centered about the queen ant in the center. I understood that this image must refer to the intense work that my unconscious and I would be engaged in for the next years. This was presented in the symbolic form of a mandala (the rectangle). Whether the queen represented a deeper level of the mother complex that I needed to work with—I had done a lot of such work in my preceding, first analysis, several years earlier—or was a hint of the anima, the inner feminine, or even the feminine part of the Self, I did not know. At that time, I was not aware of Jung's work on the alchemy of the transference, in which the mandala of the beginning carries the image of divine darkness in matter as Mercurius. As I reflected on the dream, however, I saw that this biological collectivity was a deep compensation to the images of individuation that I had come to Switzerland to work with. The soul is truly collective, apart from all of our individual aims and pretensions, like those marvelous ants, and I needed to know that, too.

Satisfied with this interpretation, I went off to my analyst's office, pausing to sit on a bench in a little park nearby. As I sat there, writing my reflections, a whole stream of ants walked up onto my notebook and traveled firmly but confidently across it and me, continuing on to the other side. I noted this coincidence, but thought it might be just that, not a synchronicity. One usually needs three such "coincidences" to be convincing. I then walked up to my analyst's office and met him in his outside but closed-in porch, overlooking a small copse. This served as his work place during the spring and summer. As I related my ant dream, there appeared, on the little table between us and coming from his side (making sure that no little creature remained from my park bench encounter), another stream of ants marching carefully across. When the analyst remarked that this had never happened before in his office, I knew that a true synchronicity had occurred. Such an acausal and meaningful association of dream and concrete event made it clear that I was now on what the Hindus called Indra's Web, the connections among events and beings in time and space that relate to a higher unity, an *unus mundus*, where both dimensions are transcended. And so it was during the next three-plus years of my intense stay in that blessed city and institution which welcomed all of us foreigners to study, permitting us the introversion, time, and protected space to devote to psyche.

This particular kind of synchronicity, showing me the power of the collective and the truth of psychic reality via the presentation of animal and image, took place again many years later, but with a different twist. It was now almost 20 years later, 1956 was long gone, and I was back in my hometown. I had long since become an analyst, had a family, a good practice, friends, and a meaningful life. I had resigned from my local Jungian society, however, and felt somewhat isolated professionally. Even more important, I had completed writing several volumes of psychological fiction that had failed to find a publisher. I was distraught with questions about both my aloneness and whether the Self had indeed, as I thought, directed me to write such books and, if so, why that same Self had not helped me get a publisher. Frustrated and restless, I got on my bicycle and started to ride, as I often did, in the hills near where I lived. No sooner had I arrived at the long winding road at the crest of the hills, when I saw a man walking with a dog, something unusual in itself. Coming closer, I saw that he was an old high school comrade whom I had not seen in many years. He, too, had become a psychologist, I knew, and had written a very successful book about his work. He was famous. Well, I thought, here is the man with the fame and recognition for which I had longed! We chatted amiably for a few minutes. The content of our conversation was largely about how he had been betrayed by publishers and by colleagues (so had I, but on a much smaller scale!). He had a home in the south of France and commuted back and forth to the States, but he seemed to be not very happy with his life.

Continuing onward on my bicycle, I felt rather as I did years before, when my dream ants were matched by palpable ants on that park bench. But now it was my psychic conflict about fame and longed-for recognition meeting an outer, negative image. I traveled onward for a couple of miles when I suddenly saw a large stag in the road. Now I often hiked in those hills and occasionally saw deer there, but I had never, in all those years, seen a stag and certainly never an animal that would remain on the road. The stag remained still and, to my mind, demonstrated great natural dignity. I got off my bike and bowed to this creature, as if he were a king. I even imagined a crown on his head. The stag seemed to bow in return and very slowly moved off the road, back into the hills. Deeply moved by this encounter, I felt strongly supported in my aloneness, independence, and individuation. This grand creature, symbol of the Self in an individual way—as the ant colony had been in a collective way—managed to live in the city, but not of it. I was not aware, at that moment, of the alchemical significance of the stag as a symbol of the Self, but I knew it as a mark of the divine and was comforted. It was only six years later that I found my publisher, which made possible an outpouring and publication of some nineteen of my books to date. Perhaps it takes such an amount of time to truly cement one's individuality and aloneness and "get the point."

Such synchronicities are clearly related to the individuation process. They happen at deeply significant times and somehow give us the sense that our own psyche is more than personal. It is connected to the larger soul of us all and even of the world, the *anima mundi*, yet we are truly on our own path. Of course, I have often experienced synchronicities, both for me and for analysands with whom I have worked, and these have always been meaningful—by definition, of course—but these animal appearances remain in my memory as particularly signatory of my path.

Notes

[1] Christopher Isherwood, *Ramakrishna and His Disciples* (Hollywood: Vedanta Press, 1965), pp. 28–29.

[2] Quoted in Trebbe Johnson, "Redefining the Bond Between Religion and Ecology," in *Sierra Magazine* 83, no. 6 (1998):52.

[3] His All Holiness Bartholomew I, Archbishop of Constantinople and New Rome, during the symposium, *Caring for God's Creation: Science, Religion, and the Environment*, held at the St. Barbara Greek Orthodox Church, Santa Barbara, California, November 6–8, 1997.

[4] Pope John Paul II, "The Ecological Crisis: A Common Responsibility," message of His Holiness for the celebration of the World Day of Peace, January 1, 1990 (Rome: Vatican, December 8, 1989), § 8.

[5] Moses Maimonides, *The Guide for the Perplexed*, M. Friedlander, trans. (New York: Dover Publications, 2000), III:13.

[6] Black Elk, *The Sacred Pipe: Black Elk's Account of the Seven Rites of the Oglala Sioux, Civilization of the American Indian Series*, vol. 36, Joseph E. Brown, ed. (Norman: University of Oklahoma Press, 1989), pp. 5–6.

[7] Sun Yu-chi'n, "No Need to Listen: A Conversation between Sun Yu-chi'n and J. L. Walker," *Parabola* 23, no. 2 (1998): 62.

[8] Ilene Serlin, "Root Images of Healing in Dance Therapy," *American Journal of Dance Therapy* 15, no. 2 (1993).

[9] Sister Wendy Beckett quoted in Mary Rourke, "Apostle of Art; Sister Wendy, a Recluse-Turned-Commentator, Is Making It Her Mission to Demystify Great Paintings of the World," *Los Angeles Times*, 2 December, 1998, home edition, p. 1.

[10] Mary Dougherty, "Duccio's Prayer: Mediating Destruction and Creation with Artists in Analysis," *Journal of Analytical Psychology* 43 (1998): 479.

[11] Ibid.

[12] Vincent van Gogh, *The Complete Letters of Vincent van Gogh* (London: Thames and Hudson, 1958), Letter 531, p. 25.

[13] Martin Mondrus, privately printed prospectus, 1995.

[14] Clint Brown and Cheryl McLean, *Drawing from Life* (New York: Harcourt, Brace, Jovanovich, 1992).

CHAPTER 8

Can Science Be a Spiritual Path? Jung's Inner Way

In the previous chapters, we have explored various spiritual paths as they have existed historically in the various faiths, as well as some occult or out-of-the way methods. We have also tasted a bit of the spiritual or religious experiences found in Nature or in pursuit of the arts, whether as creator or consumer. Now we need to consider whether science can be pursued as a spiritual path. "Is this a legitimate question?" you might ask. Most scientists are atheistic or agnostic, and historically, religion and science have often been enemies.

The answer to this question is more difficult to arrive at than is apparent at first glance, I think. Actually, science has not always been antireligious, and it was religion itself, since Galileo, which sometimes felt threatened by science and did the rejecting. The greatest scientists, moreover, until the 19th century, were quite religious and also broad-minded. Sir Isaac Newton, for example, discoverer of the natural laws of motion that are specific in establishing the deep truths of Nature, was also a spiritually devoted alchemist. Most people are unaware that he experimented and wrote voluminously on that topic and even believed that his alchemical researches were his main contribution to science itself. Kepler, the great astronomer who was similarly pioneering in his own field, was also a noted astrologer. He saw no discrepancy between these two disciplines, each having a totally different foundation while apparently examining the same subject matter. Both men were deeply spiritual and saw their work as exploring what God has brought to pass in the world. Nature's laws were God's laws.

Even in the increasingly skeptical 20th century, many physicists have often continued to be quite religious. Albert Einstein, for example, never foreswore his natal religious faith and even had great difficulty accepting the results in quantum physics that revealed uncertainty and probability, rather than cause-and-effect, in existence itself. "God does not play with dice," he declared, perhaps forgetting that in many cultures (e.g., the use of the oracle, *I Ching*, in China), it appears that the Lord surely does so.[1]

In fact, studies of the religious attitudes among scientists, which I read about in my graduate school days in the late 1940s and early 50s, suggested that religious beliefs decreased as one went from the physical sciences to the biological sciences to the social sciences. The latter scientists were particularly opposed to any *deus ex machina*, following Descartes. They seem to have forgotten that even that great philosopher, who was the father of the subsequent split between mechanism and mind, continued to have faith in God and located the mediating place of soul and the divine in the pineal gland! Psychologists also overlook the fact that Gustav Theodor Fechner, 19th-century psychologist and author of the Weber-Fechner law in psychophysics, was a mystic, and that William James's main interest in parapsychology and in *The Varieties of Religious Experience*[2] rested on his deeply spiritual orientation.

But it is also true that the later 19th- and 20th-century view of science, partly as a consequence of the rejection of the authority of church dogma, tended toward agnosticism or atheism. Hinduism, though, sees atheism itself as a legitimate spiritual path to God! One Hindu tradition has it that it takes fewer incarnations for an atheist to find God than it takes a religious person, since the former is so passionately connected to the divine, albeit negatively. It also may be true that one can approach science as a spiritual path, aimed at finding God's laws or, alternately, as a path that requires no such beliefs or spiritual aims at all.

I remember my Zurich teacher, Dr. Marie-Louise von Franz, saying that the main thing for us all is the pursuit of truth, whether we find it in the natural sciences, the psychological sciences, or in religion. To think that all truth or no truth resides in either path is foolish, in her view. What Western civilization has experienced—and what is now taking place in Asia as well—is that the spread of science and technology has accompanied, if not caused, a lessening of faith in the various religions. Unacknowledged here is the possibility that science itself is the current myth, with the status of a religion, for many "modern" men and women, some of whom, Jung thought, were in search of "soul."

I suspect that those who rejected religion in favor of the rationalism of science merely traded in the "old" god for the new goddess, Reason, emerging after the French Revolution. A fairly recent poll among Americans published by the *Los Angeles Times*, July 12, 1999, revealed that although about 44 percent believed in the biblical narrative of creation, the same number accepted evolution as a scientific fact with God having a hand in it as well. Only about 10% embraced "creationism," the literal interpretation of Genesis.

One important aspect of any spiritual path is that the seeker aims at self-transformation. Whatever good such a person might accomplish in the world—such as social service or advancing knowledge—must also entail significant self-examination. In the deepest sense, the person needs to connect his or her worldly "vocation" with what the divine will within him or her desires. Surely, there are such people in science and social service, just as in art, who are so committed, but their number is probably not large.

In the 20th century, we have seen the emergence of one psychological perspective that aims to be scientific yet takes the experiences of religion and faith seriously: that is the work of C. G. Jung and some of his followers. Rather than reducing religious experience and belief to "illusion," as Freud suggested, Jung was struck that such beliefs occur everywhere and at all times, thus indicating that they emerge out of the psyche itself. This suggested to him that there is truly a religious instinct, expressing itself in myth and ritual, dogma and belief and, above all, in experience. His work with his own dreams and fantasies, as well as those of his patients, drove him to go ever deeper into such material, maintaining a scientific attitude toward understanding what the unconscious produced, yet allowing himself to be affected and changed by this experience. In short, he found that for the "modern man in search of a soul," including himself, the religious impulse had withdrawn itself from focusing on outer and institutional symbols and signs, only to be powerfully reawakened, for some people, within the psyche itself. That, he thought, was the consequence of the loss of faith in the 20th century: the images and symbols that carried the unconscious, via projection, in the outer world were fading and dying, only to be reborn within.

Jung came to these conclusions while doing analysis, just as other clinicians were also discovering unsuspected depths in the unconscious. His work went beyond the parent/child image that has been so central in all analytic work. (Why that image has been so pervasive is a topic that asks for further understanding, as well.) Jung discovered the "collective unconscious," the layer of the psyche from which arise the myths, images, and religions the world has evolved. Indeed these are variations of structures that mirror the nature of the psyche itself. Through this discovery and work, Jung had essentially come upon the possibility for modern people to pursue an individual spiritual path. This could constitute a kind of yoga (a discipline) for those who could no longer find solace, meaning, or containment in the faith into which they were born or in materialistic science. Instead they had to rely on the hallmark of science, namely, empiricism, but now needed to investigate the divine as it manifested in their own experience, particularly in the study of their dreams and imagination.

In the early days of analysis, some practitioners even thought that anyone who "remained" in his natal faith was unable to attain to this level of work. I recall, for example, a respected Jungian analyst in Zurich having the opinion that my friend and colleague, Dr. Arwind Vasavada, was too "contained" in his Hinduism to truly grasp analytical psychology. Her opinion was understandable (some believers cannot symbolize, are too literal), but she was mistaken in his case. My experience, and that of other analysts as well, is that many modern religious people, including priests, nuns, ministers, and rabbis, can indeed maintain their faith, undergo deep Jungian analysis, and even become analysts, themselves! This capacity has to do with a readiness to embrace freedom of exploration in one's own soul, a willingness to endure conflict (such as faith vs. experience) long enough and courageously enough to arrive at one's own experience of the divine, the Self, both within and transcendent.

Jung's Stages of Individuation

Jung tried to define certain stages of such development in his book, *Two Essays on Analytical Psychology*,[3] which he revised several times. It should be understood, however, that these stages do not happen as if one were going on a road trip, stopping sequentially at various cities, but that although there is sequence, there is also simultaneity, regression, and chaos. The general development is neither a straight line of travel, nor a circle including various stages as in the hero myth (which resembles the process of individuation and may be its origin), but it is more similar to a spiral. One surely goes from stage to stage, but one also continually returns to the beginning, often, but not always, at a higher or deeper or more whole level. This process is life-long. Sure enough, there are plateaus and many people undergoing analysis, having "solved" the situation (symptom, blockage, etc.) that brought them into therapy, pursue their lives without continuing so much soul-examination. All forms of psychoanalysis, of course, are fundamentally ways of healing and may never entail spiritual questions at all. Many other people, however, who have realized that the process of psychological growth may also entail spiritual growth, do indeed continue to maintain an analytic attitude toward themselves long after they have completed a course of analytic work. Jung thought that perhaps analysis itself might one day become a kind of Western yoga, but he had no particular stake in that. His goal remained that of truth-seeking. His autobiography, *Memories, Dreams, Reflections*, is a marvelous portrayal of just how his own life reflected that path.

If we turn now to the stages Jung describes in the second of his *Two Essays*, we find six of them: ego, persona, shadow, anima/animus, old wise man/woman or mana personality, and Self. Keep in mind that these stages are based on images and experiences rather than firm and circumscribed intellectual ideas. They are symbolic (capable of many understandings) since the psyche is like that, but they are also concepts that Jung coined with the aim of establishing a scientific basis for what he called the individuation process. My descriptions are not exactly those of Jung but I believe they are true to his intentions and do not violate any of his ideas.

First, of course, we come upon the ego, or that which we (I) experience our self to be. Freud called this *das ich*, or "the I," but later usage, intending to be more scientific and abstract, has rested on the familiar Greek term. Depth psychologists understand the ego as being the center of consciousness at any moment, yet they also notice that the ego appears in dreams, for example. This contrast is itself a useful source of discussion. Thus we can also speak of an unconscious ego, but Jung refers to another psychological experience when we come to examine this paradoxical idea. Usually, however, it is sufficient for us to understand that our ego is the center of our consciousness, informed by sensations coming from the body and the world, as well as from memory and, according to Jung, from the development of the functions of thinking, feeling, sensation, and intuition. The nature of this ego, usually just assumed as "natural," can be a source of new understanding and consciousness when we begin to reflect on "it" and how "I" approach the world and my inner life (for example, introverted or extraverted, with which most highly developed function, etc.).

This "I" becomes immediately differentiated from the concept of the persona, a word that means, also from the Greek, mask or role. The persona, in contrast to how I see or experience myself as an ego, is what I show the world. Socially, this is often informed by professional roles or by socio-economic factors, so that the question, "Who are you?" is answered with a statement about what our vocation is: I am a lawyer, or a housewife, or a son of a congressman, or a thief, for example. Naturally, all these categories are not mutually exclusive, and one's persona can include several such definitions. They are all related to external images or effect, however, and we are quite startled, for example, when we have dreams in which we behave quite differently from our customary role. It is even more painful to have trouble with our role in the world, to experience a discrepancy between what we feel our self to be and how we manifest "out there." Such conflicts often appear in dreams as being naked or wrongly dressed; clothes are indeed wonderful carriers of persona images and their absence makes such definition particularly poignant. Can I survive being who I really am, "naked," in the world? Usually not; we need some way of both hiding and mediating what we are in order to be in some kind of not-too-violating harmony with what we want to be and what the world expects or permits.

Sometimes our role, or persona, has the debilitating effect of deforming us, what the French call *déformation professionelle*. This refers to the lamentable condition in which being a mechanic or salesperson or scientist or psychotherapist brings only a narrowing of consciousness. That is to say, others and the world might be seen only mechanically, as objects to make money, as causal conditions, or as needing help or correction, respectively. For example, a friend of mind, formerly a kindergarten teacher, once found herself at a dinner party, wanting to cut up one of the guest's meat for him! She decided on the spot to change her class at elementary school to the third grade. Usually, though, the self-definition by role serves useful functions for ourselves and others, provided that we don't deceive ourselves into believing that this is what we truly are.

A contrast to both ego and persona in relation is provided by the shadow: that which I am that I would rather not be. This has to do with traits or motives or qualities in our inner being that are negative to our self-image (e.g., the ego ideal) and are often qualities that are repressed. At this point, we are really beginning to deal with the unconscious. We are approaching the level that Jung called the personal unconscious, which is the central work of most psychoanalysis. Here lurk all the unacceptable or repressed aspects of our self, residues of childhood experiences, impulses or attitudes, but we are also reaching deeper into more primitive aspects of our self. The seven deadly sins are appropriate here, as well as the "super-ego's strictures," such as the Ten Commandments, to deal with them. Religions have always found ways to relate to greed, lust, dependency, hard-heartedness, and the rest. When our dreams present such material to us, we need considerable moral courage to honestly confront our personal darkness without totally sacrificing our conscious attitude or morality. This phase usually begins with dreams of overflowing toilets or unacceptable homeless vagrants, robbers, whores, etc., along with images of baths or showers as vehicles for their cleansing or transformation. As we work with such shadow material by confrontation and reflection, however, there is a process of cleansing and transformation, but paradoxically, as mentioned at the beginning, an even deeper presentation of such darkness appears. Trickster and devil images arise, which tell us that our personal shadow leads to or is contaminated by the collective shadow, that belonging to family, nation, and humankind. The overflowing toilets in the park, for example, surely refer to our collective darkness, and the image of the devil belongs to the same societal level, as Jung showed us. Such confrontation can be quite challenging and we are usually profoundly changed by this encounter. Not only do we need to work with childhood suffering and our remaining childishness, but much of what our culture as a whole has rejected presents itself as tendencies and behaviors of our own that we need to cope with individually.

This confrontation with "that which I am that I would not be" leads directly onward to the realization of the anima or the animus, or that which is truly "Other" in ourselves. Rather than devil or witch as archetypal shadow, we face our own contrasexual side, based on early experiences of family, as well as a consequence of genetic qualities of the opposite sex that we inherited. Our genetic maleness and femaleness, after all, is based on only one chromosomal pair and the "other side" is also at least latent within us. Equally important are the cultural images of masculine and feminine, subject to change and development, but still both potent and limiting, as any modern man and, especially, woman, knows all too well. The ideal images that we fall in love with are also a contributing source of these contrasexual images. Imagine a cartoon in which a man and woman are holding hands, each looking into their own mirror and seeing the partner therein. That, in a nutshell, is what this experience is: unconscious of our contrasexual nature, we see it and adore it in a partner. This romantic attraction continues until that partner no longer fits the image and then the struggle begins. Heated conversation about disappointed relationship and the misunderstandings that arise go on every day in every language and civilization in the world.

But it is not only the positive, ideal image that we "project"—as the psychological concept terms this—it is also its opposite. Indeed, Jung, Emma Jung (1957), and Toni Wolff (1951) have described how these internal, archetypal images develop during the course of life and the growth of consciousness.[4] In men, for example, the inner images develop from mother and mother-substitute (e.g., maid, aunt) onward to the prostitute and then to the nun or spiritual woman, followed by the *femme inspiratrice* and, finally, to Sophia or Wisdom, the Divine Feminine. In women, this process develops from father and father-substitute images at the beginning to the athlete or hero, followed by the lover and then the teacher, priest, or spiritual man and, finally, to the God-man and the Divine Masculine. Sure enough, the dark sides of all of these, such as the witch and succubus for men and the tyrant/Bluebeard for women, are regularly encountered, as well.

Jung talks about work with the anima and animus as central to the spiritual path when approached analytically, but relatively few people really take on this encounter with their inner opposite to the "end." Dialogue and the capacity for such work, undertaken as active imagination (inner relational encounter with these figures that affirms both our opposites and our ego) are essential for this. Most of us usually perform only the outer half of this work by engaging with the opposite sex concretely in the external world. That, too, is painful and rewarding work, but it lacks the consciousness that brings one to union with the inner opposite.

Some contemporary women have been critical of Jung's psychology of anima and animus, stating that these terms are too culturally biased, based on patriarchal assumptions. They believe that in addition to being inaccurate, the terms contribute to the suppression of women and their freedom to develop. There is surely some truth in this claim. Yet I have also noted that often a woman's animus is heavily involved in this criticism of Jung and Mrs. Jung's concepts and it is not always just. It is difficult, therefore, to be sure, for example, whether the woman should fight with the inner male tyrant, as Marie-Louise von Franz suggested,[5] or take up the cultural battle of feminism in the outer world. I think that the external struggle is essential, on the grounds of human development as well as that of simple justice, but unless a woman takes up that same struggle and relationship with the inner male, she will lack an integration of those qualities that the archetype carries. Ultimately, it is the cosmic significance of Meaning, in the spiritual and religious sense, that is the challenge and reward. This struggle is equal for men, of course; if they do not take up the relationship with the anima, they will not discover the importance of relationship and love (Eros) in the divine scheme. Those men who do this inner work become, as Jungians say, "animated" or full of life energy connected with relationship, among other things; women who do this inner work become "spirited" (translation of *animus*) or fully capable of carrying their own, individual meaning and action. Surely the entire libido is genetically based, despite the exaggerated American extraverted emphasis on cultural effect, but its manifestation in behavior and life is equally potent. We also have to acknowledge that relatively few people will feel called or inwardly compelled to take up such an *auseinandersetsung* (confrontation).

The relational struggle of anima/animus leads, in time, to the encounter with another archetypal image, that of the old wise man, old wise woman, or mana personality: that within us which transcends the ego in wisdom and power. The shadings are subtle, but the effect is profound. It is quite amazing to be able to encounter such dream figures, to engage them in conversation in fantasy, and discover that there is unexpected wisdom or power lying within our self, not consciously attained. We also learn that it is deadly when we try to exploit such wisdom or the unconscious generally. This material is there to relate to in order to build up our unique philosophy of life. Naturally, there are lots of people who get identified with such images and become walking bores of wisdom. The "trick" in the development of consciousness is to realize that the archetypal images are not just personal, that we can learn to relate to such figures without being possessed or identified with them. Usually, however, first encounters lead to identification, an inflation that gets knocked down by our spouse, neighbors, friends, or life itself. But that battering can then result in deeper relationship with these powers of the unconscious, which does indeed make life much more profound. Our own achieved wisdom then transpires naturally.

Now this experience of the Other, which transcends the ego in wisdom and power, shades readily into an encounter with what is called the Self, namely that within and encompassing us which is experienced as both center and totality, a union of opposites. To encounter such images as mandalas, God, the divine Feminine, etc., is either to recover the religiousness we have lost or to find it for the first time. This is the goal of the psychological spiritual path; its phenomenology is widely amplified in the writings of Jung and Jungians.

This is the God-within that we have explored in several of the spiritual paths in previous chapters, but is discovered in the strictly empirical—thus "scientific"—work with our own soul or psyche. On this path, we become our own experiment and experimenter, and we must prove or disprove our experiences and beliefs to ourselves alone. Naturally, whatever we turn up, should we wish to present such material to the outer world, it is subject to the criticism, rejection, and noncomprehension that individually religious people have always encountered and that, too, is part of the process. Madness cannot be ruled out, after all, as we saw when examining the path of Kabbalah.

I am reminded of Jung's experiment when he worked at the Burgholzli psychiatric hospital in Zurich as a young man. He had three patients, each of whom thought he was Jesus Christ. Jung brought them together in a room and later questioned each of them about their experience. Can you imagine what they reported? All three said that each of the other two was crazy! Their madness consisted, in part, in not being able to be true to their own experience while recognizing that others may also be "divine." Suppose one of them had said: "Well, think of that! All three of us are Jesus Christ! I wonder how that could be and what it means?" They could have discovered that Jesus did dwell in each of them, expressed himself differently in each, that all three could be "God-men," yet they would need to find a way to let each other exist as such without hegemonic pretension. They might even discover that the divine transcended them, both within each of them and among them. Such a consciousness would not be possible in madness, for then they would no longer be possessed by this archetype of the Self and could thus relate to it, both within themselves and among others. Perhaps that is a path—out of ordinary "madness"—for the future.

Such a fantasy, I have to admit, is far-fetched. Can we imagine multiple gurus living together in some kind of harmony, recognizing the divinity within each? Alas, this is not likely. Those who pursue such a path of individual spiritual growth, e.g., Jungian analysts, discover that it is quite difficult to have group organizations in which all such members truly respect each other and get along well. It is as if all the individual work on one's own psyche does not readily transfer to the capacity to deal with groups. We Jungians have noted that Jung's own antipathy to group psychology and therapy may be a heavy inheritance for us. He noted how groups oppress the individual, and said that ten geniuses in one room constituted one big idiot. I think, though, that the possibility of being with both the divine "within" and the divine "among," especially when not in a traditional context, is truly a task for the future. It is hard enough, we have to admit, to find people to even take up the inner path and carry it onward far enough to be fully related to the Self. Jung thought that even one such person, so engaged in doing the work of consciousness-raising in our time, could help change the world. Perhaps the traditional Christian belief that, at the End of Days, 144,000 people will ascend to heaven is a symbol of that process. Collective redemption of consciousness is possible if enough people can carry that task for the rest of us. Similarly, there is a Jewish tradition of the *Lamed Vovnikim*, the 36 Just Men who exist in the world at all times and carry its suffering, some of them not even knowing that they are such saints! Yet it is Jung's great contribution to show us that each of us carries such a saint and devil within us and to the extent that we can become conscious of our own darkness and our own light, we do a great cultural service. Minimally, isn't it surely a great help to project less, of both good and evil, on our fellow humans? Such individual struggle can help us appreciate the tremendously long heritage of humankind's building up the images of the Divine Among and making it possible for group life to continue meaningfully and with fulfillment. We can also appreciate the devastating effect of the loss of these traditional collective paths. All the same, once we have "left the fold," only our individual, painstaking struggles with our soul and the soul of the world can bring us back to that sense of wholeness that those original myths brought us. Don't the paradoxical truths of the last oxherding pictures make more sense now?

At this point, I am having an uneasy feeling that you might be thinking that all of these spiritual paths have a specific sequence of growth. This may take place despite my assurances at the outset that these are merely convenient classification systems, meant to provide a rubric for understanding the variety of experiences seekers have, rather than being a kind of script. In this context, I remember the early months of my first analysis, in my mid-twenties. Many of my fellow graduate students in psychology were undergoing analysis, mostly Freudian, and we would talk with each other about such things as whether one had begun to deal with the Oedipus complex, as if this were indeed a badge of honor on the psychological path. Believing in the great wisdom and knowledge of my analyst, I, too, wondered where I was, in relation to Jung's *Two Essays*, and the stages I have just described. I did not have the courage to ask, however. Finally, I had a dream about being immersed in a flood and undergoing powerful experiences. In the dream, I returned to my parents' house, trying to tell them what I had experienced, but they did not understand. I then tore off my "white coat" (future doctor!) and threw it down on the floor. My parents then said, "How about the pants!" I awakened realizing that I had to give up my "innocence" (white clothes) and parental orientation at last. This flood dream came a year after dreaming that my university, UCLA, theretofore enjoying Southern California sun-bright skies, was being flooded. At that time, I was only interested in the white caps of the sea (the "foam" of Aphrodite) and peacefully climbed onto higher buildings when threatened. The unconscious had not yet become quite "real" for me. It took another year of work for the depth of the flood experience (immersion in the unconscious) to fully take hold. When I became really flooded, I no longer wondered or even cared about what stage I was in! So, the conclusion that I hope you will draw is that it is the genuine, individual experience of the unconscious that matters in such a path; anything else is just tourism!

On Physics and Psychology

I shall close with a few words about recent research in quantum physics that brings it nearer to the findings in depth psychology, particularly those of Jung. The relativity of space and time discovered by Einstein has been extended to the same relativization of matter in connection with psyche. The Nobel prize physicist, Wolfgang Pauli, was deeply impressed by Jung's work, as well as by his own experience in analysis[6] (Pauli's dreams are discussed in Jung's *Psychology and Alchemy*).[7] Jung's concept of synchronicity, the acausal connection of events though meaning, occurring simultaneously in psyche and matter, found support in Pauli's work, as well. Findings in quantum physics, further developed by John Stewart Bell and David Bohm, have demonstrated that causality does not exist as such at the quantum level. Such stalwart experiences as local causation, independent existence, etc., are negated at the smallest, particle level of creation as well as at the universe level in its most vast reaches. These findings are beginning to be embraced by psychologists working with transference, as I mentioned in chapter 6. In the concept of the "field" I discussed there, these extremely disparate sciences—studying the ultimate opposites of matter and psyche—do indeed begin to coalesce. It is exciting to visualize a union between the Western achievement of science and the Eastern pursuit of the spiritual path. Perhaps the very pursuit of analysis will provide such a vehicle.

Notes

[1] The Chinese might argue that there is nothing random, in a larger sense, about the *I Ching*. The oracle's response gained from gathering yarrow sticks or tossing coins is based on the patterned manifestation of yin and yang existing in the environment and within the seeker. Chaos theory adds insight to this in that up close, it may be impossible for us as individuals to see how one small event leads to a series of bigger events, but from a larger perspective, it can all be seen to make sense, the way a city is a mass of confusion up close, but from an aerial view, its order is discernable. On the other hand, the Lord may not play dice, but certainly does have fun with us, maybe if only for His own amusement, which has a purpose, itself.

[2] William James, *The Varieties of Religious Experience* (New York: Modern Library, 1902).

[3] C. G. Jung, *Two Essays on Analytical Psychology*, CW 7.

[4] See Emma Jung, "Animus and Anima: Two Essays," originally published in 1931 and 1934 (New York: Analytical Psychology Club of New York, 1957) and Toni Wolff, "Structural Forms of the Feminine Psyche," 1934 paper (Zurich: Students Association, C. G. Jung Institute, 1951).

[5] Marie-Louise von Franz, *The Cat: A Tale of Feminine Redemption* (Toronto: Inner City Books, 1999), p. 89.

[6] See Wolfgang Pauli, "The Influence of Archetypal Ideas on the Scientific Theories of Kepler," in C. G. Jung and Wolfgang Pauli, *The Interpretation of Nature and Psyche* (New York: Pantheon, 1955).

[7] See Jung, *Psychology and Alchemy*, CW 12.

CHAPTER 9

Combining Types: Stages in Hinduism and Catholicism

We have now explored some examples of the Divine Within, Between, Among, and Around, plus investigated the idea, in various ways, of there being stages on the spiritual paths, culminating in the work of C. G. Jung. I believe that it would now be valuable to examine some of the ways that the institutional religions—the Divine Among—have made use of the idea of stages to combine the various types. If we think of Stations of the Cross in Christianity, for example, we realize that the person of faith who visits each of these stations in his or her church is performing an *imitatio Christi*. That is, she or he is imitating or reenacting the "Passion" of Christ, while circumambulating the stages of the Savior's exemplary life. In this way, she or he experiences the Divine Within, Among, and Around: even between, if we think of this as a simultaneous, two-way dialogue with Jesus, and not just one-sided. I have myself made good use of such stages, in an internal way, in my exploration of several religions, even Greek paganism, in my book, *Jungian Psychology and the Passions of the Soul*.[1] Here, I want to use just two illustrations of the combination path, one from Catholicism and one from Hinduism.

The Stages of Hindu Enlightenment

In *Tripura-Rahasya*, Dr. Arwind Vasavada details the stages of the path to enlightenment in the Hindu tradition, showing us that the "within" is facilitated by the "between," which arises from the *guru-chela*, or teacher-pupil, relationship.[2]

Process of Enlightenment in Hinduism

1. Contact with Saint—living embodiment of truth and reality.
2. Faith in God as something higher and transcendent to the ego but also immanent in it.
3. Detachment from involvement in the opposites by learning to see imperfection in all things.
4. Search for the Self through analysis of the I and Mine—path of discrimination.
5. Realization of the Self—pure consciousness—as the reality and the illusory character of the ego.
6. Realization that the soul and the Self are identical.
7. Realization that everything is the Self; therefore, there is neither the seeker nor the sought; everything is ablaze in Light and Love—the ultimate synthesis.

Contact with an Embodiment of Truth and Reality

The first condition, contact with a saint, requires that the seeker find a guru, a teacher, with whom she or he can experience such "embodiment of truth and reality." This is easier for Hindus, with their receptivity to spiritual teachers in a powerfully religious culture, than it is for modern Westerners, so soaked as we are in the skeptical spirit of science. All the same, this seeking and finding of a teacher does happen in the West as well. For the East generally, and especially India, this is even a fundamental necessity on the spiritual path.[3] Usually, a guru "accepts the projection" of the Self, as we would say psychoanalytically, not for self-aggrandizement but for the sake of the spiritual growth of the seeker, who now becomes a chela. The guru knows that he is both embodying the Self for the chela and that this is a projection. Most Western psychoanalysts, on the other hand, may be aware of this kind of projection, occurring problematically in deep analytic work, but they eschew such identification as inflationary and dangerous for the analysand, as well as for the analyst. There is something to be said for both views, however. At best, either "teacher" would be well advised to allow the projection to "incarnate," as we say, namely to be embodied in the analyst and in the relationship, yet maintain the dual perspective of being "it" and not "it." One way to do this is to realize that the Self of both parties is embodied in the relationship itself, and that the embracing of this path can lead to what the Hindu guru is ultimately seeking, as in the sixth and seventh stages.

Faith in God

The second stage—having faith that God, the Self, is both transcendent and immanent in the ego—is already quite difficult, since who can command faith? We can, however, consciously surrender the ego, allowing experiences to ensue that involve embracing conflict. The chela, like the analysand, discovers that he or she is no longer undivided, but finds him- or herself torn by conflict among diverse inner tendencies. This discovery of personal division in turn leads increasingly toward investing the guru with special powers, especially as a carrier of wholeness, unity, and enlightenment—all that the chela is not. This step is implicit in analytic work, as well, but much more subtly. The analysand submits him- or herself to the process and trusts that healing and consciousness-raising will be accomplished. Resistances arise in the form of skepticism, criticism and doubt, all of which are valuable if they do not overpower the process. These range from mild to serious questioning as to what is illusion and what is reality, all the way to destructive impulses that try to deny and annihilate the analytic process itself. There is difficult work here: respecting resistance yet analyzing it, thus integrating the valuable parts. The Western mode of analysis, of course, does not require or even ask for faith in God. Is that why relatively few on the analytic path have religious experiences? Some Reichian therapists, engaged in nonverbal body work, believe otherwise, since these mystical events can occur spontaneously, as I, too, can attest from my own eight-year Reichian analysis.[4] A religious temperament seems to be important, in either mode of work, for such events to occur. Reich, himself, however communist and atheist he was at the outset of his career, became deeply spiritual later on.

Detachment from Opposites

Stage three, the detachment from the opposites in order to achieve perspective, is surely found in both analysis and the guru-disciple path. The analysand grows in capacity to look at him- or herself and impulses objectively, without being merely defensively intellectual, and thus enters into the "therapeutic alliance," since both analyst and analysand have the same aim of advancing consciousness, thus enhancing freedom. The Hindu way of doing this, by "seeing the imperfection in all things," is rather different from the Western way, because the latter mode fosters objectivity and aloofness. A parallel in analysis is a working through of our tendencies to idealize (including idealization of the analyst), but the consciousness of the shadow "in all things" brings a realization of the mixture of good and evil in all aspects of life and of our own self. This understanding is found more readily in Eastern thought (especially in Taoism) than in the West, where we continue to maintain a stringent differentiation between dark and light, good and evil (especially rooted in Puritanism). Yet that Eastern capacity for accepting wholeness in this way can also be achieved in the West, particularly in Jungian work.

Search for the Self

Stage four is a "search for the Self through the analysis of the I and the Mine." This "relativization of the ego," as a Jungian would put it, goes well beyond most Freudian-derived analytic work, which focuses upon infancy and childhood conditions. The latter usually shies away from religious issues, but those who have deeply experienced the potency of the unconscious, the Freudian "id," come away with an awareness of the ego's relativity that cannot be gainsaid. Freud may have been an atheist and pessimistic about civilization, yet no one can deny that he had a deep and abiding experience of the unconscious and its "vicissitudes." This phase of ego relativization and relation to the Self within is readily found in deeper Jungian work. It usually results from accepting the challenge of dealing with the collective unconscious, anima/animus and the rest, as we saw earlier when we looked at Jung's "stages." Those who use the technique of active imagination, involving a direct confrontation between ego and unconscious,[5] become fully aware of this dilemma and how it only gradually works itself out. Unlike in the Eastern tradition, this type of involvement usually occurs only after extensive work with the personal unconscious is accomplished (as with the Freudian-derived schools), and the ego is strong enough to take on such mind-breaking energies and conceptions. At this level, however, for both East and West, we are truly engaged in the religious or spiritual work of finding the right relationship to the unconscious, prescribed in the East and discovered in the West.

Self vs. Ego

Stage five, the realization of the reality of the Self and the illusory nature of the ego, reveals the difference and dividing line between Eastern and Western consciousness. Dr. Vasavada argued with Jung on this matter, but failed to convince him. For the East, the statement that the ego itself is an illusion is both true and necessary. For Jung, the statement itself was illusory since, he claimed, for consciousness to exist there has to be an ego. There has to be an agent for consciousness to occur, for experience to be registered. Yet, later in life, Jung dreamed that he discovered a yogin meditating or dreaming and that this yogin not only had Jung's face he was aware that when the yogin awakened, Jung would die. "Am I the one who dreams he is a butterfly? Or am I a butterfly who dreams he is a man?" asked the great Taoist, Chuang Tzu,[6] and so asked

Jung, too, at this stage of his life. Jung's answer, relativization, was still intact, but at least he had the experience that Vasavada and the East were talking about!

The Soul Is the Self

Realization that the soul and Self are identical, the sixth stage, is where the two types of consciousness come together once more. "I and the Father are One," says the Christian; "Ego and Self are One," says the realized individuator. Yet both know that such unions are temporary, that fall back into separation of the opposites and their need for each other. Indeed, this is necessary, from a psychological point of view, for further development of consciousness to take place, which also results in deeper union. The unconscious, says Jung, is never "emptied out."

Everything Is the Self

The seventh stage, like the seventh stage in Kundalini Yoga (as we saw in chapter 4), brings the mystical realization that "everything is the Self, therefore there is neither the seeker nor the sought, everything is ablaze in Light and Love—the ultimate synthesis." Such realizations are both ecstatic and calming, occur only infrequently in people's lives, and yet are life changing. One does not ordinarily experience such things in Western psychoanalysis, but even Wilhelm Reich, who began as a materialist-atheist-communist, speaks in this manner in his later years, and his work was primarily with the body! Few of us can live at this level even some of the time—except for saints and arhats—yet this is the ultimate realization. The spiritual path has found its goal. Those of us who rarely or never experience this can, however, take sustenance in the realization that the path itself is the goal and that most paths bring us back into ordinary life as both the testing and fulfillment of where our spiritual efforts have brought us. Recall the last picture of the Zen oxherding series.

The Path of the Rosary

The Rosary, like the Stations of the Cross, is undertaken by groups in church as an instance of the Divine Among (when churchgoers chant it together), but also is a kind of Christian mantra that can be repeated as a solitary practice. I use this as an example here for several reasons. First, the coming aeon is one in which the feminine principle in the divine, worshipped in the saying of the Rosary, will be surely renewed and deepened. Second, the Rosary, like the Stations of the Cross, gives us a nice picture of an individuation process (parallel to the categories we examined in Jung's *Two Essays*) undertaken as a collective event. This seems to be a contradiction in terms, but when we understand individuation as a natural development of the psyche in all of us, yet not frequently undertaken in a conscious way, we can see more clearly how this works.

We begin the Rosary, holding the beads lovingly in the hand, by reciting the Apostle's Creed, an affirmation of faith. We then grasp a bead for each of three repetitions of: "Hail Mary, full of Grace! The Lord is with thee; blessed art thou among women, and blessed is the fruit of thy womb, Jesus. Holy Mary, Mother of God, pray for us sinners now and at the hour of our death, Amen." After this comes, with the next bead, "Glory to the Father, and to the Son, and to the Holy Spirit. As it was in the beginning, is now, and ever shall be, world without end. Amen."

These are potent words, recited daily by millions of voices over many centuries, as they call out in need and appreciation, in agony and joy. It is in the human heart to so call out, whether in the mantras of the East or the prayers of the West. It is both a summoning of the divine and an expression of that same divine existence, arising from the soul itself. *Hare Krishna, Shema Israel*, Hail Mary: the exclamation calls and affirms, reminding us of the motto carved on Jung's home in Bollingen, "Summoned or not, God is always present." Yet we need to call out and to be called, to carve out a space and time for this special act. This amounts to nothing less than making use of our birth-given connection with the divine, which is always there, always calls upon us and always responds. God always answers our prayers, remarked former U.S. President Carter, but not always in the way that we would like. The process of individuation begins with the call to connection to the Self, whether initiated by the ego or by the divine, arising from a dream or numinous event, whether by means of a hallowed repetition of a given collective story or by embarking upon one's own path. We may note that this particular form of "re-collection" begins with a *quaternio*, a foursome that repeats a mandala of wholeness: We begin with the threesome of Mary plus God manifesting as both Father and Son, then joined by the Holy Spirit as a fourth. Now, with our beads, we begin:

The First Joyful Mystery: the Annunciation

"The angel Gabriel was sent from God to a virgin, and the virgin's name was Mary. 'Hail, full of grace, the Lord is with thee. Blessed art thou among women.' When she had heard him she was troubled at his words, and kept pondering what manner of greeting this might be. And the angel said to her, 'Do not be afraid, Mary, for thou hast found grace with God. Behold thou shalt call his name Jesus. He shall be great, and shall be called the Son of the Most High; and of his kingdom there shall be no end.' But Mary said to the angel, 'How shall this happen, since I do not know man?' 'The Holy Spirit shall come upon thee and the power of the Most High shall overshadow thee. And therefore the Holy One to be born shall be called the Son of God.' 'Behold the handmaid of the Lord: be it done to me according to thy word.'"[7]

The beginning of the story finds Mary modest, humble, and spare in speech. A Catholic nun in the Order of the Immaculate Heart of Mary once explained to me her contemporary understanding of her vows of poverty, chastity and obedience, modeled on Mary and surely, in my experience, making her "full of grace." She understood this as the necessity for her becoming a worthy vessel for the divine-man to be born within her. Poverty, said the nun, is modesty, lack of arrogance, quiet recognition that one is a "handmaid" of the Lord, open to God's spirit. Isn't this proper psychological receptivity to the Self, to be aware and to accept being chosen, but not inflated? We are ordinary mortals, yet singled out in the soul by this event.

Regarding chastity, the nun continued to explain that Mary is pure and ever alive to the Holy Spirit speaking within her. She is not pure as an angel is pure, because angels have no flesh, have nothing to be pure about. Her chastity is ever renewed, open afresh to spirit. This reminds me of the Abyssinian woman who once told a scholar, that a good woman is always renewed: before every love she is a virgin and pure; after every love she is a mother and committed; only in this way can you know whether she is a good woman or not.[8]

The vow of obedience models Mary's attentiveness to the Holy Spirit. She listens to the angel of God and inquires as to how things are to be done. She neither fights nor falls over in submission; she is attentive, and thus obedient to the movement of the spirit as it comes to her.

Psychologically, we understand this relationship of our souls to the divine. Mary is the model of how to receive this possibility of the miraculous birth in ourselves: between flesh and spirit, mortal and divine, we come to the psychic reality of awareness of the birth of the God within. The ritual raises this possibility, in its equally miraculous brilliance, to a collective event. Some may also ultimately come to know this divine authority in themselves.

The Second Joyful Mystery: The Visitation

After saying ten more Hail Marys and the Glory Be to the Father, we continue the story: "Now Mary went into the hill country. And she entered the house of Zacharias and saluted Elisabeth. When Elisabeth heard the greeting of Mary, the babe in her womb leapt. 'Blessed art thou among women and blessed is the fruit of thy womb! And blessed is she who has believed because the things promised her by the Lord shall be accomplished.' And Mary said: 'My soul magnifies the Lord, and my spirit rejoices in God my Savior, for he has regarded the lowliness of his handmaid. For, behold, all generations shall call me blessed; for he who is mighty has done great things for me. And holy is his name; and his mercy is from generation to generation on those who fear him. He has shown might with his arm, he has scattered the proud in the conceit of their heart. He has put down the mighty from their thrones and has exalted the lowly. He has filled the hungry with good things, and the rich he has sent away empty.'"

Mary, the blessed one, now sings a song and we may be reminded of the *Magnificat*, Bach's tremendously moving musical accompaniment to this verbal expression of the great event that has occurred. She rejoices in God's choosing her and speaks of his deeds and attitudes. He is fearsome but merciful, turns things upside down, raises the lowly and puts down the mighty. This Lord in Heaven changes history, making new values and goals, for he wants to become human, to find a home in ordinary flesh and bone by being born therein. That within us which was kingly and proud, seeking and using power for its own selfish ends, will be deposed, for the ordinary, lowly humans that we are now can become a dwelling place for the divine image, the Self. Mary, as the first of these ordinary human beings, second only to Jesus to experience this humanization/divinization, proclaims it and is blessed. So, too, we even more ordinary humans are blessed as a result of her consciousness. We, too, will be nourished in the old, weak, impoverished places of our being that hunger after God. And we, too, in our false riches, our power-hunger and conceit, will be deprived and "sent away." This is the message, which also reminds us of a previous prophet, Moses, who was said to have been the most humble of men. The Talmudic sages, when asked why no one like Moses had appeared again, replied that no one had been able to sink low enough to let God fill him. But Mary is a new image: an ordinary woman, yet destined to rise into Heaven with her body (according to the 1950 dogma of the Assumption), thereby adding a feminine fourth to the divine Trinity, with both body and full humanity, as Jung realized in his *Answer to Job*.

Here, too, we find a mandala, in the symbolism of the four participants: the pairing of Mary and Elizabeth, along with Joseph and Zacharias. The latter did not believe and was made dumb by the spirit, whereas Joseph had faith and was patiently devoted, despite the obvious scandal that the world would see. That pair of opposites is matched in Mary and Elizabeth, the latter as mother to the forerunner of Jesus, John the Baptist. Do we not become, like Elizabeth, mother to that intuitive anticipation of the divine which endures and wonders, needing patience in the process, even beforehand? And is not our old and critical spirit struck dumb when psychic reality overwhelms us? Part of our spirit, like Joseph, can only stand by, enduring events, letting the feminine principle carry the burden of this new message in its simplicity and complexity. That is why this is seen as a mystery.

The Third Joyful Mystery: The Nativity

"It came to pass while they were in Bethlehem, that the days for her to be delivered were fulfilled. And she brought forth her firstborn son, and wrapped him in swaddling clothes. And she laid him in a manger, because there was no room at the inn. And there were shepherds in the same district. And behold, an angel of the Lord stood by them. 'Do not be afraid, for behold, I bring you good news of great joy which shall be to all people. For today in the town of David a Savior has been born to you, who is Christ the Lord. Glory to God in the highest, and on earth peace to men of good will.' And behold, Magi came from the East, and entering they found the child with Mary, his mother. And falling down, they worshipped him. And they offered him gifts of gold, frankincense, and myrrh. And Mary kept in mind all these things, pondering them in her heart."

The new image of the divine is born in a stable—no room at the inn. Perhaps it is always so, the changing image of the Self is usually a challenge to the established order, there is no place for it there, and it has to emerge among the lowly aspects of ourselves, close to our animal nature, which makes it alive, vital, organic. Despite this origin, the three Magi greet the new Self-image, representative of the best wisdom of the time, yet open to the new. I am reminded of my dream, which I presented at the beginning of this book, of the new and unknown image of a divine child being attended by a Jewish rabbi, a Christian priest, and a Buddhist priest. These, no doubt along with others, carry the spiritual wisdom of our own times and must find their inclusion in any kind of encompassing world spirit which can contain them, and us.

Mary ponders all these things, we are told; she tries to assimilate all that this might mean. And so do we, when the divine center emerges from within our souls and commands our complete attention and service. Hail Mary, full of grace!

The Fourth Joyful Mystery:
The Presentation at the Temple

"According to the Law of Moses, they took Jesus up to Jerusalem to present him to the Lord. Now there was in Jerusalem a man named Simeon and this man was just and devout, looking for the consolation of Israel. And it had been revealed to him that he should not see death before he had seen the Christ of the Lord. And when they brought in the child Jesus, he received him into his arms and blessed God. 'Now thou dost dismiss thy servant, Oh Lord, according to thy word, in peace. Because my eyes have seen thy salvation, which thou hast prepared before the face of all peoples. A light of revelation to the Gentiles and a glory for thy people Israel.' And he said to Mary, 'Behold, this child is destined for the fall and for the rise of many in Israel, and for a sign that shall be contradicted. And thy own soul a sword shall pierce, that the thoughts of many hearts may be revealed.' And there was one Anna, a prophetess. She was a widow of about four score and four years, who departed not from the temple, but served God with fastings and prayers night and day. And she coming in at that instant gave thanks likewise unto the Lord and spake of him to all that looked for redemption in Jerusalem. And when they had performed all things according to the law of the Lord, they returned to Nazareth. And the child grew and became strong and the grace of God was upon him."

The divine child is initiated into the traditional religion, by means of naming and circumcision, although the latter is not mentioned here since this was a particularly difficult custom for the Gentiles to accept and was later rejected by them. There are always the stages of life to be celebrated, in every faith, and the role of the new hero, the savior, is not to "reject the law" but "fulfill it," meaning that at that time the new image was not meant to overthrow the old, but to provide continuity. This, of course, was ultimately not possible, and we see the two prophets, male and female, announcing such sad tidings in the midst of a joyful mystery. The male, Simeon, now understands and foresees, no longer skeptical as was the silenced Zacharias. The female is now spiritualized and profound, a step forward from the merely devoted Elizabeth. We see the psychological drama of the development of the soul continuing. Yet dire but unspecific suffering is also predicted at this presentation, "thy own soul a sword shall pierce." For suffering is already given: we no sooner give birth to the Self in ourselves when we must sacrifice any natural maternal possessiveness we feel for the sake of the higher aims of that same Self. We see here a hint of the comparable sacrifice asked of both Abraham and Sarah, whose awesome shock from God's command continues on in this far later tale of the Judaeo-Christian spirit. Internally, in our own psyche, there is usually a similar history of joy, followed by suffering, followed by redemption and higher meaning.

The Fifth Joyful Mystery:
The Finding of Jesus in the Temple

"When Jesus was twelve years old, they went up to Jerusalem according to custom of the feast. And when they were return-ing, the boy Jesus remained in Jerusalem, and his parents did not know it. They returned to Jerusalem in search of him. And after three days, they found him in the temple. He was sitting in the midst of the teachers, listening to them and asking them questions. And all who were listening to him were amazed at his understanding and his answers. 'Son, why hast thou done so to us? Behold, in sorrow thy father and I have been seeking thee.' 'How is it that you sought me? Did you not know that I must be about my Father's business?' And he went down with them and came to Nazareth and was subject to them. And Jesus advanced in wisdom and age and grace before God and men."

We are here made aware that the gift of God to us, of the Self making a home in our own souls, is to be given back to God as a willing sacrifice. We saw this also in the previous Mystery, but now we are faced with our unwillingness to sacrifice. We must not only lose what we have gained and go in search of it, but we also must accept that the Self's aims are not our own, even though we have been the vessel for it. In so understanding, we learn that the Self is in the service of God and we mortals must bear this truth in non-understanding and in pain. But God, too, submits, the story says. After asserting his task, the God-man is voluntarily "subject to them" and goes on learning. We see what happens, even now, to the boy and girl, from all the Abrahamic religions, who continue to be "presented at the temple" for initiation at a still youthful age, and what happens to that Self within us as well. We learn, like Mary and Joseph, that the Self does not belong to us but to Itself and has Its own path. We must learn and experience, while It also learns and experiences, what this world—and all of us humans—are really like. This is a hard lesson for both the human and the divine in us.

We continue with our beads and our prayers, now beginning the five Sorrowful Mysteries. Our Father . . . Hail Mary . . . Glory be.

The First Sorrowful Mystery: The Agony in the Garden

"Jesus came with them to Gethsemane, and he began to be saddened and exceedingly troubled. Then he said to them, 'My soul is sad, even unto death. Wait here and watch with me.' And going forward a little, he fell on the ground, and began to pray. 'Father, if thou art willing, remove this cup from me; yet not my will but thine be done.' And there appeared to him an angel from heaven to strengthen him. And falling into agony, he prayed the more earnestly. And his sweat became drops of blood running down upon the ground. Then he came to the disciples and found them sleeping. And he said, 'Could you not, then, watch one hour with me? Watch and pray, that you may not enter into temptation. The spirit is willing, but the flesh is weak.'"

What sorrow is this that God, the Self, must suffer and be afraid like an ordinary mortal? That he calls out to us to share his prayer and struggle to do that which he must? And, finally, that we fall into unconsciousness, into a sleep that leaves him to carry the whole burden alone? Furthermore, where was Mary in this trial of "spirit willing, flesh weak?"The meaning must be that the spirit is willing to sacrifice, serve, even to die, in order to carry the burden of God (the personal Self in service of the larger collective Self), but the human-animal-mortal flesh, with its instincts, grows fatigued and falls into unconsciousness. It is just so; no blame. Christ, too, the God-man, was afraid of suffering, as he and we should be. Mortal-animal-Jesus-man fails the immortal-spiritual-Christ-God. But the two are one and this paradox of a God-man conjunction, a Self-ego union, is fundamental. At this moment, Mary the Mother-container is absent and even the Self asks that"this cup pass from me."But, as Jung has profoundly shown in his *Answer to Job*, it is in this moment, in particular, that God (the Self) learns what it means to be human and mortal, suffering the fate that He had permitted to be inflicted, without cause, on poor Job. And He will suffer even more later on, as we know. Here it is fear of suffering, later it is the actuality of conflict regarding His dual nature, endured on that same cross reserved for outcasts and criminals. Hail Mary, whose furthering suffering is also reserved for that later event.

The Second Sorrowful Mystery:
The Scourging at the Pillar

"They bound Jesus and delivered him to Pilate. And Pilate asked him, 'Art thou the king of Jews?' Jesus answered. 'My kingdom is not of this world. But thou sayest it; I am a king. This is why I was born, and why I have come into the world, to bear witness to the truth.' Then Pilate said, 'I find no guilt in this man. I will therefore chastise him and release him.' Pilate then took Jesus and had him scourged. Oppressed and condemned, he was taken away, a man of suffering. Though he was harshly treated, he submitted, like a lamb led to the slaughter. He was pierced for our offenses, crushed for our sins. It was our infirmities that he bore, our sufferings that he endured. Upon him was the chastisement that makes us whole, by his stripes are we healed."

What does it mean that God comes into the world as man in order "to bear witness to the truth"? The truth that God becomes human and man divine? That the kingdom of God is in the inner world, in the soul, and not the outer world? But Pilate, a king in this outer world, says he finds no guilt yet "therefore" punishes and scourges. Thus we see the truth that the world is often unjust: the guiltless are judged unjustly and punished while the guilty go free. Yet God voluntarily enters this state, to bear our infirmities, for our sake, and most important, "to make us whole, by his stripes are we healed."

How does that help us? We know that God was unjust to Job, at the behest and seduction of Satan. We conjecture, psychologically, that he entered into the human condition because of it: the Self "incarnates" (takes on our human bodily condition) in order to know what it is like, but also in order to produce wholeness, in itself and us. God took on our humanity and perhaps this is the initial marker for us all to take on our divinity, not by mere copying—*imitatio Christi*—but by suffering our own inner opposites of Self and ego, animal and human, good and evil. We thereby come to know and be known, just as St. Augustine, himself, longed for and promised Christians. In this mutuality, we find the Holy Spirit, that mediating power which reconciles and unites the divine and mortal, Self and ego, and it is this that we experience as redemption. It is also what we know in psychology about self-realization: it consists in making manifest that ego-

Self axis which we carry as potential and bring into reality by dint of life experience and hard work.

But what of Pilate, that mortal king in us who wants only peace, success, no suffering, and becomes hypocritical in punishing, thus producing injustice? The unjust judge, in both God and the world, is balanced only by forgiveness, perhaps, and it is in this act of compassion that our consciousness grows, not only in wisdom but also in love, and this is the aim.

The Third Sorrowful Mystery:
The Crowning with Thorns

"Now the soldiers led him away into the courtyard, and they stripped him and put on him a purple cloak. And plaiting a crown of thorns, they put it upon his head, and a reed into his right hand. And bending the knee before him they mocked him, saying, 'Hail, King of the Jews!' and they spat upon him, and they took the reed and kept striking him on the head. Pilate again went outside and said, 'I bring him out to you, that you may know I find no guilt in him.' Jesus therefore came forth, wearing the crown of thorns and the purple cloak. And Pilate said to them, 'Behold the man!' But they cried out, 'Away with him! Crucify him!' 'Why, what evil has he done?' But they kept crying out the more, 'Crucify him!' 'Shall I crucify your king?' And the chief priests answered, 'We have no king but Caesar.' Then he handed him over to them to be crucified. And so they took Jesus and led him away."

The crown of thorns and purple robe of kings signify, respectively, degradation and exaltation. As king of this world, he is mocked and humiliated (and the assembled people knew that this was also a trick; if they were to proclaim him their own king this was tantamount to rejecting the kingship of Caesar, causing further destruction). But as wearer of the royal-colored cloak of kingship of the spirit, Jesus is elevated. Opposites are apparent once more. But to remain with what is already known is to react similarly to those who rejected the new, who would not or could not allow the new possibility that the divine could make a home within the human soul. Isn't that often our sin and guilt—to be so afraid of the authorities of world, or so afraid of taking on our own suffering of being both divine and mortal, that we merely project this entire event and let others become either scapegoat or spiritual authority? This is as true today as it was 2,000 years ago. In the interim, many of those Christians who claimed to have taken on this newness, alas, merely continued scapegoating. But today we have the consciousness to make other choices. Doesn't the most violent and unjust century in history demand such consciousness? Are we up to it?

The Fourth Sorrowful Mystery:
The Carrying of the Cross

"'If anyone wishes to come after me, let him deny himself. And take up his cross daily and follow me.' And bearing the cross for himself, he went forth to the place called the Skull. And they laid hold of a certain Simon of Cyrene, and upon him they laid the cross to bear it after Jesus. 'Take my yoke upon you, and learn from me. For I am meek and humble of heart. And you will find rest for your souls. For my yoke is easy, and my burden light.' Now there was following him a great crowd of people, and of women who were bewailing and lamenting him. Jesus, turning to them, said, 'Do not weep for me, but weep for yourselves and for your children. For if in the case of green wood they do these things, what is to happen in the case of the dry?'"

Clear enough. We are enjoined by God to take up our own cross, our own conflicts between opposites, ultimately to endure being both a human and a divine creature, just like Jesus, the first man to do this consciously. The example, to be followed by anyone, is individuation, continuing onward right until death. But we must let others (Simon) help us and, like Simon, sometimes find that we have to take on not only our own conflicts, but also those of God! When we find that we are like God, we shiver and quake. Isn't that what Job saw, when he covered his mouth, that God Itself was a divine con-catenation of opposites? That God needed us to realize that we are meant to be God's partner in the evolution of the human spirit? That, at least, is how Jung interpreted this.

Jesus also reminds us that if he, inaugurator of the powerfully new, is condemned, they should look to their own salvation and to that of their children, for it will be even more difficult in the future. This is surely so: evolution of the spirit is not always "onward and upward"; often the best of the saviors and heroes live at the beginning of the era, the fire gradually going out over the centuries.

The Fifth Sorrowful Mystery: The Crucifixion

"And when they came to the place called Skull, they crucified him. And Jesus said, 'Father, forgive them, for they do not know what they are doing.' And one of the robbers crucified with him said, 'Lord, remember me when thou comest into thy kingdom.' And Jesus said to him, 'Amen I say to thee, and this day thou shalt be with me in paradise.' And Jesus saw his mother and the disciple standing by, whom he loved. And he said to his mother, 'Woman, behold, thy son.' Then he said to his disciple, 'Behold, thy mother.' And from that hour the disciple took her into his home. And the sun was darkened, and the earth quaked, and the curtain of the temple was torn in two. And Jesus cried out with loud voice and said, 'Father, into thy hands I commend my spirit.' And bowing his head, he expired."

Such simple words proclaimed in this terrible, wonderful event. This is how an equally simple Catholic priest expressed it: "He had such agony at Gethsemane that he sweated blood; he was betrayed, denied, deserted, arrested, falsely accused, condemned unjustly; blindfolded, spat upon, beaten; ridiculed by Herod, scourged by Pilate; crowned with thorns; loaded with the cross and then nailed to it; enduring utter dereliction of soul in the midst of terrible thirst; and even after death his side was torn with a lance."

This man of God understood perfectly well the tremendous suffering that his deity, God the Father, endured. And we, too, can understand what it means when the divine becomes totally contained with us, tortured and torturing, and even exclaiming the ancient Hebrew lament, "Eli, Eli; my God, why hast Thou forsaken me!" The ultimate cup of bitterness, the ultimate surrender of the spirit is this realization.

What of Mary in all this? We can imagine her suffering, a woman watching the total degradation and pain of her adored son, helpless and equally in agony. But he calls out to her and makes her mother of his disciples as he, himself, dies. We are to mother our brothers and sisters, those other parts of ourselves that need care and redemption, while the Self undergoes such agony. For so has Mary performed, in story and experience, for 2,000 years. And now she is appearing in greater frequency and intensity in the world, announcing a new dispensation at the end of the aeon. Perhaps we can now perform that other function requested by Jesus, that the disciple take her into his house, that we, too, mother the inner mother, care for her, let her also be both mortal and divine.

Having circumambulated the five joyful and five sorrowful mysteries, we may proceed to consider the Five Glorious Mysteries. Once again, we say the prayers and further decades of Hail Mary.

The First Glorious Mystery: The Resurrection

"'Amen, amen I say to you, that you shall be sorrowful, but your sorrow shall be turned into joy. For I will see you again, and your heart shall rejoice, and your joy no one shall take from you.' At early dawn, they came to the tomb, raking the spices that they had prepared. And behold, an angel of the Lord came down from heaven, and drawing near rolled back the stone. 'Do not be afraid, for I know that you seek Jesus, who was crucified. He is not here, but has risen. Behold the place where they laid him. And behold, he goes before you into Galilee; there you shall see him.' And they departed quickly from the tomb in great fear and great joy. 'I am the resurrection and the life; he who believes in me, even if he dies, shall live. And whoever lives and believes in me shall never die.'"

"And your joy no one shall take from you." So is Mary addressed. I am here reminded of my own "conversation," as "Daughter of Guinevere," in active imagination with Mary. When I came to this Joyful Mystery, Mary spoke, surprisingly, as the Sorrowful Madonna:

> I remember days of longing, sadness, of misery. I remember loss of faith, about which I did not speak. Better to keep silence, to carry my own sorrow, suffering, loss of conviction and meaning, than burden others with it. But I remember. And, lest others think me a Goddess, or some creature far from the laments, the pains, the doubts, the human frailties, then let them reflect again. For I was mortal and limited. My awareness of immortality came only with time. But I remember, too, the day of resurrection. When my son came to me, and proved that all was not foolishness, ignominy, and self-deception. I remember that day, too. Death is nei-ther life nor the opposite of it. Death and birth are opposed, not death and life. For there is death in life and, in the resurrection, life in death. That I learned that day. The stone door pushed away, the empty crypt. . . . Sadness is from the endless round of birth and death. . . .[9]

Mary went on to speak of the moving spirit, bringing awareness that everyone can become conscious of being a God-man and God-woman. The Self can find a home in the consciousness of us all, suffer with us and because of us, just as we can in return, in blessed partnership. The joy, the resurrection, comes in learning this truth in our blood, bones, and flesh.

The night after I wrote the foregoing active imagination so many years ago, I dreamed that "all was well in the world of the Mothers. There was great joy and homecoming." Thus is sorrow touched by joy. Yet we need to remember, as William Blake reminded us, to "kiss the joy as it flies."

The Second Glorious Mystery: The Ascension

"Now he led them out towards Bethany, and he lifted up his hands and blessed them, saying, 'All power in heaven and on earth has been given to me. Go, therefore, and make disciples of all nations, baptizing them in the name of the Father, and of the Son, and of the Holy Spirit, teaching them to observe all that I have commanded you. . . . He who believes and is baptized shall be saved. But he who does not believe shall be condemned. . . . And behold, I am with you all days, even unto the consummation of the world.' And it came to pass as he blessed them, that he parted from them. . . . And was taken up into heaven and sits at the right hand of God."

What is Jesus saying? When we are totally contained in the Christ, the Self, when consciousness has reached that level, then the power of spirit and matter is also possessed, contained. Jesus can now leave the world where man (Adam) initially fell, now helping us all to attain his redeemed state—at the right hand of God—helping others and ultimately the whole world to achieve this consciousness. Humankind can achieve this, however, only by being immersed in the water of life and emotion, the ever-encompassing waters of our own passions and desires, ultimately becoming, as was Jesus, both passionate and calm, united in a center of total freedom, total suffering, and total joy. Only then can we leave this mortal state. When I performed the active imagination many years ago, expressing myself as "Daughter of Guinevere," Mary noted that I "had grasped it but it had not grasped [me]." That experience of being "grasped" did happen afterwards and Mary then addressed "Daughter of Guinevere" as "full of Grace." Thirty years later, I can attest that such states or achievements, even in the East, are temporary. For most of us, unlike Jesus, need to arrive at this state again and again, until we, too, can leave this cycle of continuous rebirth and reincarnation, whether in one life or many lives, to achieve that other level that Jesus, and other arhats, have hinted at.

The Third Glorious Mystery:
Pentecost; Descent of the Holy Spirit

"When the days of Pentecost were drawing to a close, they were all together in one place. And suddenly there came a sound from heaven, as of a violent wind blowing. And there appeared to them parted tongues as of fire, which settled upon each of them. And they were all filled with the Holy Spirit and began to speak of the wonderful works of God. Now there were staying at Jerusalem devout Jews from every nation under heaven. And Peter, standing up with the Eleven, lifted up his voice and spoke out to them. 'Repent and be baptized; and you will receive the gifts of the Holy Spirit.' Now they who received his words were baptized, and they were added that day about three thousand souls. . . . Send forth thy Spirit, and they shall be created; and thou shalt renew the face of the earth. . . . Come, O Holy Spirit, fill the hearts of thy faithful, and kindle in them the fire of thy love."

First, we are initiated by water, by the emotions and unconscious from below. Now the Spirit from above initiates us, by air-thoughts and fire-feelings. In the former state, some could so master their passions that they could "walk on water," ride the unconscious without sinking into it or drowning. Now the immersion comes from above, there is a new initiation of the Spirit in which we know that God and human beings are co-creative partners in existence. This means that the brother/ sisterhood of humankind is our natural state, that everyone is hurt when one is hurt, that everyone is elevated when one is elevated, that this spirit dwells in all of us and needs only to be activated. Finally, we learn that the task of us all is to become like Christ, to achieve an awareness of our own divinity. We must cultivate and serve it, until the Earth is transformed, until we are all one in such divinity, servants of the One in whom we have our being and who also lives within us. Thus the three thousand Jews from all nations, representative of all humanity, are baptized—touched and initiated.

In my active imagination, upon my wondering about the necessity of repentance, Mary said (to my inner Daughter of Guinevere), "Repent that you might see God."[10] Not because of sin, she meant, but in order to experience the Self, since sin meant simply being cut off from the Self. And of what was I, acting as this inner Daughter, to repent? It was the sin of arrogance, of disease, of lack of love. The first and third were clear enough, but repenting of disease? The answer came as the disease of egoism, of "little-self" focus and involvement at the expense of "big-self" totality. This produced a powerful feeling of being "sorry", even better than repentance, since in the latter condition judgment comes from outside, whereas the former is a realization from deep within. It is upon this realization that we can "see God."

The Fourth Glorious Mystery: The Assumption

"Blessed are thou, O daughter, by the Lord the most high God, above all women upon earth. For he has so magnified thy name this day, that thy praise shall not depart out of the mouth of men. In every nation which shall hear thy name, the God of Israel shall be magnified on occasion of thee. Thou art the glory of Jerusalem, thou art the joy of Israel, thou art the honor of our people. . . . Hear, O daughter, and see; turn your ear, for the king shall desire your beauty. . . . And the temple of God was opened, and there came flashes of lightning and peals of thunder. And a great sign appeared in heaven; a woman clothed with the sun. And the moon was under her feet, and upon her head a crown of twelve stars. . . . All glorious is the king's daughter as she enters; her raiment is threaded with spun gold. Sing to the Lord a new song, for he has done wondrous deeds."

Here, at last, is the *Assumptio Mariae*, passionately declared in the Apocalypse of John and in 1950 proclaimed as dogma by Pope Pius XII, interpreted by many, psychologized by Jung. Her blessedness is our blessedness; it is the elevation of the feminine principle and the body into the highest image of God and consciousness. The Trinity of God the Father-Son-Holy Spirit becomes a quaternity. In *Jungian Psychology and the Passions of the Soul*, I wrote about a female trinity, God the Mother-Daughter-Holy Soul, balancing the male trinity. The Daughter of Guinevere had struggled with the problem of her mother's two loves—King Arthur and Sir Lancelot—and discovered that Mary also had two loves, God the Father, and the Son. This union was achieved at an etheric level, where matter and spirit are also One. Daughter of Guinevere also discovered that it was human love, Mary's, that remained present when God's love was not. Consider: God abandoned Job in His wager with the Devil; God abandoned Jesus when on the cross. So human love needed to be present even when divine love was absent! Thus are we honored to see the elevation of the ordinary woman, the ego, the person, to participate in divinity, in the Self, to endure the darkness of that self-same spirit and to mediate it in love.

The Fifth Glorious Mystery: The Coronation

"Who is this that comes forth like the dawn, as beautiful as the moon, as resplendent as the sun? . . . Like the rainbow appearing in the cloudy sky; like the blossoms on the branches in springtime . . . I am the mother of fair love, of fear, and of knowledge, and of holy hope. . . . In me is all grace of the way and the truth, in me is all hope of life and of virtue. Come to me, all you that yearn for me, and be filled with my fruits. You will remember me as sweeter than honey, better to have than the honeycomb. . . . So now, O Children, listen to me; instruction and wisdom do not reject! Happy are those who keep my ways, watching daily at my gates. For he who finds me finds life and wins favor from the Lord. . . . Hail, O Queen of Mercy, protect us from the enemy and receive us at the hour death."

Thirty-plus years ago, when I undertook the meditation upon the Rosary, at this point there came into my hands—by chance or movement of the Holy Spirit—a little brochure (which, alas or for good, I later lent away to persons now unknown) describing this image of Mary's Coronation. It contained a picture illustrating Revelation, in which there was a woman clothed with the sun, the moon under her feet, and the twelve stars of a crown upon her head. Here was a representation of a person who was totally awakened, totally enlightened. The twelve stars of the crown, the commentator thought, represented twelve body-centers, similar to insights portrayed in Kundalini Yoga and Kabbalah, that need to be awakened in human beings. Mary, with all twelve centers awakened, became the perfect type-pattern of an enlightened and "risen" woman, just as Jesus was the type-pattern for an enlightened and "risen" man.

Of these rose-like centers, there was one each in the feet, in the knees, and in the hands, tokenizing, when "opened," that one now "walked" in the way of God (on the spiritual path, we would say). One "kneeled" in meditation and prayer (conversation with God), and one's "hands" were in the service of others. Next came a spine center, suffused in red, which aided in the purification and transformation of body energies, followed by the solar plexus, green when awakened, which stimulated the life processes. These were followed by the heart center, colored a blossoming red when one loved others, and then the throat center for speech, blue in color, representing nondestructive words for the writer and for creativity. Finally, the head centers were two, violet in color, one representing image building and the other the power of the will to serve the spirit. When all twelve centers are rendered aglow in initiation, she said, from Earth (feet and knees), to Water (from knees to generative organs), Fire (generative organs to heart), Air (heart to crown of the head), the person is ready to meet the Bridegroom, God. The Marriage Feast is celebrated and the person passes into the mystic rite of conception.

Whether this woman's interpretation of the twelve centers is correct or not, surely the coronation (also appearing in alchemy), is the acceptance of the Crown of the Self. It is clearly an image of the Self for the female, and for the transfigured soul of the male, finding its parallel in the image of Jesus as the Self for the male and the transfigured spirit for the female. Their union, psychologically, is therefore a marriage of opposite aspects of the Self, both divine and mortal.

All that is missing here for totality, as Jung noted, is the inclusion of the principle of the dark side, shown in the East in the Tai Chi symbol of yin and yang (in Taoism), for example, but excluded in the West or present only as the rejected devil. So there is still work to be done, at least for those who do more regarding their "father's business." Yet the problem of darkness and evil continually harasses us, whether we want to be so occupied or not, hence the need for protection from the enemy, from within and from without. Yet who can fault this grand image from Christianity, as mirrored in the Stations of the Cross and in the Rosary, and who has truly achieved its divine level of awareness and acceptance? We are astounded, provoked, driven onward to merely match that which was given long ago. We also need to be grateful for this gift from the divine. Yet can't the image continue to develop, just as that not-so-simple woman suggested with her interpretation? This, I think, is neither disrespectful nor heretical; it merely shows that all images, the divine and otherwise, arise from the soul and she/it is our precious source and taskmistress for change. My own work with a shamanistic person who has creatively "channeled" Mary for quite some time, with impressive effect, brings fresh insights from Mary.[11] These include the observation that all good brings with it some evil, which must then be worked with and integrated as well. Such insights are profound and difficult, but indicate that Mary continues to carry a powerful collective force in the soul of the West. Together with comparable figures in other religions (Shekhina, Shakti-Kali, Kwan Yin, Kannon, etc.) this betokens a deep change in our world-image of the divine, needing to more fully include the feminine within it.

Notes

[1] J. Marvin Spiegelman, *Jungian Psychology and the Passions of the Soul* (Tempe, AZ: New Falcon, 1989). For other Jungian approaches, see J. Marvin Spiegelman, ed., *Catholicism and Jungian Psychology* (Tempe, AZ: New Falcon, 1988) and Protestantism and Jungian Psychology (Tempe, AZ: New Falcon, 1995).

[2] Arwind Vasavada, *Tripura-Rahasya: A Comparative Study of the Process of Individuation* (Varanasi: Chowkhamba Sanskrit Series, 1965).

[3] My story of Maya the yogini going her own way, in *The Tree of Life: Paths in Jungian Individuation* (Tempe, AZ: New Falcon, 1974/1993), illustrates an exception to this.

[4] J. Marvin Spiegelman, *Reich, Jung, Regardie and Me: The Unhealed Healer* (Tempe, AZ: New Falcon, 1992).

[5] See Jung, "The Transcendent Function," *Structure and Dynamics of the Psyche*, CW 8; Barbara Hannah, *Encounters with the Soul: Active Imagination* (Santa Monica: Sigo Press, 1981); and Spiegelman, *Jungian Psychology and the Passions of the Soul*.

[6] Paraphrased from Sam Hamill, trans., and J. P. Seaton, ed., *The Essential Chuang Tzu* (Boston: Shambhala, 1998), p. 18.

[7] This reading of the Rosary is adapted from Rev. J. Anthony Meis, *The Rosary, with Scripture Meditations and Practical Applications* (Baltimore: Barton-Cotton, Inc., 1970). The Dominican priests made the saying of the Rosary popular in the 13th century.

[8] C. G. Jung and C. Kerenyi, *Essays on a Science of Mythology* (New York: Pantheon, 1949), pp. 141–142.

[9] Spiegelman, *Jungian Psychology and the Passions of the Soul*, p. 206ff.

[10] Spiegelman, *Jungian Psychology and the Passions of the Soul*, p. 210.

[11] See my chapter, "Jung, Mary and the Millennium," in J. Marvin Spiegelman, ed., *Psychology and Religion at the Millennium and Beyond* (Tempe, AZ: New Falcon, 1999).

CHAPTER 10

Combining Types: Women's Mysteries

In the previous chapters, we have seen a variety of expressions of the individual spiritual search "within" and the combination of that endeavor with given collective symbols. Although these methods are "gender-free" and one of the latter (Rosary) specifically summons up an aspect of the feminine principle, it is clear that, historically, mostly men have taken up such paths. We live in a time when that patriarchal perspective is severely challenged, not only by the presence of great numbers of women actively engaged in the spiritual search, but by suggested revisions of theological formulations among the various religions, which justifiably stand accused of having practiced sexism.

Among the particular instances where women were not excluded from elite spiritual paths was the civilization of ancient Rome at its height, somewhat before the advent of the Christian era. Numerous "Mysteries" existed in these syncretistic and spiritually intense times—rather like our own situation—some of which were open to both sexes (e.g., the Eleusinian Mysteries), and some of which were exclusively reserved for women. One of the latter, of special interest for us nowadays, was that of the Villa of Mysteries in Pompeii.

This villa, apparently having become the home of an Orphic mystery cult at the time of Caesar Augustus in the first century B.C.E., was buried, along with the rest of Pompeii, under lava ash during the eruption of Mt. Vesuvius in the year 79 C.E. It remained forgotten until excavation was begun in the 19th century. The murals that adorn the large "initiation" room were uncovered only in 1930. Much study has been undertaken regarding the processes revealed in this series of murals, but all agree that an initiation process for women was the center of attention. In the following presentation, I draw on the work of Katherine Bradway and Linda Fierz-David, both first-generation Jungian analysts.[1] Figure 39 shows the Villa exterior and the north and east walls.

Historical research has established that the women who undertook the initiation provided in such a temple lived in a period of Roman history in which power was worshipped and was the center of concern, with love relegated to the background. Despite this power orientation, women enjoyed extensive social privileges, there being little difference between their rights and standing from those of men in legal, moral, or social situations. Many learned Greek and philosophy, gave lectures, practiced medicine and law, and carried on small commercial and industrial activities. Their situation was rather like that existing in the most recent times in Western countries, but was fairly well eclipsed during the two-thousand year era between then and now. Yet there was severe disparity between the sexes nonetheless. Marriage, for example, particularly in the upper classes, was only a question of money and politics; women could not legally choose their husbands. Fathers arranged such matters exclusively in terms of financial concerns. Similar disregard for relationship extended to children. Both historians and poets therefore depicted the Roman woman during this period as lonely.

The one area of life where Roman women could find solace was in cults and mysteries, which abounded. Whereas most men were connected with the cult of Mithras, a god associated with the sun and a favorite of warriors, the women maintained their devotion to the Great Mother, a carryover from Greek times, linked with the earth and

Figure 39. Villa of Mysteries exterior (top) and north and east walls
(bottom). From Bradway, Villa of Mysteries, p. 15.

nature mysteries. The only male god who carried weight for them was Dionysos, a source for both the sensual and transcendent imagination. Although their situation resembled that of the most modern of women, this establishment of women's mysteries was already old and valued, providing a sense of religious renewal and enhancing wholeness. The murals in the Villa of Mysteries give us a rewarding image and hint at how this process may have taken place, as we will now see.

Figure 40 on page 203 shows us the plan of the large room in which the initiation procedure is described in pictures and where, presumably, the mysteries took place. The arrow shows where the initiate entered and D-A, picture # 6, is the dominating scene of Dionysos seated with a goddess, generally presumed to be Ariadne. Numbers 1 to 10 indicate both placement and sequence of the stages of this initiation, with #8 constituting two scenes in itself and the ending of the rite. Numbers 9 and 10, separated from the rest and from each other by structural breaks in the wall, depict what happens after completion. Note the magical number ten as the containing symbol describing spiritual work, which we have seen earlier.

Since Dionysos and Ariadne constitute the central figures for the meaning of the initiation, we need to understand something of the story and nature of this pair. Dionysos, god of wine and ecstasy, is the most paradoxical of all the gods, since his nature brings the highest form of fulfillment but also madness and destruction, as well. Armed with his *thyrsus*, an ivy-twined staff tipped with a pine cone, he wandered the world accompanied by his tutor, Silenus (also shown in these paintings), and a group of maenads—frenzied women and satyrs who were part human and part goat. Early tribes worshipped him with exciting music and wild dancing, with phallus worship occupying a central place. Women were said to have gone mad in their worship of him, but this madness was thought to have taken place more with those women who refused to recognize his divinity.

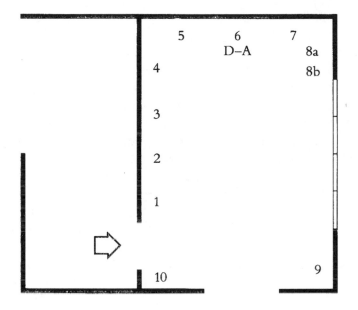

Figure 40. Plan of the initiation chamber in the Villa of Mysteries.
From Bradway, Villa of Mysteries, *p. 7.*

Like his sister, Athena, who emerged out of Zeus's brow, Dionysos was father-born. After impregnating Semele, a mortal woman, Zeus struck her dead with his lightning, snatched Dionysos from her womb, and placed him in his own thigh. Dionysos was also believed to have had a violent death, like other gods of vegetation, only to be reborn. In his resurrection, he embodied a greater and everlasting life, Zoë (Greek: *zōē,* life). He took the form of various animals, especially the snake, the bull, and the goat, all of which were sacred to him. We can think of him and his quality as ecstasy arising from nature itself, which can both integrate and disintegrate a person.

Ariadne was the human daughter of King Minos and Pasiphaë, but subsequently had attributes connecting her to the dark underworld and to love itself. The myth tells us that

Ariadne always belonged to the Bull-God Dionysos, but that she was untrue to him when she fell in love with Theseus on the Isle of Crete. She helped that hero kill the Minotaur, her half-brother, who dwelled at the center of the labyrinth, by providing him a ball of thread to lead him back out of the labyrinth. In aiding this Sun-hero, she betrayed her own dark, underworld origin.

Yet Theseus deserted Ariadne. One account has it that because of Dionysos's enraged jealousy, Artemis sent Theseus away and killed Ariadne. Another account says that Ariadne hanged herself in despair. In any case, Dionysos came over the sea to find her, embraced her as his beloved, brought her back to life, and their holy marriage was consummated. In celebration, Dionysos gave Ariadne a crown of gold, which gleams in heaven as the Corona Borealis, something we moderns can understand as a symbol of wholeness or the Self. Zeus gave her immortality and the couple ascended from the underworld into heaven.

How can we understand this myth and its importance in a mystery celebrating the initiation of women? It seems to me that we are privileged to glimpse just what an advanced woman of two thousand years ago was longing for, since it was lacking in the world, namely divine fulfillment in love. The experience of betrayal of love, of disappointment and despair, was just the condition that made possible a union of a mortal with the ecstatic god who both disintegrates and integrates. The fact that an otherwise undistinguished earthly woman was deified made possible, from our modern viewpoint, the realization of the Self, just as we have seen it earlier among other spiritual paths. The Villa of Mysteries was just the situation where this elevation of a woman's soul into wholeness could take place. We can now go through the various pictures of this spiritual path to understand how this came about.

Scene 1 (see fig. 41, top, page 205) shows the initiate, a mature woman, listening while a young boy reads from a scroll, understood as containing instructions as to what was expected of her. That the boy is naked and wearing boots was an indication, at that time, that he was divine. The wearing of boots

Figure 41: Scenes 1-8a of the Villa of Mysteries. From Bradway, Villa of Mysteries.

by tragedians in the Greek theater underscores the dramatic character of the ritual. The woman sitting behind the boy, with her right hand on his shoulder, is an officiating priestess. She, too, has a scroll, emphasizing the formality of this first stage in the initiation. The candidate is heavily clothed and wears a veil, suggesting that she is being screened from the everyday world in order to enter this inner world of mystery.

Scene 2 represents further preparation. The figure to the far left, the initiate, connects this scene with the previous one, but she is now more lightly clad and wearing a wreath of myrtle, a symbol of renewal sacred to Aphrodite, which points to the importance of love in this mystery. The initiate carries a tray holding a sacramental cake that she ritually sliced to prepare it as a sacrificial offering. The Southwest Native American women's initiation also included such an offering. The cake's purple color suggests it was prepared with wine, an attribute of Dionysos. In her right hand, the initiate holds a laurel twig, an intoxicant that was used by the priestess at Delphi to induce the euphoric trance required for her oracles. We can understand that she used the drug to help her contact her inner depths.

A priestess sitting at an altar presides over the proceedings, probably carrying the authority of the Great Mother. She, like the initiate, wears a crown of myrtle, symbol of renewal. To her left, an assistant holds a covered basket, which rests heavily on her knee. It is thought to be associated with Dionysos, possibly containing a snake, his symbol of death and rebirth and characteristic of many initiation ceremonies. To the right of the presiding priestess is a younger priestess, also crowned with myrtle, who carries a scroll and pours sacramental water over the laurel twig held in the hand of the high priestess. The image implies that she intends to lay the sprig of laurel in the basket after it has been purified with the holy water. The scene as a whole seems to represent preparation for a renewal experience in which the initiate will undergo an altered state of consciousness. The security of ego-consciousness will be sacrificed in favor of the awe-filled condition that arises in the experience of the god, the Self.

Scene 3 is markedly different from the formal ritual of the two preceding scenes. Nature and music are introduced and the initiate is no longer present, at least not in human form. Instead, there are fauns who are part human and part animal, along with the part human and part divine Silenus, tutor of Dionysos. Silenus plays a lyre and also wears a wreath of myrtle. In the background, a young faun plays a shepherd's pipe and a female faun in front of him is suckling a young female goat. Being given the breast is understood as symbolic of being accepted as an initiate, so perhaps this goat represents the woman at her instinctual level. A young male goat, Dr. Bradway thinks, may represent the initiate's own masculine aspect.[2] The goat was sacred to Dionysos and it is understood that this move toward animals and nature, paralleled in many myths, is indicative of a regression of human consciousness to a preconscious animal state, something requisite for rebirth and regeneration. Jung understood this picture as exemplifying a woman's becoming aware of her absolute connection with nature.

Scene 4 consists solely of the image of the terrified woman, behind which is Scene 5, on the back wall of the chamber, understood as the inner sanctuary where the *katabasis*, the underworld experience of the night-sea journey, can take place. The initiate has not yet reached this sphere, but her fright may be due to a glimpse of it, since she seems to be retreating, has thrown her cloak up in defense, is even coming right out of the frame, as if to run away. What does she see in that oncoming scene? Again we see Silenus, but now wearing the Dionysian wreath of ivy. Two male fauns or satyrs enact a drama: one holds a fearsome mask while the other is looking at the bottom of a wine vessel. Bradway cites Joseph Campbell and others to document the understanding that the mask is reflected in the vessel, which is associated with divine revelation.[3] All interpretations point to the woman's imminent encounter with the intoxicating God, Dionysos. Conscious control is loosened. The initiate must now decide: will she submit to a loss of conscious control or is she going to run away and break off the initiation? Dr. Bradway likens this decision to that faced by many analysands when they first emotionally confront the collective unconscious and are tempted to break off the analysis.

Scene 6 is not a stage of the initiation process itself but reveals the overall theme picture of Dionysos and Ariadne. This is the only area in the series that has suffered material damage, yet we can still make out the languid form of Dionysos lying back on Ariadne. This reversal of the usual posture of leaning suggests, according to Dr. Bradway, that the feminine is here elevated above the god, appropriate for women's initiation. But it is also here that the initiate is confronted with the profound myth of a woman, defeated in love, finding it once again at a divine (inner) level and being elevated thereby to a higher consciousness. Isn't this also an amazingly contemporary portrayal of the possibility of realization?

In Scene 7 the initiate emerges from her experience in the underworld, although what actually happened therein is not shown. This is typical of the unutterable secret of initiation ceremonies: it lies not only in keeping such knowledge safe from disrespectful and destructive hands, but also in the impossibility of truly communicating such mysteries to those who have not undergone them. Our initiate looks as if she is coming out of a trance. She carries a staff, which may be a torch. Is it a symbol of the enlightenment she has gained? It seems burdensome to her, yet she also wears a cap. This has not appeared before; perhaps it is a symbol of her new knowledge. She kneels before a basket identified as a *liknon*, used for winnowing, or separating husks from seeds of grain. It was in such a basket that Dionysos was placed after he was born and it appears in rituals pertaining to him. It commonly held the divine phallus, symbolizing the primal regenerative force. Here the initiate stretches out her arms as if to lift the purple covering, but since the contours do not conform to a phallus, it has been suggested that it may be a cult statue on which a phallus is featured. Such images are frequently seen in connection with the god.

Standing behind the initiate in the mural are two figures of women that are so badly damaged that they are hard to distinguish. One is holding a basket above the initiate's head while the other seems to be drawing back, perhaps in horror at the presumption of uncovering the phallus. Further to the right is a dark-winged female figure who looks as if she has just dropped from the heavens. Her partially clothed body identifies her as a divinity and she too, wears the tragedian boots worn by the child divinity in Scene 1. Her left hand is raised as if rejecting the kneeling woman and in her right hand she holds a long whip. Her eyes are directed toward Scene 8a on the adjoining wall. This winged figure is identified as Aidos, goddess of modesty, which suggests the interpretation that her role is to bring the initiate back to her senses after the inflationary experience of having been in contact with Dionysos. She also displaces the initiate's arrogance in attempting to unveil the sacred phallic statue. Dr. Bradway, however, suggests that this same winged goddess is the powerful feminine who leads the initiate away from being overwhelmed by the masculine power, directing her instead to reconnect with the feminine. This danger of losing one's femininity in such an encounter with the phallic male god is not trivial. The initiate submits to her, very likely with considerable ambivalence.

The winged goddess is connected to the next Scene, 8a, by the whip held in her right hand. She is clearly raising this whip to strike the shoulder of the initiate, now burying her face in the lap of another woman. The initiate does not struggle, however, but now accepts this beating, without ambivalence, as part of her initiation. This surrender is well-known in many mysteries of initiation, male and female. The older woman does not protect her from the blow, but is holding her garment back so that the whip can strike her bare flesh. Yet she also comforts her by stroking her hair. As Dr. Bradway points out, this is not a scene of a woman sinking into the lap of the Great Mother; the older woman is also human, presumably one who has already been through initiation. The initiate now gains true understanding, including the necessity of suffering, for which the previous donning of the cap of knowledge was only preparatory. Awareness in the flesh is always more complete and long-lasting than intellectual comprehension alone.

Figure 42: Scenes 8a - 10 of the Villa of Mysteries.
From Bradway, Villa of Mysteries.

The well-known theme—although often kept secret—that there may be a secret ecstasy and enlightenment connected with the infliction of pain may be traced to this profound understanding.

The initiate dancing in Scene 8b is generally interpreted as deification; she dances the dance of the arisen spirit. Unlike the previous pictures, in which music was provided, she now makes her own music with clashing of cymbals. Her scarf, representative of the feminine, flows around her, and the staff, like the thyrsus that Dionysos carries, is held for her by the priestess, who is now her attendant. She now has masculine and feminine powers as needed, but she is in thrall of neither. She is, like Artemis or Ariadne, one-in-herself and free.

Scenes 9 and 10 are not part of the ritual drama, but represent what happens after completion. Combing of the woman's hair in Scene 9 suggests preparation for return to the outer world, just as Scene 2 provided preparation for the inner world via purification and sacrifice. The mirror, reflecting consciousness of herself back to the initiate, is held by a young Eros figure. This Eros was exactly the active love and relationship energy that was most lacking in the existence of the Roman woman. Perhaps the initiate now has the capacity to at least relate to her deepest self, no matter what the outer world presents to her. In addition to the Eros figure, there is another winged figure, bringing the total to four, a symbol of feminine (even-numbered) totality.

The final picture, Scene 10, is a portrait of a lady, the only image on the outer narrow wall. She is elegantly dressed, sits serenely on a richly ornamented chair, and wears a ring on the fourth finger of her left hand. She is understood to be the lady of the house or a high priestess of the cult, probably both, who may have commissioned these murals. Her picture directly faces the back wall where Dionysos and Ariadne prevail. She is seated in a way that permits a view of all the scenes. Can she be a symbol of the enlightened woman, now aiding the enlightenment of others? In any event, we are now in a position to put all the scenes together in a continuous story. Dr. Bradway does this in a direct way:

The woman who comes for the initiation rite comes alone. She is received by a priestess and listens to instructions read impersonally to her by a child who is partly divine, adding to the numinosity of the experience and implying the possibility of rebirth [spiritual, we would add]. Certain preambles are necessary so that the initiate can develop both an awe of and a trust in the process. She proceeds to an inner chamber where formal preparation includes the initiate's making an offering as a sacrifice prior to continuing the initiation. Further preparation includes the purification of an organic, once living object. What else is included at this stage is hidden from view, but is evidently related to, or looks ahead to, the inducement of a lessening of ego consciousness in favor of renewal and transformation through the Self.

The setting now becomes less formalized, more dreamlike, with the introduction of nature and music and the disappearance of humans. Connection with both masculine and feminine instincts is made, and the connection with a divinity is anticipated. With the sudden realization of the coming encounter with a divine power, the initiate is alarmed. Her fright causes her to doubt whether she should continue on. She knows she might become lost, overpowered, and permanently separated from the world she knows. However this journey requires courage, and she must not refuse to submit to the heroic conditions of the task. Submission, an essential part of all initiation rituals, is wondrously represented by the acceptance of even further lessening of consciousness. Yet, this further, deeper state of altered consciousness puts the initiate into an ever more perilous condition, in which something happens that involves an encounter with the powerful forces of the archetypal masculine. The initiate is overwhelmed by this encounter, becomes magnetized, and presumptuously seeks to unveil the concretized phallic power. A force of an archetypal feminine strength coming from above counters her inflated enchantment; she must now submit to the pain of being struck by a whip wielded by a goddess. She yields to it. She reconnects with her own feminine being through bodily contact with another woman who supports her through the ordeal, a woman who has been through the initiation and can offer empathy and comfort—but not, significantly, protection. [Dr. Bradway here draws a parallel with the containment for such events provided by the analytical relationship.]

Once through it, the initiate is finally liberated and dances in exaltation. Like Ariadne, on whose head Dionysos placed the crown of gold as she rose with him to the heavens to be deified, the initiate fully experiences the majesty of the Self. Now she must return to her usual outer life, but inwardly she is changed, enhanced. She has been transformed into one who has been twice born.[4]

With these simple and direct words, Dr. Bradway summarizes what this series of powerful pictures conveys and shows us what one image of feminine spiritual initiation can entail. That she herself underwent such an initiation is hinted at here as well. What is startling here is how vividly contemporary these murals are for modern women, despite the obvious differences that 2,000 years of development have brought. The simplicity of the words belies the power of experience that those who have undergone such initiation understand. Perhaps, in our modern situation, new, even individual, rituals or murals will be created, just as we saw when examining the Zen oxherding series. In any case, it is well for such modern women to know that such events took place long ago and can be renewed at any time.

If we try to be more specifically contemporaneous regarding the enlightenment given by this particular path, I think we need only examine the powerful current problem of drug and alcohol addiction, something that has increased markedly over the last half century. Women, in particular, addicted only rarely before the 1960s, have become a significant part of that suffering group. How does the story of Dionysos and Ariadne apply? First of all, it is part of the general anecdotal evidence that women who have successfully gone through programs of detoxification and recovery from their addiction are at particular high risk for recidivism if a relationship has broken off. Is this not Ariadne, having her whole meaning in an outer human relationship, becoming suicidal when she is deceived or betrayed? Rather than just getting angry at a deceiving lover, many a woman feels totally broken and in ruin, secretly blaming herself for her incapacity to keep her lover, lacking in sufficient love or attractiveness. Women do this, I think, because they are more identified than men are with the image of the Divine Between; God is to be found in the relationship and to have the latter end is simply to die or want to die.

What our myth and mystery teach us, however, is that there is another possibility than to be totally identified with an outer relationship as the sole source of union with the divine, however we might term it. There is the additional image of the Divine Within, alone with the Self, something often alien to the path of many or most women. Nor can many of them fully embrace the masculine path of striving for meaning or power without losing themselves. No, it is Dionysos who brings the solution. He is a god of ecstasy and fulfillment, but is not related at all in the way that Eros or Aphrodite or Mary or the Woman of Valor in the Torah would be. He is impersonal and transcendent. To unite with him in ecstasy is to risk fragmentation and dismemberment, but to survive is to become whole and elevated into the divine kingdom. Drugs and alcohol are part of the god's way, of course, and this may be exactly what addicts seek, without knowing it. Sure enough, we are all aware of the opposing effects of reduction of pain provided by the drugs, versus the intensity of stimulation and sensory awareness, yet the ultimate cost can be, as it is with the Maenads, total and mad ruin. The solution might then be to find a way, as in this ancient mystery at Pompeii, to undergo such an initiation and come out whole afterwards.

There is the rub; how to emerge whole? The image of being beaten in this mystery is salient here. In my clinical experience, I have been surprised to find how many women have a secret desire of being spanked severely as part of a sexual fantasy. This fantasy beating is both painful and pleasurable. I think this may be a hidden summoning of Dionysos, clearly demonstrated among the stages of the Pompeiian mystery. To simply view such desires as masochistic, in my opinion, is rather inadequate. I am reminded of the story my own Reichian therapist told me about what the great master had to say about this psychopathology. A patient of his, a male, announced that he was masochistic and, when Reich hit him, he grew enraged."But you said you were masochistic," observed Reich, and the patient became bemused. Reich then said that the patient's true need was for great intensity, in order to overcome his own emotional and physical deadness. A physical beating was as good a way as any to achieve this. So it may be, I think, in the mystery and in clinical practice, although concrete hitting, like concrete sexuality, often destroys what is truly being looked for. The longing and fear of the extremes of the Dionysian experience are behind such pathologies and modern life does not know how to achieve such ecstasies apart from drugs or risky behavior. The path of addiction includes a hitting bottom—a certain, identifiable "beating" that's the last straw that galvanizes the addict to "reform." To be sure, a drug was also part of the ancient initiation mystery, but this was in—might I call it Apollonian?—moderation and was linked with a religious attitude and event. It is in this region that our reflection might profitably dwell.

Notes

[1] See Katherine Bradway, *Villa of Mysteries: Pompeii Initiation Rites of Women* (San Francisco: C. G. Jung Institute of San Francisco, 1982) and Linda Fierz-David, "Psychological Reflections on the Fresco Series of the Villa of Mysteries in Pompeii." MS (Zurich: Jung Institute, 1957).

[2] Bradway, *Villa of Mysteries*, pp. 19–20.

[3] Bradway, *Villa of Mysteries*, p. 21.

[4] Bradway, *Villa of Mysteries*, p. 28.

CHAPTER 11

A Modern Woman's Initiation onto the Shaman Path

In previous chapters, we pursued examples of the spiritual path largely via the traditions of the "world religions," as they are called, hardly noting that the majority of humankind belonged to what we can call the pagan religions, which are largely animistic. For many in Africa, Oceania, and elsewhere—let alone the many peasants and "simple" folk everywhere who actually engage in similar religious practices—life is always and everywhere an encounter with spirits and gods, in animals and plants, in Nature's events, and in the magical power of sorcerers. As we know from analytic work, almost all of us, just beneath our esteemed rationalism, are indeed "primitive" in that regard and surprisingly superstitious. There is a story about an eminent physicist who had a horseshoe nailed to his barn door and, when queried about it, replied that he had heard that the vaunted "good luck" accruing to the person who hung it took place whether the person believed in it or not! Indeed, everyone's psyche works that way and it is only when we take up a relationship between our rational consciousness and the irrational unconscious that we become aware of the conflict and need to work to resolve it.

The individual spiritual path has been limited, however, among many of our ancestors and in contemporary folk cultures, to special persons who are "called" to be shamans or medicine men/women. Surprisingly, there has been a renewed interest in the shaman's way over the last half century, beginning with the major work by Eliade[1] and brought to contemporaries in the form of workshops and training by the anthropologist Michael Harner.[2]

A moment's reflection tells us that the shaman is the precursor of many differentiated vocations in the modern world—whether it be doctor, healer, psychotherapist, prophet, teacher or priest—since all such functions were initially combined in such a man or woman called to this path. It is indeed right that we refer to both sexes in so naming the shaman since that calling has always been relatively "gender-free" and, therefore, carries particular appeal for contemporary women. These "specialists in the sacred" have always been particularly important for the culture as a whole. This is so because they are able to see the spirits, go into the sky to meet the gods or down into the underworld to fight demons, as well as answer the ever-present need to heal sickness or provide instruction.

Eliade tells us in fine detail how the shaman is "called" via dreams or sickness, is initiated by means of ritual tree-climbing or journeys of various kinds, wears special clothes and uses drums and other instruments to effect power and healing.[3] He or she is a soul-retriever and guides the tribe. We shall explore the contemporary practical teaching of the anthropologist, Michael Harner, as he describes it in his book, to get a sense of how the shaman operates.

> A shaman is a man or woman who enters an altered state of consciousness—at will—to contact and utilize an ordinarily hidden reality in order to acquire knowledge, power, and to help other persons. The shaman has at least one, and usually more, "spirits" in his personal service.[4]

Both Eliade and Harner point out that it is from a state of ecstasy, wherein the whole world is animated and each animal, stone, plant or person has a spirit with whom the shaman can communicate, that the shaman attains his or her capacity for teaching or healing. The shaman, unlike those who train in formal religious traditions, undergoes initiation alone, conducted by—what Jung would call—archetypal forces in the psyche, which are independent of institutional conditioning and therefore hold greater possibility for individual development. Yet, there is formal structure, of course, to be found in a second kind of teaching for most shamans. The latter training, conducted by the elders or other shamans in the initiate's culture, includes techniques, names and functions of spirits, mythology, etc. Personal transformation plus a return home with boons for the community are required for the shaman to complete the call. It is also this function of true mediation, coming back whole and useful, that distinguishes a shaman—in all cultures—from those who are merely dissociated or mad.

Harner describes some of these teaching methods as follows: For the first journey, the apprentice shaman needs to beat a drum (205 to 220 beats per minute), to put him or herself into the proper consciousness.[5] The apprentice is then asked to visualize an opening into the earth or other entry into the ground (a hollow tree stump, or spring, for example) and note details of what happens as he or she enters. Ten minutes for this first journey is required, after which four rapid beats of the drum by the teacher is the signal for return. The apprentice then reports on the experience.

Another training involves a stone divination.[6] The apprentice looks for and finds a meaningful stone, one that attracts him or her strongly. After reflection and careful study of the stone, seeing animals and faces, for example, the apprentice poses a question and awaits the result. With a satisfying answer, the apprentice puts the stone back where it was found, along with thanks for the spirit's help.

A further task is that of the Calling of Beasts.[7] First, the apprentice stands erect, facing the east, and shakes a rattle four times (for beginnings and endings). He or she is then to think of the rising sun for some twenty seconds. Second, the apprentice shakes the rattle while facing each of the other directions and thinks of plant and animal "relatives." Returning to face the east, the apprentice holds the rattle above his or her head for a half minute, while imagining sun, moon, and stars, followed by holding an awareness (for about three minutes) of the earth as the apprentice's home. Third, the apprentice is to take two rattles and shake them while dancing (jogging in place for five minutes), thereby showing sincerity to the animal and a willingness to sacrifice energy to it. At this point, the apprentice stops dancing and repeats the first step, indicating a readiness to begin a prolonged dance with the apprentice's animal. This accomplished, the apprentice now shakes the rattles loudly and slowly (60 beats per minute), moving slowly in free form, feeling the animal to which he or she has connected, and accordingly, making the animal's sounds while his or her eyes are half-closed. After five minutes of such slow movement, the apprentice increases the speed, going faster and faster, for about eight minutes. Finally, the apprentice stops dancing and welcomes this power animal to stay in his or her body, shaking the rattle again four times, drawing the energy toward the chest. In conclusion, step one is repeated.

By this point, the apprentice is ready to work with another person in order to restore the "patient's" lost power.[8] The novice shaman lies down beside the patient and journeys with him or her, seeking the latter's power animal and bringing it back. When this animal is found, the shaman blows this energy into the patient's chest and then on the top of the back of the patient's head.

Another instrument that the novice shaman acquires is a unique power song.[9] To accomplish this, the apprentice must fast all day, find and identify with the animal he or she previously discovered and then ask for the particular magic words, music, and chant.

A more elaborate ritual for the recovery of the power animal involves a third perso and permits the use of all techniques achieved at this point.[10] Harner is careful to admonish the new shaman to "Avoid any ominously voracious nonmammals you may encounter, especially spiders and swarming insects or fanged serpents, teeth. If you can't pass, return to upper world."[11] When the shaman has solidly contacted the power animal, he or she may consult this animal guide but only for him- or herself, accepting whatever language or nonlanguage that is offered.[12] The shaman may also ask for or attempt a vision of the future.[13]

Harner suggests that the shaman perform weekly renewal rituals and pay special attention to Big dreams.[14] At this point, he claims the shaman apprentice can now attempt restoring power at a distance to help people, but he or she must send power from his or her own power animal only to the power animal of the other. "Don't send your own energy," he warns.[15]

Finally, Harner teaches the use of quartz crystals and plant helpers for healing.[16] We can see that the training is quite specific and detailed, a far cry from that intuited or imagined by most modern people.

A Woman's Shamanic Initiation

Healing work has a long history of calling many women to the spiritual path, particularly in the pagan tradition. Lisa Sloan's own initiation, which she described as part of her doctoral dissertation at the Pacifica Graduate Institute,[17] is a vivid illustration of how this ancient spiritual path is very much alive, even among people in sophisticated countries. Early in her life, Lisa had a sense of a healing vocation, but she instead pursued a successful life as an actress, wife, and mother. In mid-life, she decided to undertake the shamanic journey both alone and with the guidance of Michael Harner.

Lisa's first journey, while in training with Harner, began in a darkened room, wherein she was instructed to meet her power animal. Only one small candle was lit in the center of the room, serving as the "home fire" for the community. Lying on her blanket, she listened to the drumming:

> I am swept into another realm. . . . drawn to a tree near my home . . . a large hollowed out core in its center. . . . entrance to the lower world . . . I cry out with my heart that if I meet with my power animal that it might so teach

me how to help other persons. . . . [The tree's] body opens into a tunnel. . . . and I begin to fly down through the darkness, feeling the moisture of the earthy sides, smelling and sensing the damp darkness surrounding me. . . . I emerge at last, out of the tunnel into brilliant white light. . . . I am standing in snow. . . . mountains in the distance. I am immediately met by a beautiful, stately animal who . . . welcomes me . . . deep dark eyes . . . ancient soul communicating with my own. The animal tells me [without words] that it will be able to carry me anywhere in the universe I need to go to help another person. It then brings me back to the entrance to the tunnel. . . . telling me that we are in Lapland. That is its home. . . . I am startled to think that I may be in an actual place on Earth as I thought this was simply an imaginary dreamscape. . . . The drums signal my return.[18]

Lisa reflected on this first journey, which cemented a sense of a reality that was separate from yet only accessible by imagination. Darkness, most unlike the New-Age consciousness that dwells in the light, seemed central and included danger. Learning divination and healing techniques during the workshop came naturally to her. She also honored the requirement that she not reveal the type of power-animal she encountered, but she did describe her sacred teacher from the "upper world" whom she met next. After an hour's walk from her tree in her inner world, she met "a muscular, darker skinned male . . . bare-chested . . . wearing a leather loin cloth and thongs."[19] In response to her question about making her healing work effective, he replied with one word, "Smile." She felt let down, but when she smiled, powerful energy moved through her body. The teacher then took her on a journey that she continues to reflect upon, years later. He carried her to the top of the tree, where a beautiful bird was singing. He said, "Tell everyone how the birds are singing just for them." He then repeated "just for them," while carrying her to a river, and then, inside a cave, told her that she must take people into the darkness, "the darkness is where the magic lies."[20]

At this point, Lisa beheld a dragon, sitting on a dark river flowing through the cave. The dragon had one ruby eye and its mouth was wide open. The teacher walked into the mouth and Lisa followed, thus descending together into the belly of this dragon, which was lush and warm, dark and sensual. Hearing the continual drumbeat from the workshop, she realized that drumming was a natural part of her vision, that the darkness of the belly of the beast was a crucial part of the answer to her question about healing. After a time, the dragon disgorged both teacher and Lisa and they emerged into the blinding white light of an exquisitely bright city made of crystal and light. Going to a palace on the city's edge, she was informed by the teacher that the castle was her home. Lisa, overcome by this experience and information, felt weakened, but when her teacher reminded her to smile, she did so and was filled with energy to go into this castle, where the teacher may not tread. There, she was met by many women who tended to her needs. She felt awkward about this service, wanting equality, but they laughed and reminded her that this is how things are supposed to be (implying, I think, that since she serves others with this vast energy, she therefore needs such renewing and service for herself as well). All the women were dressed in garments of pastel pink and blue. Massaged and loved, she then danced and joined them in circles of movement, resulting in ecstatic connection.

Lisa then left her castle, again meeting her teacher, who kissed her passionately, and then showed her a wedding band. They connected in a mystical and sacred inner marriage "within my soul, which I have been preparing for a long time."[21] This was the prelude to the healing work and its relationship to her life that she had been long awaiting. The union of the male and female within herself was the balance making this possible. The teacher then told Lisa his name, three times: Dakota, Dakota, Dakota. This was something more than an imaginal creation. Lisa then returned to her tree, stunned by all that had happened.

Lisa had much to think about, thus far. "The residence in the belly of the dragon would have an effect of slowly reforming all my ideas and perceptions . . . over the next few years, which would make and form me anew."[22] She had never read any dragon tales and had no knowledge of what meaning this creature held for humankind. Reading and study informed her that such entry into primordial animals was found in many puberty rites, in which isolation and facing darkness in the Underworld resulted in the metaphorical death of childhood.[23] She found that the Celestial Home in the upper world, with its crystal palace, was echoed in fairy tales and myths such as "Beauty and the Beast" and "Psyche and Eros," which she had not read previously. She was also warmed by Eliade's assertion that it is the primordial archetype that provides the ideal form that later translates into reality, and that it is the "divine marriage" archetype itself which makes human sexual union possible. It was then that Lisa realized that in marrying Dakota, "I was giving myself over to the vocation of healing," something also experienced by shamans.[24] This is indeed what Jung, following the ancients, termed the *mysterium coniunctionis*, a union of earthbound consciousness with the transpersonal source.[25] Dakota, however, was more than a concept for her, he was a "real presence and the spark of spiritual life."[26] From the Jungian point of view, she experienced the living reality of the animus (see chapter 8, page 163) in depth and thus achieved "psychic reality" (see comments on the Kundalini path in chapter 4, pages 82–84). She kept silent about her experience but continued to dwell on it and study.

Lisa's next workshop course taught "soul loss and retrieval," which we can understand psychologically as the listlessness and depression consequent upon dissociation and depersonalization. Lionel Corbett lists the various ways Jung understood soul loss and presents a useful comparison between the ideology of retrieval in shamanism and its counterpart in psychotherapy.[27] Lisa's power animal and Dakota presented this work as a living reality to her, which was painstaking and difficult, both in tracking a soul that had been lost in the vastness of the other world and bringing it back. This required the shaman, as well as the psychotherapist, Lisa discovered, to maintain emotional stamina, concentration, and courage. Her reported experiences while practicing in class are convincing. In one session, she became clairvoyant and found a patient's lost childhood soul in the attic of his childhood house, something that no one but the person himself knew!

As Lisa continued her studies and experiences in shaman-ism, she realized that she was increasingly faced with the theme of death and rebirth, the necessity of relinquishing her ego's hold on her identity, so that the larger Self could be available to her. She noted Jung's experience of his own almost fatal illness in his 60s and his consequent "glimpse beyond the veil," wherein he felt more whole than ever in his life. He also realized that this experience of wholeness and ecstasy, in individuation, is the modern variant of the shaman's quest.[28]

During Lisa's subsequent training, while her inner teacher was taking her on a personal journey to the sun for an impor-tant part of her initiation, she became frightened and fought against it. The closer she came to the sun, the more her own consciousness began to disappear, "in favor of another which was seeking to be born."[29] Unable to block this, later, while driving to an advanced training session in the flood-swept and hazardous Big Sur area of California, she found that her car engine surged forward on its own at 40 miles an hour, unless her foot was on the clutch. This automaticity foreshad-owed Lisa's being gripped by psychic forces erupting from the unconscious that made her realize that she was entering into chaos, a common motif within shamanic initiation. It is this immersion that is the source of the kinds of psychopathology to which future shamans are heir, and for which they are often labeled mad or crazy.

Lisa's first meeting with the advanced group was quite exciting, encountering 50 experienced people from all over the world, each of whom had brought a drum. Spontaneous drumming was followed by soul songs emerging from everyone in the circle. Then people began to dance, in which helping spirits and power animals were invited to join in. Lisa felt that, "Finally, after twenty years of searching, [I] found the union of the most precious and important forces that were central to my life."[30]

After days of further training in divination and healing techniques, she undertook a "journey to the ancestors," during which an Aztec brought her to ancient Mexico. There she participated in an archaic Sun ritual and learned that one "must design the place one is living in while in a visionary state, that one must mold the earth from one's visions, with the heartfelt intention of creating forms that will support one's spiritual life while doing everyday activities."[31] She returned with the eerie feeling that this could have been a past incarnation of her own. She was struggling with the question of boundaries regarding this experience, which she resolved when returned to Los Angeles. Her next-door neighbor (who knew nothing at all about Lisa's shamanic studies) telephoned her and said that she had had two unusually vivid dreams about her, which came to her in what would have been the evening following Lisa's journey. In the neighbor's first dream, Lisa was climbing a giant mound made out of dirt and sand and at the top there were some dark-skinned people. The neighbor was with her. The whole village was looking up to Lisa as if they needed her for some reason. The neighbor was there, she thought, to encourage the help. This dream repeated the next night, so she felt compelled to tell Lisa about it. This was a strong affirmation of Lisa's experience. Lisa's subsequent research on the Aztecs, about which she had known nothing, also supported this affirmation.

Back at the workshop, however, she had no time for reflection about the Aztec adventure, because she discovered that the sounds of drumming and singing had become painfully loud. Michael Harner gave her some ear plugs and she later on read that he, too, among the Conibo, had a heightened sensitivity to sound, and even feared he was becoming mad.[32] The plugs, however, did not help very much and she ached deeply through the night and the next day, discovering for herself how the shaman finds extension of the senses. This heightened sensitivity helps a shaman find healing properties in plants, herbs, and flowers.

In her next journey to the plant world, Lisa found herself merging with the plant, following its form down into the earth, into its roots and up to the leaves. In answer to her question whether the plant would reveal a deeper level of its spiritual existence, she heard a loud voice say that the deepest secret could be revealed if she were ready. In reply to her shout of "Yes!" she felt a power moving toward her both from within herself and without, receiving the thought that in the flower are "codes of knowledge" and "codes of power." The "secret of being" was revealed though the composition of the flower, encoded in each part. She felt her body becoming the yellow center of the flower, and her solar plexus moving like the flower's center, toward the sun. She now felt that this was the "sacred geometry," the patterns revealing universal wisdom, but she could not quite decipher what all this geometry meant, needing time to translate the code. At this point, she felt and heard the words "I AM" echoing all around her, as all of her awareness was completely filled by the light of the Sun. Upon her return to the group, she was told that the Aztecs had decoded some of the secrets held within the flower and which are revealed in the geometrical relationship the flower has with the Sun. Lisa now had the ability to retrieve and decipher this information.

The gradual deepening led her to realize that it was too difficult to assimilate all that was happening and that she needed to connect with a deeper and stronger part of herself that could do so. For her following journey, therefore, she sought advice from Dakota and her power animal about what needed to happen next, in order for her to deepen her capacity to help others. In response to her request, Dakota and her power animal brought her to the "middle world," the realm of everyday existence. There, to her surprise, she encountered dismemberment. She was beaten up severely by both her teacher and power animal, but sensed that she needed to surrender rather than resist, in order to ascertain their purpose. She realized that the dismemberment was helping her have compassion for those who have been abused and emotionally beaten and that she needed to undergo this to gain that understanding. Torn apart, she looked inside her body and saw a tiny identity tag, like those that soldiers wear. She realized that this had to be "tossed"; her limited ego had to give way to her larger Self. She was then told that there is no identity and no ego in healing work. The tag with the name "Lisa Sloan" was hurled into outer space and she was told that she must open her heart completely to the pain and suffering that is part of the work that she was committing to. She agreed and then felt her whole being opening and a simultaneous deepening of her solidarity with her teacher, while he and her power animal carefully put her back together. Re-membered, she then stood face to face with Dakota, who presented her with a simple, round stone on a natural cord. It was reddish brown, about one and one-half inches in diameter, and looked like a river stone or a barren planet or moon, round and with craters. She recognized this stone as representing her soul, but that it was also everyone's soul in some sense (all have such stones). This stone's craters represented her soul's unique journey and replaced the identity tag she had tossed away. It signified that she was willing to commit herself to a path of working for and giving her heart to all beings. The stone had power for this work and was a sacred responsibility. Dakota tied the stone around her neck as they stood, side by side, to do their work.

Suddenly, she experienced a profound loneliness, realizing that the journey is largely solitary, without much camaraderie or understanding from others. She was (and is) a naturally joyful and ebullient person and, questioning why she did not feel the joy, was informed that since she already knew the joy, she must know the other side, as well. Further reflection over time revealed to her the importance of this dismemberment in the "middle realm": conscious integration, the experience of transformation, is absolutely central for the work. Without this and without bringing this transformation back to everyday life, the shaman only has a dissociative disorder, no healing or meaning for herself or others. That was the reason for the dismemberment, making it not only intellectual or just personal.

The stone, as she later verified in alchemy, represented her new spiritual identity, the center around which her life would now revolve. The "great solitude," she discovered, is also central, far from the communal joy, dancing, and singing that brought her onto this path. She later read an account of a shaman Inuit speaking to Rasmussen, that "a real shaman does not jump about the floor and do tricks. . . . True wisdom is only to be found far away from people, out in the great solitude, and is not found in play, but only through suffering."[33]

Her next journey, in which she asked for a deeper answer to her question, "Who am I?" found her standing on earth that cracked open, revealing a giant egg that hatched a dragon, upon whose head she then stood, leaving her speechless and astounded. The dragon completely filled the earth and revealed itself to be a god, both male and female, with great majesty. It had one ruby eye and one emerald eye, which were magical, ancient, and clairvoyant, as its head was filled with the intelligence of the universe. That this came in response to her question was puzzling, but she was then flooded with knowledge and realized that she had the opportunity to have every bit of knowledge about her life and the collective unconscious, all revealed in an instant. She learned that the dragon "owns" all human beings, that all life has evolved from it. She then saw it had wings and a reptilian belly with golden scales, filled with enormous energy and power. It was the most vivid vision she had ever seen and she was mesmerized, realizing that this same belly contained every desire she had known, as well as the essence of all humankind's urges and passions. She heard: "I am the creative force of the universe. I own all human life. I am responsible for everything that exists in a form, that has an identity, all life forms on earth originate in me."[34] It was the original "I."

The dragon then swept Lisa up and flew into space, to the depths of the universe, taking her HOME. At first exhilarated, Lisa then grew doubtful and realized that she was leaving the Earth, perhaps forever, and wondered whether this was a good idea. Torn, but unable to contact her teacher or power animal, she grabbed hold of herself and pulled herself back to her earthly home. She felt ecstasy and joy upon her return, a love and openness with all about her, knowing that she is part of every mountain, rock, tree, and everyone she loves. Eventually back on the ground at the foot of her tree, she was shaken, but glad to be back. She had learned that "I am you," namely that she is, in some way, part of the rock, mountain, and dragon. But the spirits then shook their heads and shouted "NO" in unison, and tossed her into the air again. She then sensed that each time that she was thrust up and out of sight, they were helping her understand that an alchemical change was being ignited in her consciousness, happening between ascent and descent. She then recognized that she is also "I AM," meaning that she is ultimately identical to the source of being that is without form or identity, the same source she experienced on her journey to the sun, which precedes even the form of the dragon. To this realization, the spirits shouted, "YES!" Dakota then came to her and his breath brought her his spiritual vitality.

Lisa later read that the dragon is a personification of Nature, itself, the power of primordial life stuff, which, when appearing in a modern person, indicates that life energies are stirring in the psyche. This energy, containing archaic material, can overwhelm the personality with its incomprehensible contents. Lisa realized that this danger was present, but the dragon's awakening also represented a "birth of a spiritual, divine factor within my consciousness that had been gestating. . . . This dragon was surely a symbol of the Self, its golden belly and wings communicating to me its earthly connection with matter and the body as well as its spiritual and divine nature."[35]

After reflecting on her need to understand—but perhaps without the frameworks usually given in the West, including psychotherapy—Lisa then climbed her tree once more to see her teacher, but found that it was a huge struggle. Her teacher, seeming to test her, contributed to her sense that she needed to use all of her strength, and focus on her vow. When she reached him, he looked at her with dark and electric eyes, pressing his tongue on her until she understood that she could look at his tongue and see implanted in it a raised, three-dimensional, white city, surrounded and filled with white light. She realized that he was giving her the spiritual power to communicate, to translate the spiritual knowledge that this city contained. They began to dance wildly, until he said, loudly, "You can go out and do this work on your own now!" He then pushed her off the cloud. The ground beneath her shook, and she saw the dragon flying up toward her. Dakota shouted, "Disengage from the Dragon!" And then he was gone.[36]

The dragon roared and she felt it almost overwhelming, enveloping her ordinary reality. She accepted this contact but didn't know how to follow her teacher's instruction. She realized that she had to do this on her own, as a test, and sensed that it was oddly life threatening. Yet she submitted totally, understanding that she needed to do so in order to disengage. She realized that she was being offered access to unbelievable power, to control weather and other forces of nature, and sensed that this was the power that many shamans have quested after. "It is exhilarating and incredibly seductive. . . . With the dragon, I have become a god."[37]

The dragon then returned to the workshop room with Lisa and, perched on the head of a man in the group who was recognized as a master shaman, announced that the man needed healing. This was so absolute that Lisa wondered if this might be her new power animal, and lost sight of Dakota's directive to "disengage." Instead, she surrendered to the force, and the man was fully opened up, from skull to feet. "'Our' claws touch every organ, filling each with a beautiful, radiant energy and white light. There is a deep sense of the dragon loving this man, concerned for him, and through the healing is giving him what he needs."[38]

The dragon then closed up this master shaman and flew away, as Lisa then easily disengaged. Dakota reappeared, transferred more power from the city to her while she heard the roar of the dragon. Lisa felt solemn, unsettled, jangled, deeply changed, as if her very brain had been cracked open and something awakened. She later read that Michael Harner experienced a similar brain change.[39] She also learned that Dakota's transference of power was common in shamanic initiations. The shaman's tongue, for example, becomes one with the spirit realms, so that during a healing séance, speech can become a magical display of the mythic world. She also realized that each sequence became a test of her capacity to hold the opposites, make decisions, both submit and resist. In order to follow Dakota's directions, she had to reach beyond her capacity to understand "disengage." He did not say "slay the dragon," since that would be a superficial fulfillment of an old hero task. She also realized that the dragon, like any archetype or spirit, "can never be fully known or assimilated into consciousness. It is too large. We can only come into relation with it, a moment at a time."[40]

Once the session was over for the night, Lisa felt that she needed to tell the master shaman what had happened. When she did so, the shaman told her, very kindly, that before healing a person, she must always ask that person's permission. Lisa felt like she was hit by bricks and asked his forgiveness, but she realized that one always has a choice. She had not yet learned to "disengage." Long ago, she realized, this kind of individual consciousness was not so important, but modern freedom and individuality required this conscious advance and choice. The shaman kindly but firmly advised her that she had to take that energy out of him. She fully understood, but she was nonetheless surprised when this same teacher told her that he had stopped working with the dragon. What did it mean?

The creative force of the dragon also contains its opposite, namely destruction, Lisa realized. Moments before, she felt that the whole world would benefit from her new healing powers. She now realized that destruction could also occur, thus the necessity of "disengagement." She suddenly felt like a failure, having made a devastating error. With the shaman's help, she looked inside him for the bright light of the dragon and pulled it out, after which the shaman said, "Ah, that feels better."[41]

With her new-found understanding, Lisa decided to take a journey to the dragon and have a conversation with it, letting it know how she felt and to see if a working relationship was possible, respecting the standards of the 20th and 21st century.

This was a bit grandiose, she later recognized; she could not compel the dragon into a relationship based on her needs. Yet she was desperate to find any relationship at all between her ego and this archetypal presence.

She began by planning to ascend to the upper world via her tree, but it was gone! This tree, sustaining and nourishing her life, a teacher and equilibrium-bringer, symbol of her deepest structure, had vanished. Her power animal, however, appeared and encouraged her to continue. She followed this advice and used her own energy (rather than the tree's) to get to the upper world. This was very difficult, armed as she was with only integrity and spiritual purpose. Suddenly the roar began, the earth shook, and the dragon was present.

Lisa shouted at the dragon, "I will not work with you unless it is for the benefit of all!"[42] Noting that the dragon healed without the person's permission, she added that their work must always be with love and compassion. At this point, the dragon transformed into a sweet and innocent small being with a cute face. Not impressed or convinced by this change, she again demanded to feel the compassion, after which she heard a low rumbling roar and truly felt its warmth and vibration. She remained for a long time in this condition of feeling and hearing "this ancient Earth mother."

After a time, Lisa began to experiment with the dragon energies, becoming one with it, flying, and then disengaging. After many such attempts, trying to gain skill and mastery, she realized that the dragon wanted to take her HOME, but she managed to stop it. Most importantly, she realized that she was simultaneously trying to gain mastery over her own desires and emotions, even her ego, through this "symbolic exercise of coming into relation with its power." Returning from this journey, she felt that she had indeed come into some relation with the dragon. She wrote in her journal: "I know I am drawing on its power but it is in coordination with the heart."[43] But her tree was still gone. Something was amiss.

One morning, the friend who had dreamed about Lisa before told her that she had dreamed of the dragon. Lisa at first thought that this was very nice, but then realized that while she believed that she was exercising control in daylight consciousness, she had no control during sleep. She felt that she had once more violated another person.

At this point, frayed and fragile, Lisa had a deep massage, during which the resolution came:"I decided to completely and totally sever from the dragon."[44] She understood the great loss of connection with these primal energies and that she would have to exist by the grace of some other source. She realized that this was a form of self-sacrifice, designed to remove her further from the battle between the ego and larger forces of creation. She slowly realized that this sacrifice was akin to Eastern traditions, wherein the initiate detaches from earthly desires in order to attain enlightenment. It was also another version of the hero slaying the dragon, but in her case, she was neither slaying nor submitting. A psychologist might say that she sacrificed her own power drive and ambition, thus was able to relativize the ego. She knew nothing, at the time, about hero myths or Jung's work in this area, nor how religious doctrine related to her understanding. Rather, her insight arose from two sources: first was from "an intuitive guidance system" within her heart which "seemed to be following and deciphering an ancient map of spiritual transformation."[45] A Jungian might add here that it was the Self that gave her this guidance. The second source came "from the forces within the story itself, which were seeking my participation and urging me toward action." A Jungian would also see the dynamics of the Self here, seeking a relationship with the mortal ego, just as the ego seeks the blessing and guidance of the Self.

With this decision and sense of peace, Lisa "experienced the action of my severance with the dragon as more than a personal victory over attachment to my desires. . . . It was also a victory over an identification of my psyche with the collective psyche of the world."[46] She was astonished to read an affirmation of her experience, over a year later, in which Jung notes that anyone who identifies with the collective psyche lets him- or herself be devoured by the monster and vanishes in it. Whatever treasure he or she attains brings harm. Lisa returned to a sense of peace and joy.

Lisa was astounded to learn that the last journey in her shamanic initiation was that of discovering her spiritual home in the Upper World. She had known nothing of this typical shamanic dwelling, but it was extremely important since the dragon was going to take her to its home, which would have meant death for Lisa, physically or psychologically. Now she would need to find her home without the dragon and perhaps even without Dakota.

When she began this new journey, surprise! The tree had returned! But now it was bigger, stronger, and lusher; it had more branches and leaves. The unconscious had responded to her actions. She saw that she was now carrying a large, beautiful, quartz crystal as a present for her teacher. She realized that she and Dakota were indeed heading toward her home. They flew over the dragon's cave and Dakota put her down at the front walk to her home. She knew that this was her soul's home, the same beautiful, white crystal palace infused and radiating white light that she had first seen on Dakota's tongue. Dakota left her at this point and she walked along the path, made of clear glass, under which were shining rubies and emeralds. She was amazed to recognize them as the same jeweled eyes of the dragon! Separated from him and sealed under glass, their power no longer controlled or overwhelmed her; instead, their radiance was helpful. The thought occurred to her that her human existence had passed and that these jewel "eyes" represented her many identities, as a human who has loved and learned and lost, has suffered and has overcome. She deeply felt that her victory over the identification with the dragon's power brought this sweet fruit of consciousness.

Continuing on her path, she noticed that there were two dragon forearms, with claws forming a gate, before the entrance to the door. This is a prestigious symbol, announcing her achievement, but here, too, she renounced this prestige by unscrewing and discarding each claw. She also realized that she was letting go of what she thought was the goal of the shaman. She now felt a quiet power, more ascetic but not limiting, filled with devotion and a wide-open heart. She continued on her path and entered her home, where all the women rushed to greet her and take care of her, eager to hear her stories and her experiences on earth as a human, for they did not travel in that realm. But Lisa again said that she must go and then reunited with Dakota in great joy. He took the crystal that Lisa had carried for him, and said, "We do not need that kind of power either," throwing it into heaven, where it became a star. Dakota had also changed; not only was he more beautiful but he was truly an angel! Dakota affirmed that he was, indeed, Raphael, and showed her his wings. Lisa discovered that she, too, had wings, realizing that it would be in this form that she would be able to continue her service to others and to God, for eternity, now "filled with a joy and a love that are indescribable."[47]

Returning to her group, Lisa tried to describe her experiences, but could not speak. Michael Harner validated this by saying that this proves that something indeed happened. Lisa understood that her future task would be exactly that of trying to communicate, to function as a healer by being "an intermediary between the two realms, restoring a patient's lost personal connections with the mythic dimensions of the soul."[48]

Upon her return to Los Angeles, Lisa opened her Bible to read about the only dragon story she was familiar with—the Book of Revelation. She indeed saw similarities, but was disturbed to see that John saw the dragon only as a representative of the devil and only a struggle between good and evil. For Lisa, "the dragon was like a crystal revealing one facet after another, wherever light was reflected from it."[49] It clearly had its source in the Divine. It had affected and challenged her precisely where she needed transformation, thus teaching her about the deepest aspects of human nature. She could now understand why the East, unlike the West, saw the dragon as a symbol of the highest spiritual essence, with wisdom and power, enabling transformation.

Before her journey, she did not know that Raphael was the archangel of healing and is sometimes depicted with a dragon's tail. The Bible did present her with a phenomenal passage, which stunned her: "And I saw as it were a sea of glass. . . . and them that had gotten the victory over the beast, and over his image, and over his mark . . . stand on the sea of glass, having the harps of God" (Rev. 15:2). Wasn't this identical to her own glass walk on her way home?

It was only after these powerful experiences that Lisa was able to undergo an intense period of research, learning all that she could about the dragon and about initiation, from depth psychology and anthropology, from myths and religious stories around the world. On one level, she had completed her initiation, but she realized that on the second level she was unfinished. She would have to spend time in her community, learning from her elders, and integrating what she had learned so as to make use of it for others and herself.

Finally, back with her training group, she underwent the "power dance" with them. One at a time, as individuals stood and sang, a power began to flow throughout room. She, too, was moved, and this time a deep song emerged from within her, swelling her voice. She twirled and danced, drummers accompanying her, until she lost consciousness, being supported by others as she again found her breath and awareness. A psychologist might remark that this loss of consciousness and this need for others was a most potent antidote to the possible inflation and aggrandizement that could easily emerge from her previous powerful experiences.

At their final meeting, all the initiates walked together on the land, honoring it and the spirits there, giving their thanks. With a closing prayer, they exchanged names and addresses for mutual support and community. Lisa got into her car, which still surged unexpectedly, and drove back on the highway to her earthly home.

★ ★ ★ ★

I have described in some detail Lisa Sloan's shamanic initiation in order to give you a sense of what can and does happen, both in a general way and individually. This description is particularly helpful because it not only demonstrates that path, but illustrates much of what is often found in the individuation process of long-term analysis. We could easily "analyze" Lisa's experiences in terms of Jungian concepts such as shadow, animus, wise man/woman, and Self, but I am inclined to agree with her that this "Western" approach may do this experience a disservice at this time. What good is it, after all, to merely label various experiences? Such "labeling" or naming is often used in long-term analysis, but its function is to assist the person (just as Lisa did for herself after her experiences) to place these profound events in context, to help humanize them. A post-mortem analysis of this experience—at least since Jungian concepts are now generally known—seems unnecessary, even destructive. Rather, I would like to suggest to you that this is one—important—form of the individuation process and spiritual path, joining it to the several from the various religions we have already explored, and has the virtue of including the age-old pagan beliefs as well. A particular aspect of such experiences is their great intensity, which goes beyond what people usually experience in analytic work, although part of the same general continuum. Naturally, all such experiences are individual, and this is a *desideratum* for the modern shaman or analysand.

Perhaps it is of special interest to consider what we can conclude about the place of such a pagan path at the end of the 20th century. First, the work of Eliade, Harner, and those who have had such experiences and undergone training, shows us that the pagan psyche is still very much alive. A modern person, armed with useful, rational self-criticism (as Lisa courageously embraced) can bring such events and experiences into modern life as well.

Second, the healing done by shamans seems to be a form of brief psychotherapy, something that contemporary culture, especially in the United States, seems to need. Critical of long-term analysis, in terms of money and time as well as results, academic psychology and psychiatry have embraced the quick cure: six sessions with Madame Lazonga and you can do the conga. This aim of relief of symptoms and suffering, quickly and cheaply, certainly has merit. The prevailing cultural mode, however, is still highly behavioral in orientation, even though the psyche might be included, but only as something to be "fixed." Imagination and meaning, the hallmarks of the soul, remain, in our extraverted culture, like the alchemical sludge and detritus ("it's only fantasy"). Thanks first to Freud and then, more deeply, to Jung, we now know that this very fantasy, found in the "gutter" (repressed or ignored), is the source of the "gold" of greater consciousness and the capacity to love more deeply.

The shamanic path does indeed embrace fantasy. It also fulfills that deep longing of people to be "fixed," for someone to do it for them. Long-term analysis, on the other hand, is a process whereby the individual profoundly participates actively in his or her process. Since most people, for a number of reasons, are not called upon to engage in such long-term work, the shamanic path at least provides an introverted balance to the engineering endeavors of "fixing" people, allowing the "fix" but honoring the soul, which much psychotherapy does not do. It is on this ground that I think that the shamanic path, renewed at the end of our century and the beginning of the new one, will have an increasing place in our culture in the future. For many who read this book, the longer-term spiritual path will be their way and, if they are not shamans themselves, they will be able to turn to what Jung called, we remember, the "Western yoga" of deep analytic work. Of course, the paths we have already investigated in the various religions are still richly and deeply available to those who want them. What the world will look like, after another "hundred years of psychotherapy" is beyond my small prophetic capacity, but it will surely be influenced by all those people—analysts, therapists, and seekers—who take up that inner path with integrity and devotion.

Notes

[1] Mircea Eliade, *Shamanism: Archaic Techniques of Ecstasy*, Bollingen Series LXXVI (New York, Pantheon, 1964).

[2] Michael Harner, *The Way of the Shaman* (San Francisco: HarperSanFrancisco, 1980).

[3] Eliade, *Shamanism*, pp. 43–67.

[4] Harner, *Way of the Shaman*, p. 20.

[5] Harner, *Way of the Shaman*, p. 37.

[6] Harner, *Way of the Shaman*, p. 69.

[7] Harner, *Way of the Shaman*, p. 84.

[8] Harner, *Way of the Shaman*, p. 92.

[9] Ibid.

[10] Harner, *Way of the Shaman*, p. 98.

[11] Ibid.

[12] Harner, *Way of the Shaman*, p. 122.

[13] Harner, *Way of the Shaman*, pp. 123–124.

[14] Harner, *Way of the Shaman*, p. 127.

[15] Harner, *Way of the Shaman*, p. 130.

[16] Harner, *Way of the Shaman*, pp. 138, 146.

[17] Lisa Sloan, "Shamanic Initiation: Map of the Soul: The Actor-Healer Archetype Revealed" (Ph.D. diss., Pacifica Graduate Institute, 1999).

[18] Sloan, "Shamanic Initiation," pp. 113–114.

[19] Sloan, "Shamanic Initiation," p. 121.

[20] Sloan, "Shamanic Initiation," pp. 121–122.

[21] Sloan, "Shamanic Initiation," pp. 125–126.

[22] Sloan, "Shamanic Initiation," p. 130.

[23] Eliade, *Shamanism*, p. 36.

[24] Eliade, *Shamanism*, p. 120. Sloan, "Shamanic Initiation," p. 134.

[25] See Jung, *Mysterium Coniunctionis*, CW 14.

[26] Sloan, "Shamanic Initiation," p. 135.

[27] Lionel Corbett, *The Religious Function of the Psyche* (London and New York: Routledge, 1996), pp. 121–125.

[28] Sloan, "Shamanic Initiation," p. 149.

[29] Sloan, "Shamanic Initiation," p. 150.

[30] Sloan, "Shamanic Initiation," p. 153.

[31] Sloan, "Shamanic Initiation," p. 157.

[32] Harner, *Way of the Shaman*, p. 7.

[33] Sloan, "Shamanic Initiation," p. 178.

[34] Sloan, "Shamanic Initiation," pp. 182–183.

[35] Sloan, "Shamanic Initiation," p. 188.

[36] Sloan, "Shamanic Initiation," p. 195.

[37] Sloan, "Shamanic Initiation," p. 199.

[38] Sloan, "Shamanic Initiation," p. 200.

[39] Harner, *Way of the Shaman*, pp. 4–6.

[40] Sloan, "Shamanic Initiation," p. 212.

[41] Sloan, "Shamanic Initiation," p. 219.

[42] Sloan, "Shamanic Initiation," p. 221.

[43] Sloan, "Shamanic Initiation," p. 223.

[44] Sloan, "Shamanic Initiation," p. 225.

[45] Sloan, "Shamanic Initiation," p. 229.

[46] Sloan, "Shamanic Initiation," p. 230.

[47] Sloan, "Shamanic Initiation," p. 241.

[48] Sloan, "Shamanic Initiation," pp. 242–243.

[49] Sloan, "Shamanic Initiation," p. 244.

Epilogue

Thus far, this book has taken up divine manifestations among a variety of spiritual paths. In the previous chapter, I reported on the remarkably individual journey taken by one such "ordinary" person. Without the benefit of Jungian analysis or other typical spiritual teachers, she was called to experience the shamanic path in modern life and, with some assistance, was able to come through unharmed and greatly helped. But what about the many people who have labored in less spectacular fashion?

Sure enough, there are many heroes and heroines of the various religious traditions we have learned from in the previous chapters, but one might expect a psychologist and Jungian analyst to present "clinical" (that is, individual "case study") examples of how this takes place in analytic work.

The problem with case studies—which are the evidence that psychotherapists adduce when writing their clinical papers—is that they are highly selective and clearly affected by the subjective inclinations of the therapist-investigator. An additional criticism of such studies—which I have often thought about over years of clinical practice—is the absence of the co-participator in the clinical events described. That is to say, what did the patient/analysand think about these events and their portrayal? I have often had a fantasy of writing a joint paper or book with one of my analysands about their process—or, indeed, our "mutual process" as I have termed it—but this worthwhile endeavor has its own problems, e.g., the need to maintain confidentiality for such personally intimate events.

One solution to this dilemma is for the investigator (i.e. ,myself) to write about his/her own path. A difficulty here is that it smacks of self-centeredness and can become an "advertisement for one's self," in addition to the obvious limitations of further compromised objectivity. You can also look upon the published case material of psychotherapists as revealing aspects of their own psychology, willy-nilly, but that remains peripheral to the attempt to advance understanding and consciousness. Subjectivity, perforce, reigns supreme in this area. If you would like to know what this kind of pursuit of the spiritual path has meant for me, I can suggest that you read some of my books along this line. For a beginning, I can recommend the psychomythology trilogy that I wrote, beginning at age 40. *The Tree of Life: Paths in Jungian Individuation* includes ten fictional stories of individuation from as many different religious and spiritual perspectives. Its two sequels, *The Quest* and *Jungian Psychology and the Passions of the Soul*, round out the trilogy which deeply occupied me for four years.

A second solution is to recommend other books along this line, which I have occasionally done in the text thus far. There is much literature in this field, beginning with Jung himself. These studies, however, focus more on the individual path and use the spiritual material of religions as background. One fairly recent book that successfully combines several spiritual paths is Caroline Myss's *Anatomy of the Spirit*. She has usefully combined these in an interesting figure (see fig. 43 on page 243).

Dr. Myss employed the symbol of the Tree of Life, as is typically found in the various Kabbalistic texts, in her work. That ancient diagram was initially meant to serve a variety of uses. For one of the more complete yet accessible presentations I can recommend the readable and accurate work of Zev ben Shimon Halevi,[1] which contains many pictures and diagrams, as well as presenting a clear and useful text.

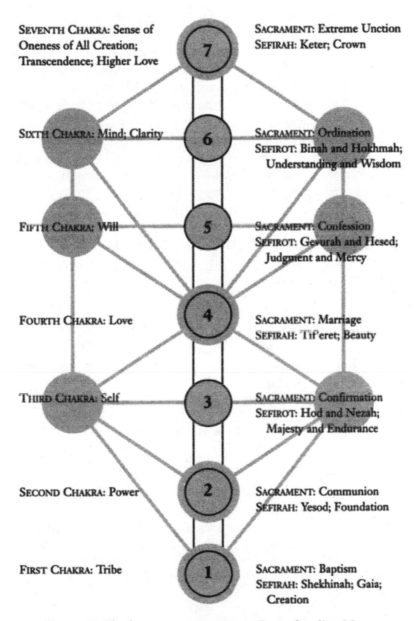

SEVENTH CHAKRA: Sense of Oneness of All Creation; Transcendence; Higher Love

SACRAMENT: Extreme Unction
SEFIRAH: Keter; Crown

SIXTH CHAKRA: Mind; Clarity

SACRAMENT: Ordination
SEFIROT: Binah and Hokhmah; Understanding and Wisdom

FIFTH CHAKRA: Will

SACRAMENT: Confession
SEFIROT: Gevurah and Hesed; Judgment and Mercy

FOURTH CHAKRA: Love

SACRAMENT: Marriage
SEFIRAH: Tif'eret; Beauty

THIRD CHAKRA: Self

SACRAMENT: Confirmation
SEFIROT: Hod and Nezah; Majesty and Endurance

SECOND CHAKRA: Power

SACRAMENT: Communion
SEFIRAH: Yesod; Foundation

FIRST CHAKRA: Tribe

SACRAMENT: Baptism
SEFIRAH: Shekhinah; Gaia; Creation

Figure 43. The human energy system. From Caroline Myss,
Anatomy of the Spirit *(New York: Harmony Books, 1996), p. 287.*
Used with permission.

Having the above-discussed dilemma in mind, I decided to present just a few dreams, representative of many, which I have received from a variety of analysands, over the years. I have selected those that point to various spiritual paths, combine them in modern syncretistic fashion, yet result in individual expression. They thus portray what I call "the psychoecumenical spiritual path." The examples that I now present are largely drawn from a paper I have included in one of my recent books on psychology and religion, *Psychology and Religion at the Millennium and Beyond*. Other examples can be found in my book, *Psychotherapy as a Mutual Process*. All of these converge on what I conceive to be a psychoecumenical vision. It seems to me that there are many such individual myths, just now, all of which connect to a slowly forming collective one on which many people are working. Only a few of these people manage to find their way to my door, of course. Other analysands reconnect more exclusively with their religion of origin or with no organized religion at all, but almost everyone has truly been engaged in working on their own path. This condition is quite modern, even postmodern, and essential for the continuing development of the larger collective spirit of our time.

Ecumenical Dreams

A score of years ago, a middle-aged American woman, of Protestant background but long-since only mildly observant, had the following dream after several years of analysis:

> I am standing in an enormous church. There are several people with me looking over the church. The ceiling is vast. It is made of thick glass: each pane is connected in a cellular pattern. It is very futuristic although along the sides there are some very old glass designs. Someone on my left says that all the bells will ring together here. I notice that there are old Hindu, Buddhist, Christian, Jewish, Moslem and Pagan artifacts around the side of the building. The thought of "all the bells" fills me with great joy. The man on my left says that the clarions are

here. I awaken feeling that I have just been in a very ancient
yet modern place.[2]

The symbol of a holy place, a church that can contain all
the religious artifacts, is itself deeply ecumenical. The ceiling
with many panes of thick glass, in "cellular pattern," suggests
the "Many" combined harmoniously into "One," both symbols
of the Self. The sound of the bells, so numinous in many
faiths, brings great joy—as we can readily understand—and
helps resolve opposites, such as the church being ancient and
modern at the same time. In ancient times, furthermore, sound
seemed to be more important religiously than it is today (e.g.,
Moses and Abraham and Muhammad are "called" by God; an
angel speaks into the Virgin's ear, as "Annunciation"). The sense
of sight has more modern appeal. But this dream combines
modalities, therefore contributing to its feeling of deeper reality. Doesn't such an image, furthermore, coming after much
inner disunity and hard work for the dreamer, suggest healing
and wholeness for her? It also hints at a collective possibility
coming in the future.

★ ★ ★ ★

A Roman Catholic nun, while participating with a mixed-faith
group of clergy (all of whom had undergone Jungian analysis),
dreamed that she and all of the group members were meditating together deeply (as they usually did in actuality). While
in meditation, a blue-violet light appeared in their midst and
rested lovingly upon each of them. She awoke from this dream
in a wonderfully blessed state.

★ ★ ★ ★

Another ecumenical dream, relying on the "within," comes
from a forty-year-old Irish-American man:

I am at a Ferbrungen [a Jewish religious celebration along
with joyful dancing and singing]. I go into a levitation trance,

spinning, eyes closed, balancing on one foot, arms extended but bent at the elbow in a 90-degree angle. I close my eyes and ask myself if God exists and answer, "I believe so." Opening my eyes, I've traveled a quarter length along the circumference of the circle we are dancing in. I bring my hands together in gassho *[prayer] and bow to the circle of people, half of whom respond by bowing back; the other half are passive.*[3]

In this dream, a person who was raised as a Catholic and was soon to become a Buddhist priest achieves an ecstatic experience in a Jewish religious celebration, doing a dance that has Muslim origin (the spinning and trance of the dervishes) and, after acknowledging his belief in God, comes to a Buddhist experience, bowing to a circle of the Self. At this point, he has gone only one-quarter of the way to wholeness! Many years before, he had been addicted to drugs, and so it is not surprising that the same night he dreamed that a shadow figure, an addict, was transformed into a poet/troubadour, wearing a madrigal costume, playing a lute, and leading a group of people in song. A modern, truly ecumenical spirit has found his way!

★ ★ ★ ★

Two quite recent dreams come from a man who first came to see me as a vital and gifted American Jewish youth of 19. We worked successfully for a fairly short time and he terminated, to return some 20 years later, now a successful businessman. After a year or so, we again terminated. He came again to see me at the age of 50, having lost his business, his long-term relationship, and his sense of fulfillment in life. He soon reported two dreams that reflected light on his past and on his path. In the first of these, a wise man from India showed him three banners or symbols that pointed to different aspects of his life and also to several women to whom he had been attracted. One was from India, one from Africa, and one from the central United States. The last was of similar ethnic/religious background to the dreamer, perhaps to become his wife. The African had been a close friend in the past who had introduced him to art, while the Indian person/quality was an attractive "unknown." These three aspects of the anima clearly brought him to his own multiplicity and need to continue developing different aspects of his soul. The next dream found him looking at an austere and ascetic group of people who were wrapped in a huge *tallith*, a Jewish prayer shawl. He felt excluded from this group and lonely, until he realized that the name of the group was the same as that of a powerful business organization that had roundly cheated him. The aim of the business—unlike the image of the devout Hassidim he admired—was sheer power and egoism, something unacceptable to the dreamer. The contrast of the "many" of the feminine in his dreams versus the power/devil of the distorted "one," proved to be a very rich source of reflection for this man on his identity, his people, his faith, and his path. How to maintain his roots and his self-expression—without succumbing to the temptation of mere power-grabbing in the business world and still honoring his soul—is a very contemporary issue, indeed.

★ ★ ★ ★

On the issue of maintaining one's individual relationship to the divine while also honoring group and institutional connections, or from another perspective, working totally alone within one's self versus seeking out a teacher, I am reminded of an ancient story told by a Korean Buddhist:

Fourteen hundred years ago, two Silla monks, Wonhyo and Uisang, set out to study in Tang China, known for its advanced development of Buddhism. Night fell as they traveled toward China, so the two monks scurried into a cave to sleep. During the night, Wonhyo woke with a great thirst and found a bowl of water beside him. He drank the water, which had the most marvelous taste, and slept soundly through the rest of the night.

The following morning Wonhyo woke to find the cave was filled with dead bodies and the bowl from which he had drunk was actually a human skull filled with rainwater! Wonhyo vomited in disgust, but then realized something.

"The water was so sweet and my sleep so restful when I didn't know where I was. Ignorance can be medicinal and knowledge can be harmful. Everything depends on one's mind. Water from a skull can be sweet and fresh water can be bitter. A skeleton can be beautiful and a beautiful woman as hideous as a skeleton. It is all in the mind. I can understand the world if I study the mind, so why do I need to go all the way to China?"

And so Wonhyo returned to Korea. Later he became one of Silla's greatest monks, as did his companion, Uisang, after he returned from his studies in Tang China. The experiences of these two great monks help us realize that there is more than one way to come to the truth. They also show us the power of legend in the Korean Buddhist search for enlightenment.[4]

It was Uisang who, in contrast to his friend Wonhyo, continued on his path of study with outer teachers, and provided an astonishing solution (because it was so early) to the problem of individual versus collective or "The One and the Many." According to this also prominent Silla monk of the Northern Kingdom (620-702 C.E.), the world is a totality that cannot exist without individual units, but when the individuality of the units is emphasized, that totality disappears. The relationship between a group and its individual members is inevitably the same. An efficient group is one that respects the unique abilities of its members, while at the same time promoting the good of the whole.

However, if something is to be called "a whole," its individual units must share a certain quality. Uisang called this quality "identity" (*tongsang*). The unique characteristics of the composite parts must be able to mold into a unified identity. The whole, in turn, must strive to achieve a perfect harmony among its individual units, a goal that cannot be achieved without self-sacrifice on the part of the individual components.

When seen from this dialectic perspective, the relationship between the state and individual citizens is much like the relationship between the one and the multitude as defined in the Doctrine of the Six Phenomena: the one (the state) contains the multitude (individuals) and yet the multitude is as one. This doctrine defines the attitude that the state and individual citizens should take toward one another. The code of action it provides can be applied to the king, his court officials, and the people at large. This dialectic regulating the relationship between the state and the people is the essence of the historical consciousness that fueled the Silla Kingdom's unification of the Korean peninsula.[5]

On Closing This Book

After writing the foregoing, I struggled with how to end this chapter and this book. I did not want to end it so cursorily and academically, yet I was reluctant to use my own experience as one of the "personal examples" that the chapter was supposed to be about, for the reasons that I have previously given. I also was loath to multiply dreams in the service of this ending. With this dilemma in mind, I went to bed, silently asking for guidance from the Self as to what I should do. I then dreamed:

> *I am at a double wedding celebration, as a witness. The two couples getting married are from four different nations, four religions, and wear four different colors: golden and green, red and blue. After the wedding, my wife joins us and we celebrate a joyous wedding feast.*

The dream, I felt, certainly gave me the sense of union and fulfillment, of completion of the task for which I had dedicated myself. Such a union, *coniunctio*, is all that one can ask for such a work. Yet there did not seem to be an answer to my question as to whether I should share my own dreams and experiences as a culmination. Inner dialogue led to continuing division. The inner Writer argued for presenting my material, as did his *femme inspiratrice*. The inner Healer and the Scholar had grave doubts. So I let it simmer.

At last, an inner voice said, "Why do you struggle so? Surely it is meet that one who circumambulates the spiritual path in general must be ready to risk revealing his own struggles. And did you not already speak of your own initial 'ecumenical dream,' at the very beginning? If you are misunderstood or criticized, so be it. There will be individuals, among those who read this book, who will appreciate what you have to say, and their significant use of this example for their own paths will be reward enough, even sufficient to quell the fears of criticism and misunderstanding by your Healer and Scholar."

So with that inner direction, I agreed to present what follows:

During the summer of 1951 (I was 25 years old), during the second year of my first Jungian analysis and several months before the Christmas dream I reported at the beginning of this book, I was living practically a hermit's life. I had completed my job as a graduate teaching assistant in the psychology department at UCLA and was getting ready to begin a clinical internship for the doctoral program in the fall. I had also taken a leave of absence from my analysis, for financial and other reasons. So, for three months I was almost completely alone in my one-room apartment over a garage in the Beverly Glen area, not far from the university. Only my dog, Jasmín, served as company, and that was fine with me. I was religiously attending to my dreams and fantasies, going on with the intense work I had committed myself to during the preceding year. At the end of summer, I had the following dream:

> I am traveling around the world on a ship with Marco Polo (in actuality I had been in the Merchant Marine during World War II and had really traveled the world, but without Marco Polo, of course!). Suddenly, a whirlwind sweeps me off the ship and down into the Underworld. There, I am briefly with the poet Virgil and I understand that there are tasks I have to perform. One of these is a battle with a green dragon that spits red and yellow fire. The colors grow more intense as I fight, finally overcoming but not killing this dragon, but I do not understand how I managed to accomplish this.

Now I find myself alone in a medieval European city. Virgil is gone. Also absent are the intense colors from the previous part of the dream, leaving things gray and bleak. I wander fatigued and disconsolate on a narrow brick road in this city, when a door suddenly opens and color returns. Two huge knights, dressed in green with yellow suns on their chests, drag me into a room. These knights beat me with branches from a tree, but I understand this to be an initiation rather than a punishment. I feel it strongly but not too painfully.

Inside the room, I see it to be large and circular, with many people inside, including a loving French couple, unknown to me, and the professor for whom I had been an assistant at the university the previous year. Everyone welcomes me and then I look to the far side of the room where there is a huge crown, filled with precious stones. I suddenly realize that I am to be crowned. This crown, however, is far too large for me, so I take a couple of steps backward, upon which the crowd murmurs, "He is unworthy," or, "He is too young." It is as if the answer was left open. I awaken sobbing and with the sense that never in my life did I have such a profound dream.

This dream naturally had an overwhelming impact on me and I spent a lot of time trying to understand it, including when I resumed analysis a few weeks later. What seemed clear was that the extraverted "travel" with Marco Polo, like that which I had enjoyed in actuality during the two-plus years from ages 18 to 20, was now really over and the spirit (whirlwind) had other plans for me. That the whirlwind plays such a powerful role in the Bible as a manifestation of the divine spirit was not lost on me, either. Working in the underworld (the unconscious), and my struggle with the instinctual forces to be found there (dragon) has certainly been a major theme of my life, both before the dream and subsequent to it. "Virgil," a representation of my need to be an author, was present in my earlier life (I wrote an unsuccessful book on my wartime experiences, which then led me to choose psychology as an alternate vocation), and subsequently (after much failure) led to the writing and publication of some nineteen books.

The encounters with the knights and the crown, however, were the crucial parts of the dream. I can surely say that the knights represented the heroic path, now one of individuation rather than conquest in the outer world, and that the crown symbol of the Self was surely far too large for me at the time. When I subsequently discovered, years later, that crown symbolism in Kabbalah is representative of the highest form of the Self, it became clear to me that I was not only too young, but that this form of the Self was too big for anybody! It was a "crowning" aspect of God and far from personal. I needed always to approach and relate to it, rather than be a "king." Equally important, however, was my experience that despite sometimes being a leader until then, my subsequent experience proved that my work was indeed to be largely in relation to the inner world, for myself and others, and not as a "leader of men" in the outer world. Neither Caesar nor Savior was my path, but the service of the soul.

As important as the foregoing, however, was a memory that came back to me after I awakened from the dream in 1951. Vividly returning was the experience I had when I was not yet four years old. It was mid-day and I had fallen asleep while sitting on my little tricycle outside my parents' little house in East Los Angeles. Suddenly, I awakened from a dream with a sense of something big happening, but not knowing what. I felt the warmth and power of the sun and suddenly "knew" that God was somehow connected with the sun and that I was a "son of the sun." I felt quite competent on my little tricycle, and special. Then I was aware of my house and my mother inside. She was rather dark and mysterious to me, as were the two little girls who lived next door. One was my friend, but the other one had scratched me for no apparent reason. So, there I was, simultaneously a heroic "son of the sun" and a boy frightened of both his mother and some girls!

This memory of the sun stayed with me for some years, providing comfort, yet also causing me to reflect, but I forgot about it long before I entered junior high school.

The memory returned, at age 25, with this dream, and I realized that the Knight archetype had manifested itself to the young boy that I was back then. My tricycle substituted for the horse, of course. My being a "son of sun" made me aware that my spiritual parent, in contrast to my biological parents, was the Self and that my quest had to do with such matters.

A few months after this Knight dream, I had the "ecumenical" dream I offered at the outset of this book, and I now understood that there was a personal Self and a transpersonal Self, as well. But the Knight imagery and the idea of my own "heroic path" did not stop there. Fifteen years later, when I was 40, married, a father of two, and a certified Jungian analyst, I had occasion to resign from my local professional society. I was once again alone in a professional sense, but still warmly connected to family and friends. I then had the following dream:

> *I am on a field of battle, I think in Macedonian Greece. My companion is a large knight, dressed in black but with a golden sun on his chest. He and I are aware that there is no longer a war to be fought and that even my service of the Jungian "cause," in a collective sense, is now over.*

This dream validated my solemn decision to resign from my local society and it also renewed my connection with the Knight, after having been set "aside" for some years. I did wonder, however, at the continuity of the psyche: a major theme that outlined my life path before my fourth birthday reappeared when I was 25, and was now manifesting again, at a crucial moment in my life, at age 40.

Nor was this the last of it! Some months later, again at that pregnant time of year, Christmas, I was reflecting on the year's events and working with an ongoing fantasy, in which I was in a cave with a mother, daughter, a silent wise old man, and an equally silent young boy. In the midst of my imaginative work with these figures, the famous Knight broke in and rode off on his horse with mother and daughter.

I went after him, in active imagination, and asked him why he did that. His response was that he was trying to get my attention. Well, I said, he certainly had it now. He then went on to say that he had some stories to tell, and that there were other people there who also had stories to relate. This would be both for my benefit and theirs, but might also have something of interest and value for others as well. Would I be willing to participate with him and his friends? I was not to be a mere amanuensis, he assured me; we were to engage in a mutually creative work.

I was struck by this proposal. I had always had an interest in writing, had worked on school newspapers and written stories. I had even written a book about my experiences in the Merchant Marine during World War II, as I mentioned before, but it was never published. I had the fantasy, back at university after the war, that I would graduate and, if my book were published, would return to the Merchant Marine and write stories and travel articles, perhaps writing a major work when I was 40. I rather imagined that I was another Jack London. When my book failed to be published, however, I had to look around for another career and chose psychology. But now, the writing path was open to me again, and exactly at that magical age of 40 that I had imagined when I was in my early 20s. I therefore told the Knight that I was ready to do so, but that my commitments to family and patients were such that I could devote only two days a week to such writing. Would that be all right? He agreed wholeheartedly and we set to work. As I mentioned earlier, I deeply devoted myself over the next four years to this work and I wrote three books. Once more, publication was problematic, but ultimately all that writing (and many other books!) did see the light of day.

What does all this mean in terms of our present issue of the individual spiritual path in contrast or in connection to the collective spiritual path? I understand the Knight figure as a representative of a personal Self-image, one that is also archetypal in foundation. He revealed for me the individual spiritual path in service of a higher power—God.

This Knight certainly was present in my early childhood, grew into my young adulthood, and came to fruition—carrying my personal creative task in the spiritual world—when I entered the second half of life. He presented himself as Jewish and Christian and Pagan (how "different was this Knight from all other Knights!"). The Knight's story did indeed honor all three spiritual paths, as well as pave the way for nine other tales of individuation. His qualities, of quest, service, and devotion, have been ongoing and, at last, essentially fulfilled in my life in my 70s. In addition, naturally, such a personal Self-figure has since taken other forms in which these qualities continue. It is notable, however, that in Kabbalah this kind of hero/Self figure is typical of the Tifereth Sephira of the Middle Pillar, and serves the function of relating the individual to the divine images above that center. I also learned that in Jewish mysticism, it is recommended that one not ordinarily take up such themes until one is 40! Despite differences, it is clear that my soul was with that tradition.

My ecumenical dream, however—the one of the divine child being born while rabbi and priests attend—is of a different nature. That child, I believe, is a larger Self image, both for me and for the collective, one who gives me a personal gateway into where, I think, much of the world at large may be heading spiritually. My sense is that this child—who has since grown into adulthood, even in a chronological sense—is present in many of us, centering our reflections and work on what seems to be the task of the new millennium: an ecumenical world spirituality.

The book you hold in hand, I think, is in service to both the personal Self, keeping me on my own spiritual path, and also to that larger Self, where many of us (maybe all of us in one way or another?) are being led. That larger Self, beyond both the One and the Many, is providing both the Goal and the Way. I also trust that this more popular presentation of spiritual paths will also please the Knight, who said that we all "need to know where the other is," namely to share our personal spiritual myths or stories with each other and with the larger collective. In that same spirit, we should take Rumi to heart when he advised us, 800 years ago, to unfold our own myth—something that is now possible for the "ordinary" person as well as the great mystics of the past.

Notes

[1] Z'ev ben Shimon Halevi, *Kabbalah: Tradition of Hidden Knowledge* (New York: Thames and Hudson, 1979).

[2] J. Marvin Spiegelman, ed., *Psychology and Religion at the Millennium and Beyond* (Tempe, AZ: New Falcon, 1998), p. 131.

[3] J. Marvin Spiegelman, *Psychotherapy as a Mutual Process* (Tempe, AZ: New Falcon, 1996), p. 152.

[4] Chung Byong, "Korean Buddhism: Harmonizing the Contradictory," in *Korean Cultural Heritage: Thought and Religion*, vol. 2, Korea Foundation, ed. (Seoul: Yeong & Yeong, 1996), p. 59.

[5] Byong, "Korean Buddhism," p. 51.

[6] Coleman Barks, trans., and Michael Green, illus., *The Illuminated Rumi* (New York: Broadway Books, 1997), p. 11.

Bibliography

Avalon, Sir Arthur. *The Serpent Power*. Madras, India: Ganesh
    & Co., 1953.

Barks, Coleman, trans. and Michael Green, illus. *The Illuminated
    Rumi*. New York: Broadway Books, 1997.

Black Elk. *The Sacred Pipe: Black Elk's Account of the Seven
    Rites of the Oglala Sioux, Civilization of the American
    Indian Series*, vol. 36. Joseph E. Brown, ed. Norman:
    University of Oklahoma Press, 1989.

Bradway, Katherine. *Villa of Mysteries: Pompeii Initiation Rites
    of Women*. San Francisco: C. G. Jung Institute of San
    Francisco, 1982.

Brown, Clint and Cheryl McLean. *Drawing from Life*. New
    York: Harcourt, Brace, Jovanovich, 1992.

Byong, Chung. "Korean Buddhism: Harmonizing the Con-
    tradictory," in *Korean Cultural Heritage: Thought and
    Religion*, vol. 2. Korea Foundation, ed. Seoul: Yeong
    & Yeong, 1996.

Case, Paul Foster. *The Tarot*. Richmond, VA: Macoy Publish-
    ing, 1947.

Corbett, Lionel. *The Religious Function of the Psyche*. London
    and New York: Routledge, 1996.

Corbin, Henry. *Temple and Contemplation*. London: KPI and
    Islamic Publications, 1986.

Cumont, Franz. *The Mysteries of Mithra.* Originally published in French, 1902. Thomas J. McCormack, trans. New York: Dover, 1956.

Dougherty, Mary. "Duccio's Prayer: Mediating Destruction and Creation with Artists in Analysis." *Journal of Analytical Psychology* 43. 1998.

Eliade, Mircea. *Shamanism: Archaic Techniques of Ecstasy.* Bollingen Series LXXVI. New York, Pantheon Books, 1964.

Fierz-David, Linda. "Psychological Reflections on the Fresco Series of the Villa of Mysteries in Pompeii." MS. Zurich: Jung Institute, 1957.

Funk & Wagnall's Standard Dictionary of Folklore. Maria Leach, ed. New York: Funk & Wagnall's, 1949.

Gogh, Vincent van. *The Complete Letters of Vincent van Gogh.* London: Thames and Hudson, 1958. Halevi, Z'ev ben Shimon. *Kabbalah: Tradition of Hidden Knowledge.* New York: Thames and Hudson, 1979.

Hamill, Sam, trans. and J. P. Seaton, ed. *The Essential Chuang Tzu.* Boston: Shambhala, 1998.

Hannah, Barbara. *Encounters of the Soul.* Santa Monica, CA: Sigo Press, 1981.

Harner, Michael. *The Way of the Shaman.* San Francisco: HarperSanFrancisco, 1980.

Heschel, Abraham Joshua. *God in Search of Man: A Philosophy of Judaism.* New York: Noonday Press, 1997.

His All Holiness Bartholomew I. Address at the symposium, *Caring for God's Creation: Science, Religion, and the Environment.* Santa Barbara, California, 1997.

Isherwood, Christopher. *Ramakrishna and His Disciples.* Hollywood: Vedanta Press, 1965.

James, William. *The Varieties of Religious Experience.* New York: Modern Library, 1902.

Johnson, Trebbe. "Redefining the Bond Between Religion and Ecology," in *Sierra Magazine* 83, no. 6. 1998: 52.

Jung, C. G. *Answer to Job, The Collected Works of C. G. Jung,* vol. 11. R.F.C. Hull, trans. Bollingen Series XX. Princeton: Princeton University Press, 1952.

————. Introduction to *The Secret of the Golden Flower,* by Wilhelm, Richard. London: Routledge, 1931. In *Psychology and Alchemy, The Collected Works of C. G. Jung,* vol. 12. R.F.C. Hull, trans. Bollingen Series XX. Princeton: Princeton University Press, 1968.

————. *Memories, Dreams, Reflections.* Aniela Jaffé, ed. New York: Random House, 1961.

————. *Mysterium Coniunctionis. The Collected Works of C. G. Jung,* vol. 14. R.F.C. Hull, trans. Bollingen Series XX. Princeton: Princeton University Press, 1970.

————. "Psychological Commentary on Kundalini Yoga: Lectures One and Two" (1932). In *Spring: An Annual of Archetypal Psychology,* 1975.

————. "Psychological Commentary on Kundalini Yoga: Lectures Three and Four" (1932). In *Spring: An Annual of Archetypal Psychology,* 1976.

————. *Psychology and Alchemy* (1944). *The Collected Works of C. G. Jung,* vol. 12. R.F.C. Hull, trans. Bollingen Series XX. Princeton: Princeton University Press, 1968.

————. "The Psychology of the Transference" (1948). In *The Practice of Psychotherapy, The Collected Works of C. G. Jung,* vol. 16. R.F.C. Hull, trans. Bollingen Series XX. Princeton: Princeton University Press, 1954.

————. "The Transcendent Function" (1916/1957). In *The Structure and Dynamics of the Psyche. The Collected Works of C. G. Jung,* vol. 8. R.F.C. Hull, trans. Bollingen Series XX. Princeton: Princeton University Press, 1970.

————. "Transformation Symbolism in the Mass." *Psychology and Religion: West and East. The Collected Works of C. G. Jung,* vol. 11. R.F.C. Hull, trans. Bollingen Series XX. Princeton: Princeton University Press, 1969.

————. *Two Essays on Analytical Psychology* (1916/1942). The Collected Works of C. G. Jung, vol. 7. R.F.C. Hull, trans. Bollingen Series XX. Princeton: Princeton University Press, 1953.

Jung, C. G. and C. Kerenyi. *Essays on a Science of Mythology.* New York: Pantheon Books, 1949.

Jung, Emma. "Animus and Anima: Two Essays." Originally published in 1931 and 1934. New York: Analytical Psychology Club of New York, 1957.

Kartha, D.K.M. "A Singer for Krishna," in *Parabola* 23, no. 2. 1998: 15–17.

Khan, Hazrat Inayat. *In an Eastern Rose Garden: The Sufi Message of Hazrat Inayat Khan*, vol. 7. New Lebanon, NY: Omega Publications, 1991.

Maimonides, Moses. *The Guide for the Perplexed.* M. Friedlander, trans. New York: Dover Publications, 2000.

Meis, Rev. J. Anthony. *The Rosary, with Scripture Meditations and Practical Applications.* Baltimore: Barton-Cotton, Inc., 1970.

Mondrus, Martin. Privately printed prospectus, 1995.

Myss, Caroline. *Anatomy of the Spirit.* New York: Harmony Books, 1996.

Otto, Rudolf. *The Idea of the Holy: An Inquiry into the Non-rational Factor in the Idea of the Divine and Its Relation to the Rational.* John W. Harvey, trans. New York: Oxford University Press, 1958.

Pauli, Wolfgang. "The Influence of Archetypal Ideas on the Scientific Theories of Kepler." In C. G. Jung and Wolfgang Pauli, *The Interpretation of Nature and Psyche.* New York: Pantheon Books, 1955.

Pope John Paul II. "The Ecological Crisis: A Common Responsibility." Rome: Vatican, December 8, 1989.

Regardie, Israel. *The Middle Pillar: A Co-relation of the Principles of Analytical Psychology and the Elementary Techniques of Magic.* St. Paul, MN: Llewellyn, 1970.

Rourke, Mary. "Apostle of Art; Sister Wendy, a Recluse-Turned-Commentator, Is Making It Her Mission to Demystify Great Paintings of the World." *Los Angeles Times,* 2 December, 1998.

Serlin, Ilene. "Root Images of Healing in Dance Therapy." *American Journal of Dance Therapy* 15, no. 2. 1993.

Shaw, Miranda. "Delight in this World: Tantric Buddhism as a Path of Bliss." *Parabola* 23, no. 2, 1998.

Sholem, Gershom. *On the Kabbalah and Its Symbolism*. London: Routledge, 1965.

Sloan, Lisa. "Shamanic Initiation: Map of the Soul: The Actor-Healer Archetype Revealed." Ph.D. diss., Pacifica Graduate Institute, 1999.

Smith, Huston. *The World's Religions*. New York: Harper & Row, 1958.

Soloveitchik, Joseph B. *The Halakhic Man*. Philadelphia: The Jewish Publication Society of America, 1983.

Spiegelman, J. Marvin. *Jungian Psychology and the Passions of the Soul*. Tempe, AZ: New Falcon Publications, 1989.

———. *Psychotherapy as a Mutual Process*. Tempe, AZ: New Falcon Publications, 1996.

———. *The Quest*. Tempe, AZ: New Falcon Publications, 1984.

———. *Reich, Jung, Regardie and Me: The Unhealed Healer*. Tempe, AZ: New Falcon Publications, 1992.

———. *The Tree of Life: Paths in Jungian Individuation*. Original 1974. Tempe, AZ: New Falcon Publications, 1993.

Spiegelman, J. Marvin, ed. *Catholicism and Jungian Psychology*. Tempe, AZ: New Falcon Publications, 1988.

———. *Protestantism and Jungian Psychology*. Tempe, AZ: New Falcon Publications, 1995.

———. *Psychology and Religion at the Millennium and Beyond*. Tempe, AZ: New Falcon Publications, 1998.

———. *Sufism, Islam and Jungian Psychology*. Tempe, AZ: New Falcon Publications, 1991.

Spiegelman, J. Marvin and Mokusen Miyuki. *Buddhism and Jungian Psychology*. Tempe, AZ: New Falcon Publications, 1985.

Spiegelman, J. Marvin and Arwind U. Vasavada. *Hinduism and Jungian Psychology*. Tempe, AZ: New Falcon Publications, 1987.

Sun Yu-chi'n. "No Need to Listen: A Conversation between Sun Yu-chi'n and J. L. Walker." *Parabola* 23, no. 2, 1998.

Suzuki, Daisetz T. "Awakening of a New Consciousness in Zen" (1954). In *Man and Transformation*, Eranos Yearbooks, vol. 5. London: Routledge, 1964.

————. *Manual of Zen Buddhism.* New York: Grove Press, 1960.

van der Leeuw, Gerhard. *Religion in Essence and Manifestation* (1933). J. E. Turner, trans. London: Allen and Unwin, 1938.

Vasavada, Arwind. *Tripura-Rahasya: A Comparative Study of the Process of Individuation.* Varanasi: Chowkhamba Sanskrit Series, 1965.

von Franz, Marie-Louise. *The Cat: A Tale of Feminine Redemption.* Toronto: Inner City Books, 1999.

Wieseltier, Leon. *Kaddish.* New York: Alfred Knopf, 1998.

Wilhelm, Richard and C. G. Jung. *The Secret of the Golden Flower.* London: Routledge and Kegan Paul, 1931.

Wolff, Toni. "Structural Forms of the Feminine Psyche" (1934). Zurich: Students Association, C. G. Jung Institute, 1951.

Zeller, Max. *The Dream: The Vision of the Night.* Los Angeles: Analytical Psychology Club of Los Angeles, 1978.

Zohar, The. Five volumes. Harry Sperling and Maurice Simon, trans. London: Soncino Press, 1933.

Index

Abelard and Eloise, 114
active imagination, 164
Adam Kadmon, 107–108
Adam and the pilgrimage,
    18–24
addiction, 18; and women,
    213–215
Adlerian psychology, 78
Agni, 77
Agony in the Garden, 184–185
ahamkara, 75
ahklak, 145
Aidos, 209
ajna chakra, 67, 86–87
akasha, 85
Akbar, 13–15
Akiba, Rabbi, 97
'Arafat, Al, 20
Alchemical Model, 10–12
alchemy, 10–12, 27, 41, 44, 58,
    75, 82, 91, 112–135
Alchoholics Anonymous, 20,
    27
Allah, 21
anahata chakra, 78–82, 82, 85

analysis, 118–123, 159–160; and
    clergy, 9–10; and natal faith,
    158–159; as Western yoga,
    135–136
ananda, 68
Anatomy of the Spirit, 242
anima mundi, 153
anima, 163–165
animus, 163–165
annunciation, the, 178–179
Answer to Job, 99, 133, 185
anthropos, 107
Aphrodite, 215
Apocalypse, 61
Arabi, Ibn al, 5
Arafat, Yassir, 20
archetypal pair, 119–120
Ariadne, 202, 204, 208, 211, 213
Armstrong, Neil, xiii
Artemis, 204, 211
asanas, 69
Ascension, the, 191–192
Assiyah, 103–115
Assumption, the, 180, 194–195
Assumptio Mariae, 133

Athena, 203
Atma, 87, 88
Atman, 86
Avalon, Arthur, 70, 75, 77, 80, 86
awakening, 38–39, 53
Axiom of Maria Prophetissa,
    116–117, 131
Ayin, 98
Ayin Sof, 98–99
Ayin Sof Or, 99
Azilut, 103–108
Bach, 180, 143, 144
Bal Shem Tov, 5
baptism, 6–7
Bartholomew, 142
bath, in alchemy, 123–124
beating, image of, 214–215
Beethoven, 143
Bell, John Stewart, 169
Beriah, 103–114
bija, 77
Binah, 100, 102
binarius, 116
Black Elk, 143
Black Stone, 24, 22
Blake, William, 191, 115–116
Boehme, Jacob, 5
Bohm, David, 169
Book of Job, 106
Bradway, Katherine, 200, 208,
    209, 211, 207–208
Brahma, 68
Brahms, 143
Buddha, 113
Buddha-Man, 61
Buddhism, Tibetan, 9
Buddhism, Zen, 26–64
Calling of Beasts, 218–219
Campbell, Joseph, 207
Candamaharoshanatantra, 113
Caro, Joseph, 5

Catholicism, stages in, 171,
    177–197
chakras, 68–69; table of, 70
chanting, 143
Child-Brahma, 71
chit, 68
Christ, Jesus, 127, 135, 181–184,
    185–187, 187–191
Chuang Tzu, 175
Communion, 7
Community Model, 5–10
Confession, 8–9
Confirmation, 7
coniunctio, 126, 137
Corbett, Lionel, 223
Corbin, Henry, 17
Coronation, the, 195–197
counter-transference, 121
crown, 100, 102, 251, 252; of
    myrtle, 206; of the Self, 196
Daat, 100
dance, 145
davening, 143
de Leon, Moses, 97
Decartes, Renée, 156
déformation professionelle, 161
denarius, 131
dervishes, 145–146
devil image, 116
dharma, 51
dhikr, 21
Diebenkorn, Richard, 149
Dionysos, 202–204, 206–208,
    211, 213, 215
Divine, Among, 5–10, 30, 167,
    177; Around, 12–15, 140–154;
    in art, 146–149 Between,
    10–12, 112–138, 215; Child,
    ix; in dance, 145–146; Femi-
    nine, 163; and humankind,
    repairing breach, 19; in

Islam, 17–25; in literature, 149–150; Masculine, 163; in music, 143–145; partnership, 20; synchronicity, 150–153; Within, 1–5, 26–65, 66–95, 96–111, 32, 215

Doctrine of the Six Phenomena, 248–249

Dougherty, Mary, 147–150

dragon, symbolism of, 229

dreams, of ant colony, 150–151; big, xii, 220; double wedding, 249–250; ecumenical, 255; of immersion in flood, 168; Macedonian Greece, 253; Marco Polo, 250–251; psychoecumenical, ix–xiv, 244–247

dualism, 56, 61

Duccio, 147–148

Eckhart, Meister, 5, 52–53, 62

ego, 55, 86, 127, 160–161, 176; relativization of, 174–176; vs. Self, 175–177

Ehyeh Asher Ehyeh, 100, 106

Einstein, Albert, 169

elephant, symbolism of, 71

Eleusinian Mysteries, 199

Eliade, Mircea, 217

Elohim, 106

enlightenment, 51–52; process of in Hinduism, 171–172

Eros, 112, 211, 215

Eucharist, 9

evil, 101

extreme unction, 9

faith, 173–175

fall from Paradise, 17

fana, 23

Fechner, Gustav Theodor, 156

felix culpa, 17

feminine, 58, 63, 85; in alchemy, 133–135; in Nature, 142

femme inspiratrice, 163

Fierz-David, Linda, 200

filius philosophorum, 127

free association, 45

Freudian psychology, 45, 78, 121

Gabriel (angel), as guide on pilgrimage, 18–23

Galilei, Galileo, 155

gazelle, symbol of, 80

Gevurah, 100–101

Gideon's Dew, 128

God, 103–116; image, 121; faith in, 173–174; feminine presence of, 102–103; in Judaism, 98; mystic understanding of, 53; name of, 103–110; praying to, 20–21; recovery of connection, 22–23; within, 166

godliness, 61–62

God-Man, 61, 163

Gogh, Vincent van, 148

Gopa, 113

Gorman, Paul, 142

Guinevere, Daughter of, 192, 193, 194–195

guru, 93, 172–173

Hafiz, 143

Hajj, 17–25

Halakhic Man, xviii

Halevi, Z'ev ben Shimon, 97, 242

Hannah, Barbara, 3

hara, 44

Hari, 74

Harner, Michael, 217

Hashem, 18

Hesed, 100
Hinduism, 66–93, 156; stages
 in, 171–176
Hiroshima, 57
Hod, 102
Hokhmah, 100, 102
Holy Spirit, 118
Hopper, Edward, 149
I Ching, 3, 156, 169 n. 1
Iblis, 23, 24
id, 175
ida, 68
imitatio Christi, 9, 127
individuation, 135, 159–167
Indra's Web, 93, 151
initiation, in the Villa of Mysteries, 211–213
initiation, of women, 204
intellectualization, 42–43
Ishta-devata, 88
Ishvara, 81
Islam,17–24 113–114
Itara, 87
Jacob, 46
Jacob's Ladder, 106
James, William, 156
jimrah, 23
Jung, C. G.; and alchemy, 75,
 132; and the Assumptio
 Mariae, 133; and chakra
 animals symbolism, 84; on
 chakras, 71, 73, 75, 77, 78–80,
 82–83, 86, 87–88; and communion, 8; criticism of his
 psychology of anima and
 animus, 164–165; dreams, xiii,
 87, 88, 175–176; on Eastern
 spirituality, 54; experiment at
 Burgholzli, 166; illness in 60's,
 224; on Kundalini Yoga, 90;
 and psychological perspec-
tive of religious experience,
 157–159; vision of, 57
Jung, Emma, 163
Jungian analysts, and born-into
 faith, xiv
Jungian Psychology and the Pas-
 sions of the Soul, 242
Ka'aba, 5, 17, 22, 24, 103–117
Kabbalah, 24, 27, 55, 92, 97,
 96–112
Kabbalistic meditation, 108–109
Kaddish, 36
Kalicharna, 75, 80, 81, 88
kama, 73
Kannon, 197
katabasis, 207
Kav, 99
Kelippot, 106
Kepler, Johannes, 155–156
Keter, 100, 102, 106
Khan, Hazrat Inayat, 4, 16
King Arthur, 194–195
King David, 145
King Minos, 203
Kleinian analysis, 121
klesas, 73
Knight, the, xvi–xvii, 251–253
Koran, 21, 146
Korean monks, story of, 247–
 248
krodha, 73
Kundalini path, 66–95, 90–93;
 Yoga, 24
Kwan Yin, 197
Lakini, 77
Lamb, the, 32
Lamed Vovnikim, 167
Lancelot, 194–195
laurel, symbolism of, 206
left pillar, 99
leviathan, 73

Li-Po, 145
liberation, 86
lightning path, 100–103
liknon, 208
love, 112
Luria, Isaac, 5
lust, 73
mada, 75
Maesta, 147–149
maghrib, 21
Magnificat, 180
Mahabarata, 67
Maimonides, Moses, 142
makara, 73
mala, 71, 86
malakut, 24
male principle, 85
Malkhut, 102–103
mana personality, 165
manas, 86
mandala, xv, 54, 55, 118, 181
mani, 75
manipura chakra, 75–78, 80, 82
mantra, 77, 80
marriage, 8
Mary, Virgin, 177–197, 215
Mass, 5, 9
matsarya, 75
maya, 55, 57, 58, 86
Mecca, 5, 22, 23
mechanism and mind, split between, 156
Meier, C. A., 67, 124
Memories, Dreams, Reflections, 8
Men, 36 Just, 167
Mendelssohn, 144
mercurial fountain, 30
Mercurius, 116, 118, 127, 150
Mevlevi tradition, 145–146
Middle Pillar, 99, 100
Mina, 19, 23

Minotaur, 204
Mithraic mysteries, 48–49
Mithras, 200
moha, 75
moksha, 86
Mondrus, Martin, 148–149
Morning of the Presence, 21
Mozart, 143
Mt. Sinai, 21
mudra, 71
mukti, 67
muladhara chakra, 71–73, 75, 76, 82, 86
music, sacred, 143
Mutus Liber, 114
Muzdalifah, 21
Mysteries; Glorious, 190–197; Joyful, 178–184; Sorrowful, 184–190
nadis, 68
Nagasaki, 57
Name of God, 7
Nativity, the, 181–182
Nature, 33, 58, 64; early Christian view of, 141–142; return to, 141–142
Nature, Art, and Synchronicity Model, 12–15
Newton, Sir Isaac, 155
Nezah, 102
nigredo, 126
numinosum, 140
numinous, 1, 13
old wise man/woman, 165
Om, 86
opposites, 120, 124, 126, 130, 174
Ordination, 9–10
Otto, Rudolf, 1
ox, 32, 36; catching the (Oxherding Picture 4),

39–42; coming home on
(Oxherding Picture 6), 46;
entering the city (Oxherding Picture 10), 59–64;
forgotten, leaving the man
alone (Oxherding Picture 7),
49–52; herding the (Oxherding Picture 5), 42–46; and
man gone (Oxherding
Picture 8), 52–54; searching
for (Oxherding Picture 1),
30–34; seeing the (Oxherding Picture 3), 36–39; seeing
traces (Oxherding Picture
2), 34–36; returning to the
origin, (Oxherding Picture
9), 54–59; whitening of, 44
Oxherding Pictures, 26–65, 167,
176
padma, 70
pagan religions, 216
Pasiphae, 203
Pauli, Wolfgang, 169
Pearl, 22
Pearlstein, Philip, 149
Pentecost, 192–194
persona, 161
physics and psychology, 168–
169
pilgrimage, 17–25
Pillar of Mercy, 100
pingala, 68
Plato, xiv, 8, 112
Pope John Paul II, 142
power song, 219
powers, parapsychological, 81
pranayama, 69
prima materia, 115
projection, 121, 172–173
psyche, ix, xv–xvi; collective
    Christian, 9; comparisons

between Eastern and West-
ern, 27
psychoanalysis, 159–160. *See
also* analysis.
psychology, group, 166–167
psychology and physics, 168–
170
psychology and religion, xiv
Purnananda, 70, 71, 75, 77, 80,
81, 88
purusha, 79, 80
qadosh, 1
Quest, The, 242
Rainmaker Model, 1–5, 46
Rakini, 74, 75
Ram, 77
ram, symbol of, 75
Ramakrishna, 140–141
Ramayana, 67
Raphael (angel), 235
Reich, Wilhelm, 176, 192
Reichian therapy, 173–174
religio, xiii–xiv, 141
*Religion in Essence and Manifes-
tation*, xvii, 15
religion vs. science, 157
resurrection, 135
Richter, Jean Paul, 143
right pillar, 99
Rosarium Philosophorum, 30, 63,
114, 116, 133; and Oxherding
Pictures, 27–30
rosary, path of the, 177–197
Ruach ha Kodesh, 100
Rudra, 75, 77
Rumi, 5, 113–115, 137, 145, 256
Sabbath, 5
sacraments, Christian, 6–10
saddhaka, task of, 69, 77
sadhana, 68
Sadha-Shiva, 85

Safed, 92
sahasrara chakra, 87–91
Saint Augustine, 141, 186–187
Saint Francis, 5
Satan, 24
satchitananda, 68
Saul, 145
Scholem, Gershom, 97
science as a spiritual path,
    155–169
science vs. religion, 157
Self, xv, 54, 55, 62, 68, 75, 86,
    118, 127, 152, 165–167, 204,
    206, 213; vs. ego, 175–176;
    without ego, 88; estrange-
    ment from, 32; is every-
    thing, 176; incarnation of,
    186–187; image of, 38–39;
    and objective world, 35–36;
    personal in service of col-
    lective, 185; as *purusha*,
    82–84; reborn, 131–132;
    search for, 174–175; as soul,
    176
selflessness, 52
Sephirot, 27, 99–103, 107
serpent path, 100–104
Serpent Power, The, 69
shadow, 162–164
Shakti, 68, 71, 78, 81, 85, 86,
    197
shaman, 217–218, 224
shamanic initiation, 218–220; a
    woman's, 220–236
shamanism, in modern life,
    237–238
Shams of Tabriz, 113–116,
    137–139
Shan-lin, 144–145
Shekhina, 102–103, 197
Shemittot, 103–109

Shi-en, Kaku-an, 26, 31, 32, 34,
    36, 38, 39, 41, 44, 45, 57
Shiva, 68, 71, 73, 75, 77, 81, 86
siddhis, 81, 86
Silenus, 202, 207
sins, seven deadly, 162
Smith, Huston, xvii–xviii, 15
Soloveitchik, Rabbi Joseph B.,
    xviii
Song of Songs, 114
Sophia, 163
soror mystica, 12, 30, 115, 135
soul, collective, path of, 137
soul, divine child of, 127
soul, is self, 176
soul, maturity of, 47–48
soul retrieval, 219, 223
spiritual path, 34–35, 126–127,
    254–255
Star of David, 80
Stations of the Cross, 27, 177
stone divination, 218
stone, as symbol of Self, 24
sublimation, 135
succubus, 163–165
Sufism, 4, 5, 16, 54, 98, 113–
    114, 137–139, 143
sunnah, 145
sunya, 53
sunyata, 55, 62
super-ego, 162
sushumna, 68
Suzuki, D. T., 26, 27, 32, 37,
    40, 41, 42, 52, 53, 56, 57, 62,
    60–61
svadhisthana chakra, 73–76
swastika, 75
synchronicity, 150
taboo, 124
Tai Chi symbol, 196
Tansen, 13–15, 143

Tantra, 112–113
tarot, 107
tattva, 71, 76
tejas, 75
Temple of Light, 24
Ten Commandments, 162
ten, symbolism of, 27
Theseus, 204
Thiebaud, Wayne, 149
three, symbolism of, 75
threeness, in Hinduism, 68
Tifereth, 102, 106
Torah, 106, 215
transference, 115–116
tree, 63; Zen story of, 59
Tree of Life, The, 67, 242
Tree of Life, 55–56, 63, 96–111,
    132; paths on, 107
Tripura-Rahasya, 171–172
truth and reality, contact with
    embodiment of, 172–173
twelve-step programs, 20, 27
*Two Essays in Analytical Psy-
    chology*, 159
Tzimtzum, 98–100
unconscious, collective, 158
unicorn, 18
unio mentalis, 135
unio mystica, 86
Unus Mundus, 151
van der Leeuw, Gerhard, 15
Varieties of Religious Experience,
    156
Vasavada, Arwind, 159, 171–173,
    175
veil, 21
vessel, 30, 121, 126
Villa of Mysteries, 199–200, 204,
    211–213

Virgil, 251
Vishnu, 68, 73, 75
vishuddha chakra, 82–86
visitation, the, 179–181
visitation, first devotional, 19–
    20; fourth devotional, 23–24;
    second devotional, 20–21;
    third devotional, 21–23
von Franz, Marie-Louise, 157
WABA system, xvi, 1–16
Weber-Fechner law, 156
White Pearl, Secret of the, 24–25
whitening, 127
Wilhelm, Richard, 3–4
Wisdom, 163
witch, 163–164
Wolff, Toni, 163
Woman of Valour, 215
women and addiction, 213–214
women's mysteries, 199–215
World Wide Web, as Indra's
    Web, 93
World's Religions, The, xvii–xviii,
    15
Worlds, four, 103–107
yang, 196
Yesod, 102
Yezirah, 103–113
Ygdrassil, 55–56
YHVH, 103–111
yin, 196
yogin(i), 68
Yohai, Rabbi Simeon ben, 97
Yom Kippur, 21
Zahzahot, 99
zazen, 44
Zen consciousness, 44
Zeus, 203
Zohar, 97–98